American Men of Letters

FRANCIS PARKMAN

Francis Parkman

American Men of Letters

FRANCIS PARKMAN

BY

HENRY DWIGHT SEDGWICK

Sout bien ou rien

The Riverside Press

BOSTON AND NEW YORK
HOUGHTON MIFFLIN COMPANY
Riverside Press Cambridge

TO

S. M. S.

Qual vuol gentil donna parere,
Vada con lei.

PREFACE

THE life of a scholar is almost of necessity uneventful, and his accomplished work speaks for
itself; therefore the biographer must deal in
the main with the scholar's labors of acquisition
and preparation. Journals kept on two summer
vacations, and on a trip to Europe, and several
erratic and scrappy notebooks, show Parkman's
methods of examining historic places and of collecting historical materials. These, together with
the "Oregon Trail," his own brief narrative of
his life, and an irregular correspondence, consti-
tute the autobiographical records of his life.

My thanks are due to Miss Parkman, the historian's sister, for putting those records at my
disposal; to Mr. Charles Haight Farnham, the
author of the "Life of Francis Parkman," for
his generous permission to make what use I
might wish of his biography — and but for his
labors my own would have been fourfold greater;
to Messrs. Little, Brown & Co., for their per-

mission to quote from that " Life " and from Parkman's published works; to the late Abbé H. R. Casgrain, for leave to use his unpublished " Correspondence for twenty-eight years with Mr. Parkman;" to The Westborough Historical Society, for leave to make extracts from the " Diary of Rev. Ebenezer Parkman," and to those ladies and gentlemen who have kindly allowed me to print letters written to Parkman. I am also indebted to the monographs of Mr. Edward Wheelwright, the Rev. O. B. Frothingham, Mr. John Fiske, and Mr. Barrett Wendell.

H. D. SEDGWICK.

NEW YORK, April, 1904.

CONTENTS

FRANCIS PARKMAN

CHAPTER I

ACHIEVEMENT

THERE is a fine passage in Bunyan which describes the fighting courage of the Puritan type : —

Then said Great-heart to Mr. Valiant-for-Truth, "Thou hast worthily behaved thyself; let me see thy sword." So he showed it to him.

When he had taken it in his hand, and looked thereon a while, he said, "Ha! it is a right Jerusalem blade."

Valiant. It is so. Let a man have one of these blades, with a hand to wield it and skill to use it, and he may venture upon an angel with it. He need not fear its holding, if he can but tell how to lay on. Its edge will never blunt.

Great-heart. But you fought a great while. I wonder you was not weary.

Valiant. I fought till my sword did cleave to my hand ; and then they were joined together as if a sword grew out of my arm, and when the blood ran through my fingers, then I fought with most courage.

Great-heart. Thou hast done well. . . .

Mr. Great-heart was delighted in him (for he loved one greatly that he found to be a man of his hands).

Parkman was such another Valiant-for-Truth, and with the right Jerusalem blade of character fought his victorious way. Silent in pain, patient in accomplishment, modest in victory, gentle in bearing, and yet determined to grimness, he proved himself lawful heir of the best Puritan traits. The name Puritan he disliked, but however much he might wish he could not escape his moral ancestry. He inherited not the accidental beliefs of the Puritans, but their attitude toward life, their disposition and inherent bent. " Not happiness but achievement " was his watchword. Cut off by race and temperament from those light, sunny, skeptical, feminine moods that belong to other bloods, his nature was concentrated in the pith of his race. With head erect, jaw fixed, shoulders square, he was the image of New England's best. He had New England's difficulty of self-expression, he was not without traces of her inflexibility of mind, and he was endowed, more than the measure of his race, with a proud, shy tenderness.

Nature would have made a soldier of him, but in Fortune's hugger-mugger allotment of parts, it fell to him to grasp the pen instead of the sword; his name is not written upon fort and battlefield, but it is inseparably united with the story of the first great epoch in the history of North America.

In the field of history Parkman's name stands as high, perhaps higher, than that of any other American. John Fiske, a student of the historians of Europe and America, says: "Into the making of a historian there should enter something of the philosopher, something of the naturalist, something of the poet. In Parkman this rare union of qualities was realized in a greater degree than in any other American historian. Indeed, I doubt if the nineteenth century can show in any part of the world another historian quite his equal in respect to such a union. . . . It is only the historian who is also philosopher and artist that can thus deal in block with the great and complex life of a whole society. The requisite combination is realized only in certain rare and high types of mind, and there has been no more brilliant illustration of it than Parkman's volumes afford." And he adds, speaking of Parkman's whole history: "Strong in its individuality, like to nothing else, it clearly belongs, I think, among the world's few masterpieces of the highest rank, along with the works of Herodotus, Thucydides, and Gibbon."

A writer in the "Spectator," reviewing an English edition of Parkman's works, says: "Francis Parkman long since won an honorable place among the classic historians of the world, and it is with the greatest cordiality that we welcome the present reprint of his works. Now, at last, we have a library edition which we may put by the side of Gibbon and Michelet, of Livy and Taine. For Francis Parkman need not fear the most august society; he has the true genius of history in him, — the genius which knows how to wed accuracy with romance." Goldwin Smith compares him with Tacitus. Professor Albert Bushnell Hart says: "Francis Parkman is the greatest of all the writers who have ever made America their theme or have written as American scholars, and his greatness depends upon three qualities rarely brought together in one man; he was a matchless investigator, a man of the most unflinching tenacity, and somehow he knew how to write so that men loved to read him."

These are enthusiastic praises, and Mr. Fiske, who had a warm heart and a fine capacity for friendship, might be thought to have spoken from a May morning mood, the English reviewer might be deemed over-grateful to Parkman after reviewing other historians, Goldwin Smith enthusiastic from love of Canada, Professor Hart from love of Harvard; but such conjectures fail, for these men make but the mouthpiece of the common voice. The boy who in the course of nature reads Parkman after Cooper and the Waverley novels finishes "Pontiac" or "Montcalm and Wolfe" with a "By Jove, that's bully!" The temperate person of uncertain age says, "What an admirable piece of work! how true, how just! would that our fiction had half the charm of such history!" The student rejoices in the accuracy, the impartiality, the wise correctness of this history.

It is for scholars, however, to decide whether Parkman is as great as Thucydides and Gibbon; the very suggestion is more than enough honor for any other historian; it is for readers to determine if his books are as agreeable as Michelet or Livy; the biographer can but show whether the historian has been loyal to his task, — whether he has studied, explored, reconnoitred in all those places where he might ferret out knowledge of his subject; for in such loyalty lies not only the historian's honor, but also what benefit men may derive from history.

In considering the merits of a historian, heed must be paid to the subject of the history, the theme must be looked at; a little man minces up to a little subject, a strong man strides up to a great subject. No story of Martha's Vineyard, of Dorking, or Tarascon could deserve the title of a great history. Parkman chose worthily,

sagaciously seeing clearly where other men had
only peered. His subject is universally acknowledged to be a great subject. It is the history of
Canada, it is the history of the United States as
well. The events which he recounts are the great
prologue to the drama of the American Revo-
lution ; they are the slow factors which begot
sentiments of mutual dependence among bicker-
ing colonies, and finally, forcing them to confed-
erate, enabled them to break the ties that held
them to Great Britain and to found a new nation.
Incidentally, as a story of two nations of different stocks, Parkman's history involves the contrast between two political systems, — one where
a single man holds the power of the state, the
other where the general body of citizens possess
it; likewise it involves the contrast between two
great religious systems, Roman Catholicism and
Teutonic Protestantism. The English-French conflict was the struggle between two sets of ideas
— one derived from Rome, the other from Ger-
many — for domination on the continent of North
America. In Europe those discordant ideas had
set up their respective boundaries ; in the New
World they fought not for boundaries, but for
all or nothing. The importance of this struggle
Parkman was perhaps the first fully to realize.
So great a theme imposed a grave duty.

Parkman's self-training and self-education, in

order to fulfill this duty, make the most interesting part of his life. To be sure, as a historian of past time, he had in some respects unrivaled opportunities. When Froude described Elizabethan buccaneers and Freeman the Normans of the Conquest, they were constrained to use that constructive sense which out of manuscripts, stones, and bones must create living men; but Parkman was able to live in the past, as it were, to use eyes and ears instead of his imagination. Indians, French Canadians, and American frontiersmen are his *dramatis personæ*. Fortunately for him, Indians are singularly persistent in ancestral ways, singularly incapable of adaptation to altered modes of life. What the Iroquois and the Algonkins of the seventeenth and eighteenth centuries were, such were the Snakes and the Dakotas of 1846. Likewise the French Canadian, in less degree, is rigid and obstinate; the *habitant* follows his father's footsteps with the fidelity of instinct, what he learned to do as a boy he does as a man, and unless he emigrate, he remains the same from generation to generation. Were it not for assaults from the outer world, his gun, his plough, his boat would remain as they were in Frontenac's time; so would his gayety and his politeness. In 1842 the frontiersman, also, on the borders of Vermont and Maine, was not greatly changed from his pre-

decessors of a century before. Those were still
the days before the great Irish immigration;
the frontiersmen whom Parkman met in his
undergraduate days were Yankees, handling
gun and axe very much as their forefathers
had done, theological, independent, lanky, ready,
rough, unmannerly. So, too, in the days of Parkman's roamings, the woods on the borders of
Lake George and of Lake Champlain, the forests of pine, spruce, oak, and maple, between
the White Mountains and the St. Lawrence,
had not changed since the French and Indian
wars. Here fortune favored him. Paris of the
second empire was not like the Paris of Henri
IV, London of Queen Victoria was not the
London of Charles II; but in Parkman's boyhood great tracts of the American forest were
changed only in so far as old trees had fallen to
decay and young shoots had grown up to take
their places.

All these *dramatis personœ* — the Indian, the
Canadian, the frontiersman, the forest — could
be studied in the life, and in these respects Parkman had great advantages over other historians.
These advantages he used to the full, and this
little book will, in great measure, consist merely
of Parkman's own accounts of these studies
afield. But the peculiar praise due to Parkman is that he determined, while still a lad, not

merely to write a history of the French and English war, but to be thorough in his preparation. Thoroughness ordinarily means alcoves, green shades, spectacles; with Parkman it meant not merely such "emasculate scholarship," but also hardening the muscles, aiming the rifle, riding bareback, in order to qualify the student to undertake his outdoor studies.

Fully aware of the greatness of his undertaking, ready and eager to submit to whatever schooling should best educate him, Parkman judged that history should be written with a view to being read. However accurate, however profound it be, if it remain on the shelf, whether of the bookshop or public library, it is a failure.

Parkman, too, was deeply impressed with the beauty, the color, the romance of our North American history; he believed that beauty, color, romance are not mere trappings and holiday decorations of history, but integral parts, and that to omit them is to be false to fact. To some men this world, both present and past, looks dry, dull, autumnal; to Parkman it blossomed with the bloom of spring, and he knew that, in order to gather and preserve that beauty in little black printed letters, art was necessary, and that art means training. Therefore he set himself to work to become a master of art in prose, just as he worked to become a master of art with his rifle. His diaries are sketches and studies in narrative, his reading aimed at the same end; until after long years by this patient labor he was able to produce those " glorious " and " shining " pages which, not for Mr. John Fiske alone, fill " the most brilliant and fascinating books that have been written since the days of Herodotus."

By these means, by the simple method of faithful fulfillment of his duty, Parkman accomplished his great task. " The path of duty was the path of glory," and to those who are primarily concerned with history and literature, the process of his preparation will be the most interesting period of his life; but to those who prefer manhood to history, and fortitude to fame, who are zealous for American character, to them the most brilliant parts of Parkman's story are the periods of enforced idleness. In boyhood he had some physical weakness, and throughout his life from undergraduate days till his death, there is one long record of physical ills, pausing but continuing again inexorable, of lameness that forbade walking, of almost complete blindness that forbade seeing, of insomnia that banished sleep, of pain that stopped the impatient brain.

Intense of purpose, impetuous in pursuit, intolerant of idleness, effeminacy, and indifference, emphatic in belief, dependent on himself alone, pleasant to his acquaintance, beloved by his friends, he fought his way through fifty years of achievement, a worthy comrade to those great figures in his histories whom he has lifted to fame and honor.

CHAPTER II

INDOMITABLE resolution was the chief trait in Francis Parkman. It may be somewhat fanciful to trace a single trait up the male line through eight generations, but in Parkman's case there is satisfaction in finding that this ascent takes us to Devonshire, the breeding place of indomitable spirit. Parkman's last English ancestor was William Parkman of Sidmouth, Devon, of whom we know little, yet at least that he was born and bred in Elizabethan England, in the same shire that begot Raleigh, Drake, Gilbert, Hawkins, and other freebooting buccaneers, and that he was entitled to a birthright of will and courage. William's son Elias emigrated to Massachusetts Bay prior to 1633; there he married, and begot a line of descendants, over whom — worthy people with Old Testament names — we may lightly skip to the fourth generation from the Devonshire ancestor. In that generation the twelfth child, Ebenezer, is well known by reason of a journal which he kept for many years. He graduated at Harvard College in 1721, at the age of eighteen, and three years later was elected town minister of Westborough, Massachusetts. He continued his ministry in this little town for fifty-eight years, until his death. His published journal begins abruptly on February 13, 1737, about two years after his first wife's death. The minister's second attempt at wooing is recorded thus :—

Feb. 17. Capt Foot & Sister Elizabeth & Mrs Mary Tilestone took a ride with me in a double slay at evening to Capt. Robert Sharp's at Brook-line, & Br^r Elias came to us upon my horse, after supper there. At 10 o'clock they returned in ye slay but I tarried. N. B. The discovery of my Inclinations to Capt Sharp & to Mm. By y^{eir} urgent Persuasions I tarried and lodged there. N. B. Mrs Susannah Sharp. [Mistress Susannah was twenty-one years old.] . . .

March 3^d. Towards night I rode over to Roxbury. N. B. I proceeded to Capt Sharp's. By Capt Sharp's strong Solicitation I tarried all night. N. B. Mrs Susan not very willing to think of going so far in ye Country as Westborough, &c &c &c. . . .

March 4. I returned P. M. from Town & went again to Capt Sharp's. N. B. Capt Sharp & Mm. gone to the Funeral of a Relation at Roxbury. I tarried whilst the Capt and his spouse came home. Arguments which be fruitless with Mrs Susan. I returned to Father Champney's between 8 and 9 in ye Evening.

[This rebuff was received philosophically.]

March. 18. Eve at D^r. Gott's. Mrs Gott had been very ill, but is recovering. *Mrs Hannah Breck with her*, but I spent my time with ye men. [Mistress Hannah was twenty-one years old and was a younger sister of Mrs. Gott.] . . .

March. 19. A. M. To Dr. Gott's, but a short space with Mrs Hannah. At my Request, she had (she assured me) burnt my Letters, Poems, etc . . .

March 25. I rode to Marl^b [Marlborough]. Spent ye afternoon at Dr Gott's — was at ye Coll.'s, [certain friends] but returned to Dr's. Mr Hovey there with a Bass Viol. N. B. M^{rs} H——h B——k at ye Dr's still. Our conversation of a piece with what it used to be. I mark her admirable Conduct, her Prudence and wisdom, her good manners and her distinguishing Respectfulness to me w^c [which] accompany her Denyals. After it grew late in ye Even'g, I rode home to Westb., through the Dark and the Dirt but cheerfully and comfortably (comparatively). . . .

April. 1. At Eve, I was at Dr. Gotts, Mrs H——h was thought to be gone up to Mr Week's or Capt Williams, with design to lodge there, but she returned to ye Doctor's. And she gave me her Company till it was very late. Her Conversation was very Friendly, and with divers expressions of Singular and Peculiar Regard.

Memorand^m, Oscul: But she cannot yield to being a step mother. — I lodged there, and with g^{rt} Satisfaction & Composure.

The two were married in September and lived very contentedly, yet an entry on the anniversary

of his first wife's death, forty-three years afterwards, betrays the fact that she was his real
love.

The records of this diary, brief and matter-of-
fact as they are, bring a vivid picture of the simple, frugal country life of the time. The minister's salary was eked out, or perhaps wholly paid,
by the labor and the gifts of his congregation.
For instance, in October, the month after his
marriage, occur the entries: —

6. Young men came to gather my corn. Set
   y^m to work. . . .
   About 18 or 20 hands husked out all my
   Corn. N. B. in my absence Winter Apples
   gathered in. . . .
7. Mr John Pratt brought home my cyder which
   he had made. . . .
12. Mr Lock came & carried in Corn. . . .
13. At evening Br^r Hicks helped in more
    Corn. . . .
14. Jon^n Rogers got in Pumpkins, & ye re-
    mainder of ye Corn. . . .
15. Noah How helped in with Turnips & some
    of ye Potatoes. . . .

In this Westborough minister we have a typi-
cal instance of the moral and intellectual life of
New England in that awkward age of transition
preceding the Revolutionary War, during which
Massachusetts and its fellow settlements were
passing from boyhood to manhood. Here were

still the narrow horizon, the scant intellectual
resources, and the tough conservatism of Puritan
days, but also that rigid sentiment of duty and
that desire to do well and to make the most of
granted opportunities, which have made New
England what she has been. Francis Parkman
and his great-grandfather, with the differences
appropriate to their generations, held in common this belief, that life is man's opportunity to
try his mettle, to measure himself against adverse
forces, and to determine whether he or they be
the stronger and more resolute. The minister's
intellectual life was limited, but not willfully limited. He endeavored to acquaint himself with
a wider range of thought than ordinarily found
its way into Westborough. On the 13th of July,
1779, is this entry: —

Mr Adams has brought home to me at length
Sir Wm Temple. He has led me also into an Ex-
change of a number of Books viz. For Voetius 3
vols, I have Dr Stanhope's Thomas a Kempis D^r
Calamy, of Vows : Horneck's crucified Jesus, &
Dr Goodman's Old Religion. For Monsr Boi-
leau's 2^d vol and Mat Prior's Works 2 vols, I
have Dr Hammond's Annotations in large Folio.
For the Lay Monastery, I have Herman Prudence, & Three Select Pieces of Mr Thos. Shepherd. For Comin's Real Christian, unbound, I
gave him at his proposal a Pound of Sugar. He
presented me a Pamphlet, Dr Gibson on ye Sin-
fulness of Neglecting and profaning the Lord's

Day. N. B. I returned him Drexilius on Eternity.

The Rev. Ebenezer Parkman died in his eightieth year. His successor in our story is Samuel Parkman, his son, a prosperous merchant and prominent citizen of Boston. He began life a poor boy — his father's purse was too light to pay college fees; "he did his own lugging," as he said in his opulent age, and when he came to die left a large property, a portion of which enabled our historian to devote his life to a non-money-getting pursuit.

Several of Samuel's brothers displayed their New England spirit: William, at the age of seventeen, served in a Massachusetts regiment during the French war, keeping a diary, — a family trait; Breck, a minute-man, marched from Westborough to Lexington on the 19th of April, 1775 ; a third brother also served in the Continental Army.

Samuel's son Francis, father of the historian, was born in 1788, and graduated at Harvard College in 1807. Destined for the pulpit, he studied theology under William Ellery Channing, and, in obedience to the moral law which then prevailed in Boston, became a Unitarian. He took to his grandfather's calling, and in 1813 was ordained pastor of the New North Church, where he remained throughout his active life, and

until his son Francis had grown to manhood.
He was a kind, benevolent man, esteemed an eloquent preacher with "a special gift in prayer,"
and took a prominent place among his fellow
clergy.   For thirty years he was one of the
overseers of Harvard College, and presented a
sum of money towards the endowment of the
Parkman Professorship of Theology.   His conversation was well spiced with wit and humor;
anecdotes of his high spirits in talk are still
remembered. He possessed a tenacious conservatism, and yet in spite of this their common trait,
he was very unlike his more serious son, and
did not sympathize with his literary ambition.
Notwithstanding their differences and fundamental lack of sympathy, he was a good father, and
did his duty as he saw it towards his son. To
him a noble eulogy has been paid, " he was particularly kind to the unattractive." His house
was open and hospitable, and many guests of
note in their day were entertained there. Happy
memories long lingered on of "that blessed 5
Bowdoin Square house and its radiant inmates
. . . that spacious, hospitable mansion graced
by a household into which it was an unspeakable
privilege for a child to have been born."

Francis Parkman resembled his mother more
than his father. She was a tender, loving, dutiful, unselfish woman, a great favorite in the large

family circle, whose interest in life did not often travel beyond the threshold of her home; she, too, was of Puritan stock, having descended from the Cottons, and was endowed with character, reserve, simplicity, and a certain shrewd humor. Frank was like her in many ways, and the older he grew the more the expression of his face became like hers.

Their children were Francis, Caroline, Mary, Eliza, and John Eliot; Mr. Parkman had also an older child, Sarah, by an earlier marriage.

CHAPTER III

FRANCIS PARKMAN, the historian, was born September 16, 1823, in a house on a little street which runs across the northern slope of Beacon Hill, then known as Somerset Place, now Allston Street. The Rev. Mr. Parkman lived there until Frank was six or seven years old, when he moved to a larger house, No. 1 Green Street. Town life was not suited to the boy; his health was delicate, and his woodland nature, unsatisfied with the resources of his father's yard, rebelled against the cramping streets and alleys of the city. He went to Medford to live with his mother's father, Mr. Nathaniel Hall, who, having retired from business, kept a farm about a mile from the village. Frank, as day-scholar, attended a boarding-school for boys and girls kept by Mr. John Angier, a graduate of Harvard College. Others liked the school but Frank did not, and since with boys as well as with men learning waits upon liking, he learned little; but he was constant in his attendance at another school, adapted to his disposition and well equipped to teach him the

beginnings of that knowledge which was to make
him famous, — the school of the woods. At the
distance of a few rods from Mr. Hall's farm lay
the Middlesex Fells, a capital wilderness. This
tract of six or seven square miles, of rocky,
barren soil, retained no marks of certain ancient
and vain attempts at cultivation except some old
apple-trees and tumble-down stone walls. It had
ponds, — one, half a mile across; a hill hundreds
of feet high; heaths, glens, dales, crags; thickets
full of trees too big to clasp, jungles of under-
brush; rotten stumps to be smashed by a battle-
axe; thick moss to drive a spear into; mud to
smear new clothes from head to foot; glorious
varieties of dirt, and all the riches of a wilderness. In this great school and playground the
boy spent all the time he could save from Mr.
Angier, gathering birds' eggs, setting traps for
squirrels and woodchucks, catching snakes, or
creeping on his belly with bow and arrow to
get a shot at a robin, which, in spite of the
utmost ingenuity of approach, by some chance,
miraculous in the hunter's eyes, almost always
succeeded in flying away unharmed. These days
of rambling through this trackless forest were
among the happiest of his life; he always liked
to look back upon them. No doubt they owe a
part of their joyous colors to the black background of Mr. Angier's school. In spite of a

pure and honest purpose of play, the roamings in Middlesex Fells provided Frank with some knowledge; here he began to make a collection of minerals, which gradually grew until in course of time it became worthy to be presented to the Harvard Natural History Society; here he hacked, picked, and plucked trees and flowers till he found to his surprise that he had learned a little botany; here he acquired a love of plants which in later days, when ill health chained him to a garden chair, opened to him the vegetable kingdom; here he picked up, by tail and hind legs, newts, frogs, pollywogs; and made close acquaintance with all kinds of little living creatures.

> Now things there are that, upon him who sees,
> A strong vocation lay; and strains there are
> That whoso hears shall hear for evermore.

So, in these early days, one may discover the bent of Parkman's mind towards the forest; here, to quote his words, " he became enamoured of the woods," and plainly showed that inclination towards outdoor schooling and self-instruction in nature to which he gave loose rein in college.

After four years at Medford Frank went back to Boston to live with his parents. In spite of active life in the country, his body was not robust, and perhaps physical inability to join in athletic games was the cause that turned the boy's attention to the indoor diversion of chemistry. There was a shed at the rear of the house which his father converted into a laboratory, and here Frank shut himself up too steadily for the good of his health, and devoted himself to chemical experiments. In his fragmentary autobiography he says that he accomplished nothing beyond poisoning himself with noxious gases and scorching his skin with explosions; but probably he did well enough, his years considered, for his masterful disposition always determined to have the upper hand in a grapple with any study to which he turned. He impressed his comrades with respect for his skill, and succeeded in making an electrical machine with which he administered shocks to sundry rash boys and girls. He also entertained himself and his friends with lectures, duly announced by printed bills.

In the autobiography an extreme seriousness, begotten in great part by long illness, seems to have cast a shadow backward over his youth, or at least to have left the man somewhat oblivious, or careless, of the lightheartedness of his boyhood, which, in fact, had its fair share of gayety. The records of his childhood indicate jollity and happiness; and he would have been most ready to acknowledge this and render thanks, but in his little memoir his mind was fixed upon the lessons which others might learn from his life, and therefore he passed by those details which in that view were irrelevant. For instance, at the age of thirteen, Frank and his companions turned the loft of a barn behind the house into a theatre. They were the scene-painters, costumers, and in part, perhaps, playwrights, as well as the company of players. Sometimes, in moments of greater ambition, they borrowed costumes from a theatre. Here is a copy of a play-bill, printed by one of the company: —

STAR THEATRE.

On Wednesday, Feb. 22, will be presented for the first time in this Theatre, (with new scenery, &c.,) the celebrated play of

MY FELLOW CLERK!

Mr. Hooker - - - - - -	F. MINOT
Tactic - - - - - -	WM. MARSTON
Victim - - - - - -	Q. A. SHAW
Fag - - - - - -	F. PARKMAN
Mr. Knitbrow - - - - -	C. DEXTER
Bailiff - - - - - -	P. DEXTER

AFTER WHICH

A COMIC SONG!!

BY MR. MARSTON.

To conclude with some interesting experiments in Chemistry by Mr. Parkman, being his first appearance as a Chemist.

☞ Doors open at 1-4 before 3. Curtain rises at 1-4 after 3.

The company gave performances on Wednesday and Saturday afternoons, and acted before their public for a year or two. Frank commonly played women's parts, and trailed calico skirts across the boards with great effect.

About the year 1837 the Rev. Francis Parkman left Green Street, and moved his family into the "hospitable house," No. 5 Bowdoin Square, which his father, Samuel Parkman the merchant, had built. This was a large, handsome house, in the colonial style, adorned with pilasters, which rose in dignity from the first story to the roof, with a round porch held up by Doric pillars; there was a grass plot in front, and a general appearance of prosperity. In the rear was a large paved court, and beyond that a garden sloping away in terraces, where pear-trees did their best to reconcile boyhood to the abstinences of town life. The house and its yard were characteristic of Boston, displaying the urban pleasures of retired leisure, full of unostentatious ease; it marked the change which had come over the commonwealth since the days when her clerical aristocracy dwelt in little wooden houses like that of the Rev. Ebenezer Parkman at Westborough.

Frank went to school under Mr. Gideon Thayer, and seems to have studied with diligence Latin, Greek, English, and the rudiments of science. He himself wrote long afterward concerning his experience at this school : —

When fourteen or fifteen years old I had the good luck to be under the direction of Mr. William Russell, a teacher of excellent literary tastes and acquirements. It was his constant care to teach the boys of his class to write good and easy English. One of his methods was to give us lists of words to which we were required to furnish as many synonyms as possible, distinguishing their various shades of meaning. He also encouraged us to write translations, in prose and verse, from Virgil and Homer, insisting on idiomatic English, and criticising in his gentle way anything flowery and bombastic. At this time I read a good deal of poetry, and much of it remains *verbatim* in my memory. As it included Milton and other classics, I am confident that it has been of service to me in the matter of style.

He had a boyish fancy for poetry, and put into verse the scenes of the Tournament at Ashby-de-la-Zouch in "Ivanhoe," which he and other boys declaimed with the dauntless declamation of boyhood. Perhaps the curious may here discover a touch of that fondness for rhetoric — the heart of the boy lasting on into manhood — that willingness to express with purple and gold the exaltation of a high mood which stayed with him always.

CHAPTER IV

COLLEGE

FRANK entered the class of 1844 at the age of seventeen. Harvard College in those days was as different from the University of to-day as the rivulet from the river. There were sixty or seventy students in the freshman class; most of them about sixteen years old. Frank must have been one of the older boys. The instruction was scarcely more advanced than in a good school to-day. President Quincy was not the executive head of a great corporation; he was the shepherd of his flock, the father of his children. The yard served as a garden for Holworthy, Massachusetts, Hollis, Stoughton, University, the Law School, and the Chapel. Football was played for fun or some such old-fashioned reason on the Delta, by all the boys who cared to take off their coats and kick. There were no boat-races except such as random students rowed, in antique craft, against each other; so that a lad, like Frank, bent upon gaining muscular strength, was obliged to divide his times for exercise be-

tween walking, riding, and dumb-bells. In social
matters numbers were too few to permit the
sections and subsections which now divide undergraduates into all the genera and species
between the grinds, with nose to book, and the
groups of young Pendennises — lilies of the field
— who adorn Randolph and Claverly. But the
college, both as a place of study and as an undergraduate world, by its very incompleteness, probably served Frank's purposes as well as the present
university would have done. In like manner as
when a boy at Medford he had learned more
from his own lessons in the Middlesex Fells than
in Mr. Angier's class-room, so in Cambridge he
continued to be his own teacher, and pursued a
system that, if it had been followed in moder-
ation, would have well fitted him to do his life's
work. In his freshman year that life's work
was haunting the background of his mind, not
as yet in the definite form which it took a little
later, but rather as a strong attraction which
drew him towards the forest, and persuaded him
that the way to woo her with success was to ac-
quire strength of limb and understanding of
woodcraft.

There was a holiday side to his undergraduate
life ; but usually Frank was going about his own
business in his impetuous Devon fashion ; he
tried to *cram* endurance by long walks taken at

a pace far too rapid to make his companionship
comfortable, and spent long hours into the night
reading English classics and all sorts of books
concerning American Indians. He avoided all
interests and occupations that did not feed the
sacred flame of his forest love.

Prior to this time Frank had nursed a whim
for poetry, and had entertained a notion that he
might become a poet or a devotee of literature,
half poet, half man-of-letters, for he was fond of
poetry and had a knack for rhyming. Traces of
this taste lasted up to the year after graduation,
when he published in "The Knickerbocker" a
poem of several hundred verses called "The New
Hampshire Ranger." But the whim for poetry,
like the caprice for chemistry, was quickly vanquished by the real interest of his life; and
before the end of his freshman year all thought
of poetry as a serious pursuit had passed out of
his head.

The real business of the year began with the
summer vacation, when he took his gun and
fishing-rod, and, in the company of his classmate, Daniel Denison Slade, a tall and athletic
young man, set forth on what might be called a
field course in American history. In his autobiography Parkman says, with happy recollection:
"For the student there is, in its season, no better place than the saddle, and no better com-

panion than the rifle or the oar." He kept a full diary, from which lack of space forbids quotation. The two went on foot, with an occasional "lift," to the White Mountains and adjacent regions, and Parkman enjoyed himself immensely. This year was the determining period of his life, for in it he resolved to devote himself to the task of writing the story of French colonization and empire in North America, which he at last completely accomplished after, as has been aptly said, "a half century of conflict."

We need not suppose that Frank sat in Massachusetts Hall, like Gibbon on the steps of the Capitol, and at a definite hour made up his mind to write a history ; but in his sophomore year "the plan was in its most essential features formed," and the designer immediately set to work to carry out his plan : —

Before the end of the sophomore year my various schemes had crystallized into a plan of writing a story of what was then known as the "Old French War," — that is, the war that ended in the conquest of Canada, — for here, as it seemed to me, the forest drama was more stirring and the forest stage more thronged with appropriate actors than in any other passage of our history. It was not till some years later that I enlarged the plan to include the whole course of the American conflict between France and England, or, in other words, the history of the

American forest; for this was the light in which I regarded it. My theme fascinated me, and I was haunted with wilderness images day and night.

There are few records, if there are any, of so large a purpose, conceived so young, and with such constancy executed; and when we consider the pain, the attacks of almost complete blindness, the physical infirmities that barred his way, we may excuse those who in an outburst of American enthusiasm challenge the world to show such another hero in the world of letters since the death of Cervantes.

Frank took his share in the ordinary college life of young gentlemen; he was a member of the " Institute of 1770," of the " Hasty Pudding," of a little and very intimate group called the Chit-Chat Club, whenever the mysterious letters C. C. were allowed to assume all their significance. He was a fair student, too, taking certain minor academical honors. At his commons he got the ironical nickname, " The Loquacious; " he was never that, though all life long he enjoyed talking with his friends. He was good company, vigorous even fiery in argument, entertaining, an excellent story-teller, of lively imagination and well provisioned memory, and on the whole was much more sought than seeking. Boy and man, he was a modest, unassuming, resolute, high-minded gentleman.

CHAPTER V

EXPLORATIONS

THE college term ended in July, and Frank lost no time in setting out upon his summer excursion in company with his friend, Henry Orne White:

July 15th, '42. Albany. Left Boston this morning at half-past six, for this place, where I am now happily arrived, it being the longest day's journey I ever made. For all that, I would rather have come thirty miles by stage than the whole distance by railroad, for of all methods of progressing, that by steam is incomparably the most disgusting. . . .

July 16th. Caldwell. This morning we left Albany — which I devoutly hope I may never see again — in the cars, for Saratoga. . . . After passing the inclined plane and riding a couple of hours, we reached the valley of the Mohawk and Schenectady. I was prepared for something filthy in the last mentioned venerable town, but for nothing quite so disgusting as the reality. Canal docks, full of stinking water, superannuated rotten canal-boats, and dirty children and pigs paddling about formed the foreground of the delicious picture, while in the rear was a mass of tumbling houses and sheds, bursting

open in all directions, green with antiquity,
dampness, and lack of paint. Each house had
its peculiar dunghill, with the group of reposing
hogs. In short, London itself could exhibit nothing much nastier. . . . Finally reached Saratoga, having traveled latterly at the astonishing
rate of about seven miles an hour. "Caldwell
stage ready." We got our baggage on board, and
I found time to enter one or two of the huge
hotels. After perambulating the entries filled
with sleek waiters and sneaking fops, dashing
through the columned porticoes and inclosures,
drinking some of the water and spitting it out
again in high disgust, I sprang onto the stage,
cursing Saratoga and all New York. . . .

Dined at the tavern, and rode on. Country
dreary as before ; the driver one of the best of
his genus I ever met. He regaled me as we rode
on with stories of his adventures with deer,
skunks, and passengers. A mountain heaved up
against the sky some distance before us, with
a number of small hills stretching away on each
hand, all wood-crowned to the top. . . . But as
we drew near, the mountain in front assumed a
wilder and a loftier aspect. Crags started from
its woody sides and leaned over a deep valley
below. "What mountain is that?" "That 'ere
is French Mounting," — the scene of one of the
most desperate and memorable battles in the old
French War. As we passed down the valley,
the mountain rose above the forest half a mile
on our right, while a hill on the left, close to the
road, formed the other side. The trees flanked
the road on both sides. In a little opening in

the woods, a cavity in the ground with a pile of
stones at each end marked the spot where was
buried that accomplished warrior and gentleman,
Colonel Williams, whose bones, however, have
since been removed. Farther on is the rock on
the right where he was shot, having mounted it
on the look-out — an event which decided the
day; the Indians and English broke and fled at
once. Still farther on is the scene of the third
tragedy of that day, when the victorious French,
having been in their turn, by a piece of good
luck, beaten by the valorous Johnson at his in-
trenchment by the lake, were met at this place
on their retreat by McGinnis, and almost cut to
pieces. Bloody Pond, a little slimy dark sheet
of stagnant water, covered with weeds and pond-
lilies and shadowed by the gloomy forest around
it, is the place where hundreds of dead bodies
were flung after the battle, and where the bones
still lie. A few miles farther, and Lake George
lay before us, the mountains and water confused
and indistinct in the mist. We rode into Caldwell, took supper — a boat — and then a bed.

July 17th. Caldwell. The tavern is full of
fashionable New Yorkers — all of a piece.
Henry and myself both look like the Old Nick,
and are evidently looked upon in a manner corresponding. I went this morning to see William
Henry. The old fort is much larger than I had
thought; the earthen mounds cover many acres.
It stood on the southwest extremity of the lake,
close by the water. The enterprising genius of
the inhabitants has made a road directly through
the ruins, and turned bastion, moat, and glacis

into a flourishing cornfield, so that the spot so celebrated in our colonial history is now scarcely to be distinguished. Large trees are growing on the untouched parts, especially on the embankment along the lake shore. In the rear, a hundred or two yards distant, is a gloomy wood of pines, where the lines of Montcalm can easily be traced. A little behind these lines is the burying place of the French who fell during that memorable siege. The marks of a thousand graves can be seen among the trees, which of course have sprung up since. . . . One of Montcalm's lines ran northwest of the tavern toward the mountains. Two or three years ago in digging for some purpose, a great quantity of deer, bear, and moose bones were found here, with arrows and hatchets, which the tavern keeper thinks mark the place of some Indian feast. The spikes and timbers of sunken vessels may be seen in strong sunlight, when the water is still, at the bottom of the lake, along the southern beach. Abercrombie sunk his boats here. There are remains of batteries on French Mt., and the mountain north of it, I suppose to command the road from Ft. Edward. This evening visited the French graves. I write this at camp, July 18th. Just turned over my ink bottle and spilt all the ink.

July 18th. Camp at Diamond Island. Set out this morning in an excellent boat, hired at Caldwell. . . . We landed occasionally, and fished as we went along. About ten o'clock stretched across Middle Bay and got bread, pork, and potatoes at a farmhouse, with which and our fish we regaled ourselves at a place half way down the Bay. Here I wrote my journal for yesterday; we slept an hour or two on the ground, bathed, and read Goldsmith, which Henry brought in his knapsack. At three we proceeded to explore the bay to its bottom, returned, made for Diamond Island, which is now uninhabited, prepared our camp and went to sleep.

July 19th. I woke this morning about as weak and spiritless as well could be. All enterprise and activity was fairly gone; how I cannot tell, but I cursed the weather as the most probable cause. Such has been the case with me, to a greater or less degree, for the last three or four weeks. Rowed to-day along the eastern shore. . . . But everything was obscured with mist. When the wind became less violent we rowed to an island in the middle, where we are now encampéd.

Wednesday, July 20th. Entered the narrows this morning, and rowed among all the islands and along all the shores. . . . We passed under Black Mt., whose precipices and shaggy woods wore a very savage and impressive aspect in that peculiar weather, and kept down the lake seven miles to Sabbath Day Pt. High and steep mountains flanked the lake the whole way. In front, at some distance they seemed to slope gradually away, and a low green point, with an ancient dingy house upon it, closed the perspective. This was Sabbath Day Pt., the famous landing place of many a huge army. . . . We ran our boat on the beach of Sabbath Day Pt. and asked lodging at the house. An old woman, after a multitude of guesses and calculations, guessed as how

she could accommodate us with a supper and a
bed, though she could n't say nohow how we
should like it, seeing as how she warn't used to
visitors. The house was an old, rickety, dingy
shingle palace, with a potato garden in front,
hogs perambulating the outhouses, and a group
of old men and women engaged in earnest conversation in the tumble-down portico. The chief
figure was an old gray-haired man, tall and spare
as a skeleton, who was giving some advice to a
chubby old lady about her corns.

"Well now," said the old lady, "I declare
they hurt me mighty bad."

"I 'll give you something to cure them right
off."

"What is it? I hope it ain't snails. I always
hated snails since I was a baby, but I 've heerd
say they are better for corns nor anything else
at all," etc., etc.

The old man was a revolutionary pensioner,
Captain Patchin by name, and stout-hearted,
hale, and clever by nature. . . .

Thursday, 21st. Fished for bass. . . . We
caught fish enough, landed, and with Myrtle
Bailey, one of the young Brobdignagians, a simple, good-natured, strong-handed, grinning son
of the plough, set out on a rattlesnake hunt on
the mountain back of the Point. . . . We soon
reached a still higher point, which commanded
the noblest view of the lake I had yet seen.
There would be no finer place for gentlemen's
seats than this; but now, for the most part, it is
occupied by a race of boors about as uncouth,
mean, and stupid as the hogs they seem chiefly to

delight in. The captain's household is an exception. . . . Afternoon: Fished again. Evening: Fished again, and caught a very large bass — all in company of Myrtle, whose luck not satisfying him, he cursed the "darned cussed fish" in most fervent style.

Friday, 22nd. Left old Patchin's this morning. . . . We broke an oar when within about half a mile, and paddled to shore with great difficulty through a considerable surf which was dashing against the beach like the waves of the ocean. We found the post-office a neat little tavern kept by one Garfield, entitled the Judge. He referred us to a carpenter, who promised to make an oar forthwith, and worked six hours upon it, an interval which I spent chiefly in wandering through the country. . . . Returned to Garfield's, and found there Mr. Gibbs with his wife the "vocalist." Presently the man appeared with the oar finished. White undertook to pay him with a Naumkeag Bank bill — the only bills he had. "Don't know nothing about that money: wait till Garfield comes and he 'll tell whether it 's genuine or not." "There 's the paper," said I; "look and see." He looked — all was right. "Well, are you satisfied?" "How do I know but what that ere bill is counterfeit. It has a sort of counterfeit look about it to my eyes. Deacon, what do you say to it?" The deacon put on his spectacles, held the bill to the light, turned it this way and that, tasted of it, and finally pronounced that according to his calculation it was good. But the carpenter was not contented. "'Bijah, you 're a judge of bills;

what do you think?" 'Bijah, after a long examination, gave as his opinion that it was counterfeit. All parties were beginning to wax wroth, when the judge entered and decided that the bill was good.

We pushed from the beach and steered down the lake, passed some islands, and beheld in front of us two grim mountains, standing guard over a narrow strait of dark water between. . . . One of these mountains was the noted Rogers Slide, the other, almost as famous, Anthony's Nose, Jr. Both had witnessed, in their day, the passage of twenty vast armies in the strait between; and there was not an echo on either but had answered to the crack of rifles and screams of dying men. We skirted the base of the Nose — for which sentimental designation I could find no manner of reason — till we arrived opposite the perpendicular front of his savage neighbor. About a mile of water was between. We ran the boat ashore on a shelving rock, and looked for a camping place among the precipices. We found, to our surprise, at the side of a steep rock, amid a growth of cedars and hemlocks, a little inclosure of logs, like a diminutive log cabin without a roof. We made beds in it of hemlock boughs — there was just space enough — brought up our baggage and guns, ate what supper we had, and essayed to go asleep. But we might as well have slept under a shower-bath of melted iron. In that deep sheltered spot, bugs, mosquitoes, and "no-see-ems" swarmed innumerable. . . . This morning was the most toilsome we have passed. The wind was dead against us;

the waves ran with a violence I had never seen
before except on the ocean. It required the
full force of both arms to hold the boat on her
course. If we slackened our efforts for a single
moment, she would spin round and drive backwards. We had about twelve miles to row under
these agreeable auspices.

"Well," said White, "you call this fun, do
you? To be eaten by bugs all night and work
against head winds all day is n't according to my
taste, whatever you may think of it."

"Are you going to back out?" said I.

"Back out, yes; when I get into a bad scrape,
I back out of it as quick as I can," and so he
went on with marvelous volubility to recount his
grievances. Lake George he called a "scrubby
looking place," — said there was no fishing in it
— he hated camping, and would have no more of
it, — he would n't live so for another week to save
his life, etc., etc. Verily, what is one man's meat
is another man's poison. What troubles me
more than his treachery to our plans is his want
of cash, which will make it absolutely necessary
to abandon our plan of descending through
Maine. His scruples I trust to overcome in time.

We reached Patchin's at last, and were welcomed by the noble old veteran as cordially as if
we were his children. We dined, and sat in his
portico, listening to his stories. He is eighty-
six. . . .

We consigned our boat to the captain, to be
carried back to Caldwell, and got on a stage we
found at the wharf, which carried us to the village
of Ty. [Ticonderoga]. It is a despicable manu-

facturing place, straggling and irregular,—mills, houses, and heaps of lumber,—situated in a broad valley with the outlet of Lake George running through the middle, a succession of fierce rapids, with each its saw-mill. I bespoke me here a pair of breeches of a paddy tailor who asked me if I did not work on board the steamboat, a question which aggravated me not a little. I asked a fellow the way to the fort. "Well," said he, "I've heerd of such a place, seems to me, but I never seen it, and could n't tell ye where it be." "You must be an idiot," thought I; but I found his case by no means singular. At last I got the direction, and walked about two miles before I saw the remains of a high earthen parapet with a ditch running through a piece of woods for a great distance. This, I suppose, was the place where the French beat off Abercrombie's army. Farther on, in a great plain scantily covered with wood, were breastworks and ditches in abundance running in all directions, which I took for the work of Amherst's besieging army. Still farther were two or three square redoubts. At length, mounting a little hill, a cluster of gray ruined walls, like an old chateau, with mounds of earth and heaps of stone about them, appeared crowning an eminence in front. When I reached them, I was astonished at the extent of the ruins. Thousands of men might have encamped in the area. All around were ditches, of such depth that it would be death to jump down, with walls of masonry sixty feet high. Ty stands on a promontory, with Champlain on one side and the outlet of Lake George on the other; his

cannon commanded the passage completely. At
the very extremity is the oldest part of the for-
tress, a huge mass of masonry, with walls sinking
sheer down to the two lakes. All kinds of weeds
and vines are clambering over them. The senseless blockheads in the neighborhood have stolen
tons upon tons of the stone to build their walls
and houses of, — may they meet their reward.

Wednesday, 27th. In Yankee land again,
thank heaven. Left Ty this noon — after going
over the ruins again — in one of the great Champlain steamboats, and reached Burlington at
night. Visited the college. It was term time
and the students were lounging about the ugly
buildings or making abortive attempts at revelry
in their rooms. The air was full of their diabolical attempts at song. We decided that they were
all green, and went back, drawing comparisons
by the way between the University of Vermont
and old Harvard.

Thursday, 28th. Left Burlington this morning, knapsack on back, for Canada. . . . We
followed the road through a deep wood, and
when we emerged from it the village of Cambridge lay before us, twenty-five miles from
Burlington. We stopped here for the night.

Friday, 29th. From Cambridge we walked on
to Johnson. . . . At Johnson we took the stage
for Stanstead, in Canada. The " stage " was a
broken down carryall, into which six passengers with luggage were stowed, and the thing
set in motion — under the auspicious influences
of two sick horses — over a road of diabolical
roughness.

Saturday, July 30th. Stanstead, Canada. Resumed our journey this morning in the same "stage." . . . The place is large, with several handsome churches. There was nothing in particular to distinguish it from a flourishing Yankee town till we pulled up at the tavern, where were two or three British soldiers, in their undress, standing on the porch. There were thirteen of them, with a cornet, quartered at the house, as there now are in all the border villages. They were good-looking fellows, civil enough; natives of the provinces. They were gathered round a fire in the barroom, smoking and telling stories, or else indulging in a little blackguardism and knocking one another about the room. They invited us to drink with them, and the liquor being mead — the house being temperance — we consented. They have just clubbed to buy a barrel of cider.

Sunday, July 31st. Last night we were kept awake by the din of bugles and drums with which the soldiers were regaling themselves in the entry, singing and dancing meanwhile. This morning rainy and dismal. Soldiers and all gathered round the stove in the barroom. Their conversation was about as decent and their jokes as good as those of a convocation of Harvard students. . . .

We set out on foot for Canaan, which promised land some told us was twenty miles distant, while others reckoned it thirty. The road for a few miles was good, but we were soon compelled to leave it and take a path through the woods. A beautiful river — smooth and rapid — ran across the road under a bridge of logs, between forest-covered banks. Not far from Stanstead we had crossed a furious stream, answering to the sentimental designation of the Nigger River. We had walked but a few miles when the clouds settled on the hills and it began to rain. We went to a log cabin for shelter. The " old man " was frank and hospitable like all his genus I ever met, and the " old woman " — a damsel of twenty-two, who sat combing her hair in the corner — extremely sprightly and talkative. She seemed somewhat moved at heart by the doctrines of Miller, whose apostles are at work all along the Vermont frontier. We abused that holy man to our content, and, the rain ceasing, left the cabin. Soon after leaving this place we entered the aforementioned path through the woods. Now and then there would be a clearing with its charred stumps, its boundary of frowning wood, and its log cabin, but for the most part the forest was in its original state. The average depth of the mud in the path was one foot. . . . The day was showery, with occasional glimpses of the sun ; so that we were alternately wet and dry. . . . Thence passing various dwellings, and holding various colloquies with the inmates, we reached Canaan, and a good tavern. The landlord has quartered [us] in his hall — large as a barn. Canaan is a microscopic village, the houses scattered through a valley among low mountains, all covered with forest. We saw here the Connecticut for the first time — rapid and full of rocks and foam. We follow its banks to-morrow.

CHAPTER VI

THE MARGALLOWAY

TUESDAY (2d). Weather still cold and blustering. Thick clouds all over the sky. Set out after breakfast for the Connecticut Lake, twenty miles distant. . . . White seems to have lost his apathy and is now quite ready to proceed. Reports of the Margalloway trout have inflamed him. The road was still hilly, narrow, and great part of the way flanked by woods. The valley of the river looked, as it always does, rich and fertile, but the hills and mountains around presented one broad unbroken expanse of forest, made the more sombre by the deep shadows of the clouds. In the afternoon we reached a hill-top and a vast panorama of mountains and forests lay before us. A glistening spot of water, some miles to the north, girt with mountains which sloped down to it from all sides with a smooth and gradual descent, was Lake Connecticut. As far as we could see, one mountain of peculiar form rose above the rest which we afterward learned was the Camel's Hump. Passing a river with rapids and a saw-mill, at the end of the day we reached the lake, where are two houses, Barns' and Abbot's. There are steep rapids at the outlet, with a mill, of course. We went to Abbot's house, and asked for lodging and a supper. . . . Abbot says that one of his relations, Kenfield by name, fought at William Henry, and, at the massacre, seeing an Indian about to strip a fallen officer, caught him, raised him in his arms, and dashed him to the ground with such violence as to make him senseless. Our host greatly exults in the bodily strength for which his family have been eminent — he himself noway dishonors his race in that respect.

Wednesday (3d). . . . We lived in backwoods style to-day — sugarless tea for dinner — water drunk from a mug common to all the company, etc. We liked it — I did, at least. Abbot sat cobbling his shoe against his projected expedition towards evening, but as I came up he turned round and remarked that he was not a disciple of St. Crispin but only an occasional follower. As I was marveling at this unexpected display of erudition, his wife thrust her head from the door, and exclaimed, " Here, supper's ready. Where's that other man gone to ? " We accepted the elegant invitation and walked in, where Abbot astonished us still more by comparing the democrat levelers to Procrustes, who wished to reduce all men to the same dimensions by his iron bedstead. All this was while he was squatting on his home-made chair, one leg cocked into the air, shirt-sleeves rolled up to his elbows, bushy hair straggling over his eyes, and eating meanwhile as if his life depended on his efforts. I have since found that he has read a vast amount of history, ancient and modern, and various other things — all fact, however, for fiction, he says, he cannot bear. When twenty-five — he is now thirty-six — he defended himself against a good lawyer in a court, and won his case, his opponent confessing himself outmatched by Abbot's general knowledge and quick memory.

Thursday (4th). Started this morning to strike the Little Margalloway. We proceeded first towards the north, with a path for the first few miles. It soon failed us, and we had to force our way through tangled woods. . . . White had hurt his foot the day before and constantly lagged behind, so that we had to wait for him, every minute the prey of torturing flies. At length the ascent of the first mountain made the way still more laborious. When at length we reached the top we could see nothing on account of the thick growth of trees. We passed through a singular piece of boggy ground, of an oblong shape, inclosed in a fringe of cedars rising one above the other, all hung with tassels of white moss. There was another place, partially open, near the summit. As we passed it, a large buck sprang from the ground, and leaped with long bounds down the mountain, before my rifle was at my shoulder. We heard him crashing the boughs far below. In this spot were several springs of cold water, in broad cup-shaped hollows in the ground, which had probably attracted the deer. We went down the mountain and found a little stream flowing through the valley at the bottom. Both Abbot and myself were for proceeding, but White said he could not go on on account of his foot; so we found a convenient spot and encamped. It was by the stream, flowing half concealed beneath brushwood and fallen trees, in a thick growth of firs, spruces, and birches. We made a fire, and proceeded to cook our supper. We had brought with us seven pounds of bread, six and a half of rice, and a quantity of butter. We had beside about an ounce of tea, and salt, of course.

We made our fire in the middle of the grove, cut spruce boughs for a bed, lay down on our blankets, and with our knives speedily made way with a mess of rice placed on a broad piece of birch bark amongst us. Then we heaped new wood on the fire, and lay down again, cooled by a gentle rain which just now began to fall. The fire blazed up a column of bright flame, and flung its light deep into the recesses of the woods. In the morning we breakfasted on rice, bread, and tea without sugar and cream, and then— Friday — prepared to resume our course. . . . After journeying many hours in this painful style, we heard the plunging of waters in a valley below us, and joyfully turned towards the sound. We had struck a branch of the Little Margalloway. White's lameness seemed mysteriously to leave him; he seized his fishing tackle and rushed up and down the rocks, pulling a trout from every deep hole and the foot of every waterfall. I soon followed his example. Abbot built a fire by the bank and cooked our fish. We made a plentiful dinner, and then began to follow downward the course of the stream. . . .

Saturday, Aug. 5th. The morning opened with a grand council. How were we to get down the

river? Abbot could make a raft, thought he
could make a spruce canoe, and was certain that
he could make a log one. I told him to make
a log one. We roused White from the spruce
boughs where he persisted in snoring, in spite
of our momentous discussion, and then prepared
and ate our breakfast. White went to fishing.
Abbot shouldered his axe and he and I went off
together for a suitable pine-tree to make our
canoe of. He found one to his satisfaction on
the other side of the stream, some distance down.
I built him a fire to "smudge" the flies, waded
back across the stream, and as I ascended the
farther bank heard the thundering crash of the
falling pine behind me, bellowing over the wilderness, and rolling in echoes far up the mountains. . . . As I went back to camp, I found
that Abbot was not at work on his canoe. While
I was marveling at this I stumbled upon a half
finished spruce canoe, which Abbot had set about
making, having found the pine-tree, which he
had cut down for his log boat, rotten. I was not
much pleased at this change of plan; nevertheless, as the thing was begun I lent him assistance
as I could, so that by nightfall we had finished
something which had the semblance of a canoe,
but, owing chiefly to haste and want of tools,
had such a precarious and doubtful aspect that
White christened it the Forlorn Hope. We put
it into the water. It leaked. We took it out and
stuffed the seams with pounded spruce bark,
chewed spruce gum, and bits of cloth. It still
leaked, but we hoped it would do, with diligent
baling; so, fastening it to the bank, we cooked

our supper, rolled ourselves in our blankets, and went to sleep before the fire.

Sunday, Aug. 6th. We were obliged perforce to adopt the sailor's maxim, "No Sunday off soundings," for our provisions were in a fair way of failing, and starvation in the wilderness is not a pleasant prospect to look forward to. . . . After breakfast we packed our luggage, and proceeded to make the dubious experiment of the canoe. All were embarked; White in the middle to bale, Abbot at the stern, I in the prow. "Push off!" the canoe glided with a quiet and gentle motion down the swift stream, between the tall walls of forest on each side, but soon the ripple and tumbling of a rapid appeared in front and the hour of trial came. She quivered and shook as she entered the disturbed waters; at last there was a little grating sound. She had struck upon the stones at the bottom, but the peril was past; the water grew smooth and deep again, and again we floated quietly and prosperously down in the shadows of the woods. At last another rapid came. She entered it, grated heavily over the stones, and struck hard against a large one before her. The water spouted in like a stream from a pump. It would not do. The experiment was an utter failure. We left Abbot with the canoe to conduct that and the baggage as he could down to the basin, and waded to shore ourselves to walk there through the woods. We had not gone quarter of a mile when "Hello, here," came from the river. "What's the matter now?" shouted we in return. "The canoe's burst all to pieces!" Sure enough, we found it so. Abbot stood in the middle of a rapid, up to the knees, holding our baggage aloft to keep it dry, while the miserable remnant of the demolished vessel was leisurely taking its way down the current. We pushed through the woods towards the basin, deliberating what to do next. Abbot was sure he could make a raft which would carry us down to the settlements, and yet draw so little water as to pass the "rips" in safety. The navigation would indeed be slow with such a machine, but it could be made in an hour or two, and this would more than counterbalance the want of speed. The river was high; the plan seemed eligible, and we proceeded to execute it. Meanwhile it began to rain furiously. We walked into the water to our waists and held the timbers in place while Abbot withed them together. Jerome's camp was demolished to furnish materials, his setting-poles and birch-bark vessels appropriated to our use. After about two hours of aquatic exertion, during which we were wet equally by the rain above and the river beneath, the raft was finished. Owing to the badness of the timber it drew twice as much water as we expected. We pushed from shore in a deluge of rain. Like its luckless predecessor, the raft passed the first rapid in safety, only venting a groan or two as its logs encountered the stones beneath. These rapids in the main river were of course much deeper than those of the Little Margalloway, above the basin, where the canoe had met its fate. When it came on the second rapid, the machine seemed to shiver in direful expectancy of its approaching destruction. Presently it grunted loud and dolefully. We set our poles and pushed it into the deepest part. For a while it bumped and blundered downward; at length there was a heavy shock, a crash, a boiling and rushing of many waters. The river spouted up between the logs. We were fixed irrecoverably aground. The water coursed savagely by us, and broke over the end of the raft, but it could not be moved. The result of this second experiment was more dismal than of the first. We were in the middle of the river; the trees on both shores loomed gloomily through rain and mist, and a volume of boiling and roaring waves rolled between. However, there being no remedy, we walked in, and, by dint of considerable struggling, waded safe to the western bank, where I directed Abbot to try no more experiments but to work on a log canoe till he had finished it. He accordingly felled another tree, while we were, with great difficulty on account of the rain, building a fire. Abbot worked with great perseverance and skill. Before night, his canoe was nearly hewed out. We plied him with tea to keep his spirits up, relieved him of the cooking and all his other duties, so that his task was accomplished in what seemed an incredibly short time. That afternoon I went back to the basin to get fish for the public benefit. At night the rain, which had ceased for a while, began to pour afresh. We put up White's blanket, which was wet, for a tent, and spreading mine on the ground beneath, made a great fire before it, ate our supper, and lay down. As soon as we were quiet, the continual drop-

ping and splashing of rain through the forest
had a sound singularly melancholy and impressive. White dropped asleep, after his established
custom on all occasions, but Abbot and myself,
both of us wet to the skin, chose to lie and talk
before the fire till past midnight. Our guide is
a remarkably intelligent fellow, has astonishing
information for one of his condition, is resolute
and as independent as the wind. Unluckily, he
is rather too conscious of his superiority in these
respects, and likes too well to talk of his own
achievements. He is coarse and matter-of-fact
to a hopeless extremity, self-willed, and self-
confident as the devil; if any one would get
respect or attention from him, he must meet
him on his own ground in this matter. He is
very talkative. I learned more, from his conversation, about the manners and customs of the
semi-barbarians he lives among, than I could
have done from a month's living among them.
That night in the rain, leagues from the dwellings of men, was a very pleasant one. We slept
a few hours towards day, and rose before it was
fairly light, he to finish the canoe, we to prepare breakfast. We launched the boat soon
after, embarked, and paddled down stream. . . .
At length we saw, on the left bank, a camp
built of logs for the use of " loggers." We went
ashore. The place was dry, the roof being slant
and thatched waterproof, with a hole at one side
to let out the smoke of the fire. . . . Fortunately,
I had secured my matches in a tin case, and this
in my waterproof knapsack, so that we were
able to build a fire with the aid of some dry

birch bark we found in the hut. . . . Hanging our superfluous clothing to dry, we laid down in the rest and slept comfortably all night.

Tuesday, Aug. 8th. [After a hard paddle and a long tramp they reached Brag's.]

Wednesday, Aug. 9th. Left Brag's this morning to walk to Colebrook. I had to carry about thirty pounds weight, including my blanket, which having covered White's shoulders through all the storms of yesterday, had become saturated with moisture, and was about as heavy when rolled up as a log of hard wood. Abbot carried his for him. The day was overcast and showery. When we had got about six miles, we overtook an old fellow in a wagon, who was jolting along over stones, logs, gullies, and all other impediments, towards Colebrook. White got in with him and rode the rest of the way, Abbot and I going on together, first committing the baggage to his care, except my knapsack, which I chose to keep with me. . . .

Thursday, Aug. 10th. Stayed at Colebrook today, for want of means to get off. In the villainous little hole of a tavern there, there is never anything stirring to break the dismal monotony. Every day is a Sunday. . . .

Friday, Aug. 11th. The stage came by this morning from Canaan. It is called a stage, but is in reality a milk-cart. We got in. At noon we reached Lancaster, where White stopped, being reduced to his last quarter of a dollar, to see his uncle and borrow the needful of him. I kept on to Littleton, where I now am.

Saturday, Aug. 12th. Started for home by way

of Plymouth. . . . With an accommodating driver and a pleasant party of ladies and gentlemen — one of the former exceedingly handsome, romantic, and spirited — we rode on towards Plymouth, and got there late at night. There was a general on board, — a man of exalted character and vast political influence which he exercised on the righteous side of radical democracy, fiercely maintaining that ninepence was better than a million dollars, insomuch that the possessor of the first is invariably a good man and contented with his lot, while the owner of the last is always a grasping, avaricious child of the devil. When the general alighted at his own tavern he saluted the first loafer who met him at the door as "Major," the next but one was "Colonel," while our driver answered to the title of "Captain."

Not long after his return home the autumn term of his junior year began.

CHAPTER VII

TRAVELS

In the winter of his junior year Frank made a visit to the village of Keene, New Hampshire, where his classmates lived — George S. Hale, destined to an honorable position at the Boston bar, and Horatio J. Perry, subsequently first secretary to our legation at Madrid. Here he followed deer-tracks, which lent a great interest to the snow-covered ground even without sight or smell of buck or doe, and here he forgot the ill success of the chase in the company of some attractive girls, of whom his friends often make mysterious mention in their invitations to him, — "There are some here who would not be displeased at your coming."

It is not to be wondered that girls liked him. He was a tall lad, near six feet, of strong build, straight legs, and soldierly carriage. His face was brave, open, and sunny, full of trustfulness and manhood, his brow broad and intelligent, his thick brown hair, parted at the side, curled a little where it was brushed back over the ears ; his nose was masculine but delicate, his mouth

good, and his chin the emblem of fortitude.
The garb of the period became him, — the
swallow-tail coat with big round buttons, rolling
away to show the white waistcoat and shirt-
front, a bandanna or plaid cravat swathed round
the neck, reminiscent of the stock, and knotted
sparkishly under the chin. Boyish convictions,
flashes of vehemence, good humor, and good
manners, made his conversation acceptable, even
to persons who were indifferent to the "flourish
set on youth."

The most important and the most unfortunate
event of his junior year, however, was not the
society of young women but the building of the
first gymnasium at Harvard. Frank set to work
with his usual "pernicious intensity," in order
to *cram* into six months the swelling muscles
that should have been acquired in as many years,
and strained himself; and, in consequence of
this strain, or perhaps from general ill-health,
that summer he forebore a journey into the
woods and contented himself with a tour by
Lake George, Montreal, Quebec, and the White
Mountains in search of historical information.
His little pocket diary shows his methods: —

GILES F. YATES, ESQ., SCHNECTADY.
"The best of Am. Antiquarians" — that is,
with an extensive knowledge of the colonial hist.
of N. Y.

Rev. Mr. Williams, Schenectady.

Kerney — Clergyman, Clermont, Columbia County, N. Y. A grand-nephew of Sir W. Johnson. ———

The Germans of the Mohawk know much of Sir William and family.

———

The gent. who told me the preceding told me also what follows. He was a man of most extensive and minute information on similar topics. His ancestor's house, together with one other, were all that escaped the Schnectady burning [Count Frontenac, etc., pp. 212, etc.] — for this reason. His ancestor, an old Dutchman, saved a Jesuit priest whom the Mohawks were about to burn at their " burning place " near Schenectady. The priest was secretly packed in a hogshead, boated down to Albany, and thence sent home to Canada. The old man accounted to the Mohawks for his escape by the priest's omnipotent art magic. This priest accompanied the war party and protected the house.

The grandfather-in-law of this gent. was saved when at the stake by Grant. He made the masonic sign, Grant was a Mason and so interfered.

———

Lake George. On a little hill by a pine-tree, near Ft. George, I saw a flat rough stone with an inscription as follows : " 1776. Here lies Stephen Hedges," and more unreadable. Close by, on a fresh ploughed [field] a boy with me found a buckshot and a coin about the size of a 50 ct. piece. I myself picked up a musket ball and a copper coin.

Montreal — Friday. Visited the nunnery of
the *Sœurs Grises*, Hospital for invalids, School
for children. Patients hideous to look upon —
nuns worse. Building of the same rough gray
stone generally used here. . . . Two regiments
are in town — 71st Highlanders and the 89. A
part of the 43rd are on the island a short way
off. . . .

" Hope Gate." Quebec is defended something in this manner : [Here follows a diagram
lettered] G — gate, B blockhouse, stone below,
with loops for musketry — wood above, and
portholes for two cannon commanding the street
S, which is a precipiece on one side. a a a loops
all along the wall, c two more guns on the wall,
also commanding the street. . . .

" Emily Montague," a novel to be read forthwith. Butler — Jesuits.

[The traveler then went to Crawford's, and
to Franconia Notch.]
M. S. Wars of Canada — C. F. Hoffman knows.

Hoffman's " Wild Scenes in Forest and Prairie," " Winter in the West," etc.

From Senter Harbor to Fryeburg, spent Sunday and visited the Pond. Paugus's gun, so
called, is shown at the Academy. [Half Century
of Conflict, vol. i. p. 258.]. . . Stayed a day
or two and rode on to Ethan's to spend the
night. Mrs. C. soon produced her history of her

husband's adventures, etc. — a manuscript which
she means to publish. . . .

"Captivity of Mrs. Johnson," Windsor, Vt.,
1807.

———

A book worth getting, " Frontier Life in '44,"
etc. . . .

Robert Southey had in his possession the
whole of Wolfe's correspondence.

Went over to see the Indians. . . . Saw
François and others, — some squaws extremely
good-looking with their clubbed hair [?] and
red leggings. . . . The Indians use the genuine
wampum. . . . There are a number of loggers
in their red shirts seated in the bar ; some of
them have been to see "the Lord's Supper."
One expressed his disapprobation of the character of the exhibition as follows : " G—d d—n it,
I should like to take that fellow by the nape of
the neck, and pitch him into the road. He 's no
right to serve that 'ere up for a show in that
way."

Bought some wampum of F.'s squaw which he
says he bought from the Caughnawagas near
Montreal 25 years ago. It is, however, sometimes made by the whites in Canada.

Frank picked up some bloody yarns from the
Indians, and discontinued his diary. The last
entry is, " Saturday night, had no supper."

That summer there was another visit to Keene,
and the plan at least of a visit to his classmate
Snow at Fitchburg ; the visit had to be deferred
on account of the illness of Snow's father.

FITCHBURG, Tuesday [1843].

MY DEAR FRANK, — . . . A hard thing it is for me, my friend, to have your visit delayed even for a week. I had famous anticipations of the glorious times I should have with you. And mother had no less agreeably anticipated your visit, and had baked twenty most unexceptionable mince pies, each one of which I should venture to pit against that famous one of your sister's, nice as it was. However, they will keep till you come back. — Now I stipulate most firmly that you make me the visit when you have finished your sojourn in the enchanted land [Keene], and if you don't, I shall have terrible suspicions that "your gorge has risen" at the delay. I also stipulate you use your influence to get Hale to accompany you, and I will entertain both as far as my capabilities will admit.

Yrs in great haste,

CHAS. A. B. SNOW.

Thus passed winter and summer in that happy time when a buckshot on a historic field, yesterday's rabbit-tracks in the soft fallen snow, twenty unexceptionable mince pies, and the random glance from a pair of eyes, indifferent black, will convert much poorer material than a New England village into an enchanted land. The holidays passed, as holidays will, hopping, skipping, jumping; but when college opened its lecture rooms, Frank found himself not well enough to take up college life, and it was decided to send him to Europe. He started on a dull November day; he was not well, the ship was a little craft, his fond mother and his little sisters were very unhappy to part with him, so there was very little cheer that day, but Frank was not daunted, and went off, no doubt, with boyish smiles on his face and boyish tears in his heart. He kept a long diary, — for he would not intermit his training in rhetoric, — from which I take the following pages : —

BARQUE NAUTILUS, November 16th, '43.
(Devil of a sea — cabin dark as Hades.)

Got under weigh from Central Wharf about 10 A. M. of Sunday, Dec. 12th [November 12] — fine weather, and a noble west wind. . . . Before long we were pitched up and down on an execrable swell — the fruit of yesterday's east wind. The barque tossed about like a cork, snorted, spouted the spray all over her deck, and went rushing along like mad in a great caldron of foam she raised about her. At the same time it grew cloudy, and the wind became stronger. The sea rose and fell in great masses, green as grass, the wind driving the spray in clouds from their white tops. As I came from the cabin, I beheld to my great admiration a huge wall of water piled up in front, into which the vessel was apparently driving her bows ; a moment more, and the case was reversed — her bowsprit and half her length rose straight from the waters and stood relieved against the sky. In consequence of which state of things I, like a true greenhorn, grew seasick by the time we were fairly out of sight of land. Accordingly I got into my berth as soon as it was dark, and stayed there twelve hours.

When I came on deck in the morning, the weather had changed nowise for the better. I wrapped myself in my cloak, and sprawling on the poop-deck read the "Bible in Spain." A schooner, with only topsails set, went scouring past us, before the wind, homeward bound — also, in the afternoon, a brig, tossing so that her keel was almost visible. A troop of porpoises went tumbling about us, and I ransacked the vessel in vain for a musket to get a shot at them.

The next morning opened under direful auspices. I came on deck, disconsolate with seasickness, when I was straightway saluted by about two hogsheads of water which came dashing over the gunnel, accommodating me with a most unwelcome morning shower-bath. . . . I spent most of the morning in my berth, reasonably miserable with seasickness — cogitating, meanwhile, on things human and divine, past, present, and to come. When dinner-time came, I heard the captain's invitation to dinner, and staggered to the cabin door, determined to accept it, in spite of fate, when lo! the ship gave a lurch, the plates and the rack which should have secured them slid together from the table, in a general ruin, to the floor. . . . We have a singular company on board — the three officers, "the passenger," the steward, and six men, viz.: a

Yankee, a Portuguese, a Dane, an Englishman, a
Prussian, and an old gray-haired Dutchman, the
best sailor in the ship. Of the officers, the captain is a sensible gentlemanly man ; the mate has
rather more individuality, being, as to his outer
man, excessively tall, narrow-shouldered, spindle-
shanked, and lantern-jawed, with a complexion
like dirty parchment. Mr. Jonathan Snow is
from Cape Cod, a man of the sea from his youth
up. When I first came on board he was evidently
inclined to regard me with some dislike, as being
rich(!) He constantly sighs forth a wish that he
had five thousand dollars "then ketch me going
to sea again, that's all." He is rather given to
polemic controversies, of which I have held several with him, on the tenets of sophists, Unitarians, Universalists, Christians, etc., etc. Of
course, he imagines that men of his rank in life
labor under all sorts of oppressions and injustice
at the hands of the rich. Harvard College he
regards with peculiar jealousy, as a nurse of aristocracy. "Ah! riches carry the day there, I
guess. It's a hard thing to see merit crushed
down, just for want of a thousand dollars."

Mr. Hansen, second mate, is the stoutest man
on board, and has seen most service, but being,
as Mr. Snow remarks, a man of no education, he
has not risen very high in the service. He accompanied Wyeth's trapping party to the Rocky
Mts., where he was more than once nearly starved
and within a hair's breadth of being shot. He
speaks with great contempt of Indians, but not
with quite so much virulence as I have known
from some others of his stamp. He plumes him-

self on having killed two or three. " Oh, damn it, I'd shoot an Indian quicker than I'd shoot a dog." He is now seated at supper, amusing me and himself with some such discourse as follows : —

" I've lost all my appetite, — and got a horse's. Here, steward, you nigger, where be yer — fetch along that beef-steak. What do you call this here? Well, never mind what it be ; it goes down damned well, anyhow." Here he sat stuffing a minute or two in silence, with his grizzly whiskers close to the table, rolling his eyes, and puffing out his ruddy cheeks. At last pausing, and laying down his knife a moment !

" I've knowed the time when I could have ate a Blackfoot Indian, bones and all, and could n't get a mouthful, noway you could fix it." Then resuming his labors — " I tell you what, this here agrees with me. It's better than doctor stuff. Some folks are always running after the doctors, and getting sick. *Eat!* that's the way I do. Well, doctoring is a good thing, just like religion — to them that likes it ; but damn the doctors for all me ; I shan't die," etc., etc.

By treating Mr. Hansen with brandy and water, I have got on very good terms with him, and made him very communicative on the subject of his Oregon experiences. Would that we had a consumptive minister, with his notions of peace, philanthropy, Christian forgiveness, and so forth, on board with us ! It would be sport of the first water to set Mr. Hansen talking at him, and see with what grace the holy man would listen to his backwoods ideas of retributive justice and a proper organization of society. "Shoot him over, and that damn quick, too," is Mr. Hansen's penalty for all serious offenses. . . . As soon as it was daybreak I went on deck. Two or three sails were set, the vessel scouring along, leaning over so that her lee gunnel scooped up the water; the water in a foam, and clouds of spray flying over us, frequently as high as the main yard. The spray was driven with such force that it pricked the cheek like needles. I stayed on deck two or three hours; when, being thoroughly salted, I went down, changed my clothes, and read Don Quixote till Mr. Snow appeared at the door with, "You 're the man that wants to see a gale of wind, are ye? Now 's your chance; only just come up on deck." Accordingly I went. The wind was yelling and howling in the rigging in a fashion that reminded me of a storm in a Canada forest. The ship was hove to. One small rag of a topsail set to keep her steady — all the rest was bare poles and black wet cordage. I got hold of a rope by the mizzen mast, and looked about on a scene that it would be perfect folly to attempt to describe — though nothing more, I suppose, than an ordinary gale of wind. . . .

Friday. As yesterday was Thanksgiving, I may as well record how we fared. Our breakfast was utterly demolished by the same catastrophe that overtook a former repast, that, namely, of being dashed in ruins upon the floor by an ill-timed lurch of the ship. We dined on a lump of ham, Cuffee being unable to purvey a more sumptuous banquet, because the seas put out the

fire in his galley as fast as he kindled it. As for
our supper, it was of bread, pork, and onions.
Not that this is a fair sample of our bills of fare,
which are usually quite as luxurious as any reasonable man need desire. . . .

Wednesday, Dec. 6th. We have been tormented for ten days past with a series of accursed
head winds. Here we are, within thirty-six hours'
sail of Gibraltar, standing alternately north
and south, with no prospect of seeing land for
many days. The captain is half mad, and walks
about swearing to himself in an undertone. Mr.
Snow's philosophy has given way — and I never
had any. Hansen alone is perfectly indifferent.
He sits on deck whistling and talking over his
work, without troubling himself about our where-
abouts, or caring whether we are in the North
Sea or at Cape Horn.

Thursday, Dec. 7th.

> " Day after day, day after day,
>   We stuck, nor breath nor motion;
>   As idle as a painted ship
>   Upon a painted ocean."

This has been our enviable position to-day. A
dead calm — a stupid flapping of sails and creaking of masts.

Saturday. Again a calm! The captain's signs
and portents have come to nought. A turtle
came up at the ship's side to sleep on the quiet
surface, but prudently sunk back to the depths
just as Mr. Hansen was lowering me by a rope
to take him prisoner. A few bonitos splashed
about the bow, some "rudder fish" played alongside; and a pair of "garfish" glided about in

defiance of all attempts to capture them. Before noon a breeze — a favorable one — sprang up! It bore us on a hundred miles farther, but now has subsided into the old trebly accursed calm.

Tuesday. A light wind to-day but dead ahead. More porpoises and more fruitless attempts at harpooning, on the part of Mr. Snow. I am rapidly growing insane. My chief resource is the conversation of Mr. Hansen, who has humor, volubility, much good feeling, and too much coarse rough manhood in his nature to be often offensive in his speech. Moreover, one man may say a thing with a very good grace that would be insufferable from the mouth of another. Witticisms and stories which, uttered by Snow, would make me turn my back on the fellow with contempt and disgust, sound well enough in the frank and bold accents of Hansen.

Evening. We have beat up against the wind into full view of the Spanish coast. Right and left, from Trafalgar far beyond Cadiz, the line of rugged and steep bluffs reaches, with here and there a tower just visible with the glass. But about noon our evil genius becalmed us again!

Thirty days from Boston. Old Worthington promised that I should see Gibraltar in eighteen, but he is a deacon.

CHAPTER VIII

EUROPE

WEDNESDAY evening. We have not yet reached Tarifa. Dozens of vessels come past us from Gibraltar, some of them of a most outlandish aspect to my eye.

Thursday. More delay and vexation. The captain has not slept for two nights, and is half worn out by fatigue and anxiety. For myself, I was so exasperated by our continued ill fortune that I could not stay below. We passed Tarifa light about midnight — then were driven back four miles by a rain squall. But by nine in the morning we had fairly entered Gibraltar Bay!

[Gibraltar.] Saturday. Yesterday I came ashore in the barque's boat, landed, got passport signed and established myself at the "King's Arms."

I dined at the consul's and spent the day in exploring this singular city — the world in epitome. More of it in future. This morning I set out, in company with a midshipman, the son of Captain Newton of the Missouri, to ride round the Bay to the Spanish town of Algeciras.

Sunday. . . . Sunday is the day to see the motley population of Gibraltar at one glance. Just without the walls is a parade large enough to hold the six regiments stationed here. This evening, according to custom, everybody was thronging up there. I established myself at the foot of a bronze statue of the defender of Gibraltar — I forget his name, General Eliot — but there he stands towering above the trees and aloes at the summit of a hill above the parade, with the emblematic key in his hand, and with a huge cannon and a mortar on each side of him. Here I had a specimen of every nation on earth, it seemed, around me. A dozen Moors with white turbans and slippered feet lolled one side ; Jews by couples in their gaberdines; the Spanish gentleman in his black cloak and sombrero — the Spanish laborer with his red cap hanging on one side of his head — the Spanish blackguard in bespangled tights and embroidered jacket. On benches among the trees officers and soldiers carried on successful love suits ; on the parade below English captains were showing forth good horsemanship to the best advantage. The red coats of soldiers appeared everywhere among the trees and in the crowd below. There were women in cloaks of red and black, ladies with the mantilla and followed by the duenna, — no needless precaution, — and ten thousand more, soldier and civilian, bond and free, man and woman and child. Not the least singular of the group were the little black slaves belonging to the Moors, who were arrayed in a very splendid and outlandish attire, following after their masters like dogs. Bands were stationed on the parade and around a summerhouse among the trees. The evening gun dissolved the pageant — *God save the Queen* rose on the air; then the crowd poured through the gates into the town.

I went to a diminutive theatre in the evening, to see a play performed by the privates of an artillery company. . . .

A "rock scorpion" carried me off to the frigates in the harbor, English and American. The reptile in question was a mixture of Genoese and French blood — spoke both languages fluently, besides English and half a score of others. . . .

Sunday, Dec. —. Got tired of Gibraltar — heard of a government steamer about to sail for Malta — embarked on her, abandoning my previous design of penetrating Spain immediately. . . . I was prepared for no very agreeable passage, knowing the hauteur approaching to insolence of a certain class of English naval officers, and was surprised as well as gratified by the polite attentions of Lt. Spark, the commander of the boat, with whom I spent about half the night in conversation. Unfortunately I am the only passenger. Lt. Spark seems resolved that my voyage shall be agreeable notwithstanding — certainly, he spares no pains for my accommodation, opening his library to me, producing an endless variety of wines, doing all he can, in short, to promote my enjoyment.

We have passed Cape de Got and the Sierra Nevada, which looks down on the city of Granada. The coast of Barbary is now in full sight. To-day the old man mustered his sailors and marines in the cabin — a large and elegant one — and read the service of the Church, not forgetting a special prayer for the British Navy, and the success of the British arms. He knew Sir John Moore, Sir P. Parker, and other heroes of those days, has shaken hands with Blucher, has fought the French by sea and land. Beside his manifold experiences in active life, he has been a great reader, not only of English works but of all the eminent American authors. . . . Here in this old world I seem, thank Heaven, to be carried about half a century backwards in time. As far as religion is concerned, there are the ceremonies of the Catholic church and the English litany, with rough soldiers and sailors making the responses. A becoming horror of dissenters, especially Unitarians, prevails everywhere. No one cants here of the temperance reform, or of systems of diet — eat, drink, and be merry is the motto everywhere, and a stronger and hardier race of men than those round me now never laughed at the doctors. Above all, there is no canting of peace. A wholesome system of coercion is manifest in all directions — thirty-two pounders looking over the bows, piles of balls on deck, muskets and cutlasses hung up below, the red jackets of marines, and the honest prayer that success should crown all these warlike preparations, yesterday responded to by fifty voices. There was none of the new-fangled suspicion that such belligerent petition might be averse to the spirit of a religion that inculcates peace as its foundation. And I firmly believe that there was as much hearty faith and worship in many of those men as in any feeble consumptive wretch at home,

who, when smitten on one cheek, literally turns
the other likewise, instead of manfully kicking
the offender into the gutter.

Thursday. After a passage of about five days
we reached Malta.

Friday. Late last evening I made an attempt
to see the Church of St. John. It was closed.
My servant pommeled the oaken door in vain.
He then proceeded to sundry coffee-houses in
the neighborhood, hoping to find the man who
had the doors in charge. Three or four Maltese,
all jabbering their bastard Arabic, soon aided
in the search. At length the great bell began
to roar from the church tower, an unequivocal
evidence that somebody was there. " Gulielmo,
Gulielmo! " roared my troop of assistants. After
a lapse of five minutes Gulielmo descended and
issued from a portal among the columns at one
side, summoning me in. . . . [Here he describes
the church.] Leaving reluctantly the church
where so many brave men had kneeled to God
for his blessing on their matchless enterprises,
I got into a boat, and was put on board the Nea-
politan steamer Francesco Primo, bound for
Messina, where I lay an hour or two on deck,
listening to the distant music of the English
drums and trumpets.

As I lounged about the deck in the morning,
utterly unable to hold any intercourse with any
one on board except by signs, a sleek-looking fellow came up and accosted me in English. We soon
got deep into conversation. My new acquaintance proved to be Giuseppe Jackson, a Sicilian
with an English grandfather, who had been a

cook at the Albion, and at Murdoch's tavern, had frequently been to Fresh Pond, knew some of the Cambridge students, and was now on his way to Mr. Marston's in Palermo. I was right glad to see him, cook though he was. He made me a very good interpreter. In the course of our conversation he made some remark about "the Pope, that fool."

"What," said I, "do you speak so of the Pope. Are you not a Roman Catholic?"

"Ah! I was till I live in America. I was all in the dark — you understand what I say — till I come there. Then my eyes open; I say, dat for the Pope, and his old red cap. Ah! once I was afraid to think of him."

"You are no longer a Catholic; what religion do you believe in now?"

"Oh, no religion in particular."

I congratulated him on so happy a conversion from the error of his ways.

At breakfast — a Mediterranean breakfast of eggs, fruit, and nuts — an old man, of severe countenance and tremendous mustache, sat opposite me. We made various attempts at conversation; as neither understood the other, we had to be satisfied with reiterated bowings, and mutual attentions of various kinds, in which the old man showed himself exceedingly apt and polite. I afterwards found that he was no less a personage than il Principe Statelli, a general of the Sicilian army — but Sicilian "Principes" are apt to be humbugs.

Mount Ætna is smoking vigorously in front of us. We are skirting the shore of Sicily.

We stopped at Syracuse. . . . In going ashore, a little square-built English-looking man, making a low congee, presented me with a bundle of papers, which proved to be certificates of his qualifications as a guide to the curiosities of the place. Accordingly Jack Robinson — for such was his name — and I got into a kind of ferry-boat and landed on the other side of the bay. [His guide took him to the Ear of Dionysius and other places of interest.]

Jack insisting on showing me his certificates of service in the American Navy, and I, being desirous of seeing how the Syracusans lived, went home with him, and enjoyed the exhibition of his numerous progeny, who were all piled together in bed. This done we took boat and went off to the steamer. Jack was so well satisfied with the dollar and a half I gave him for his day's services that he must needs salute me after the Sicilian style with a kiss on the cheek, which I submitted to. He then departed, kissing his hand as his head disappeared over the ship's side. The stubborn English temper was well nigh melted away with his long sojourn among the Gentiles. He had been pressed in early youth into the navy — had served both England and America (though the latter, I believe, in the capacity of a washerman). As far as I could see, Jack was an honest man, an exceedingly rara avis in these quarters.

Arriving at Messina in the morning, my acquaintance the cook — an experienced traveler — was of the greatest service to me. Indeed, without his assistance my inexperience and igno-

rance of the language would have put me to serious embarrassment. He showed me how to treat
a Sicilian landlord, and to bribe a custom-house
officer. I am indebted to him for very excellent
accommodations at a very reasonable price.

Messina, Sunday. I took my station outside
one of the gates in the rear of the city, to look
at the scum of humanity that came pouring out.
All was filth, and age, and ruin, — the walls,
the tall gateway with its images and inscriptions,
the hovels at the top of the wall and in the ancient suburb, all seemed crumbling to decay. The
orange and lemon groves in the ditch of the fortification were dingy and dirty, but away in the
distance appeared the summits of the mountains,
almost as wild and beautiful as our mountains of
New England. I thought of them, and, in the
revival of old feelings, half wished myself at
home. I soon forgot, however, all but what was
before my eyes, in watching the motley array
that passed by me. Men and women literally
hung with rags, half hid in dirt, hideous with
every imaginable species of deformity, and bearing on their persons a population as numerous
as that of Messina itself, — these formed the bulk
of the throng. Priests with their black broad-
brimmed hats and their long robes, — fat and
good-looking men, — were the next numerous
class. They draw life and sustenance from these
dregs of humanity, just as tall pigweed flour-
ishes on a dunghill. Then there were mustachioed
soldiers, very different from the stately and se-
date soldier of England. There were men bearing holy pictures and images ; ladies in swarms,

whose profession was stamped on their faces;
musicians, with a troop of vagabonds in their
rear. All around the gateway were the tables
of butchers, fruiterers, confectioners, money-
changers, boot-blackers, and a throng of dirty
men, women, and children. Shouts, yells, and
a universal hubbub.

Tuesday, Jan. 2nd. This morning I set out on
an expedition to see a little of the country, in
company with a Spanish gentleman, Don Mateo
Lopez, who speaks good English. We hired a
carriage together, and got outside the gates by
eleven, after some trouble in procuring pass-
ports. At night we reached a little fishing town
called Giardini, not far from Ætna. The weather
was beautiful, the atmosphere clear and soft.
As for the scenery on the road, it was noble beyond expression. For myself, I never imagined
that so much pleasure could be conveyed through
the eye. The road was a succession of beautiful
scenes, — of mountains and valleys on one side
and the sea on the other; but as to the people,
they are a gang of ragamuffins. . . . These disgusting holes of villages only added zest to the
pleasure of the scenery, — a pleasure not inferior
and not unlike that of looking upon the face of
a beautiful woman. In many respects our own
scenery is far beyond it; but I cannot say that
I have ever looked with more delight on any of
our New England mountains and streams than
upon these of Sicily. The novelty of the sight,
and the ruined fortresses on the highest crags,
add much to the effect. . . .

I went to the museum of Prince Boscari, a

valuable collection of antiquities, etc. In the midst of a hall, surrounded by precious fragments of statues and broken pottery, lay the skeleton of a Chippeway birch canoe. I welcomed it as a countryman and an old friend.

I bought some specimens of lava and amber of a couple of rascals who asked twice their value, and abated it at once when I refused to buy.

I went to see an opera of Bellini — a native, I have heard, of Catania. . . . Lopez had a friend waiting for him here — a light-hearted and lively young Spaniard whose youthful eccentricities sat as easily and gracefully upon him as awkwardly upon old Mateo. When we set out on our return, *il mio amico*, as Lopez called him, was rattling away incessantly, and imitating every dog, hog, or jackass we met.

We had a sort of calêche. Besides the driver, a small boy ran along by our side, or clung behind, ready to do what offices might be required of him. A still smaller one was stowed away in a net, slung between the wheels where he kept a constant eye on the baggage. The larger one employed himself in tying knots in the horses' tails as he ran along — or he would dart along the road before us, clamber on a wall, and sit till we came by, when he would spring down with a shout and run on again. . . .

The women of this country are not handsome. You see groups of them about the stone doorways spinning twine, with their hair drawn back in the fashion represented in the portraits of our grandmothers.

We stopped at night at Giardini. The " padrone" showed us with great complacency the register of his house, which, he said, contained the recommendations of the guests who had honored him with their company. One man's "recommendation" warned all travelers that the padrone's beds were full of fleas; another's that nothing in the house was fit to eat, etc. The importunate padrone could not read English....

CHAPTER IX

IN SICILY

THE Church of the Benedictines is the noblest edifice I have seen. This and others not unlike it have impressed me with new ideas of the Catholic religion. Not exactly, for I reverenced it before as the religion of generations of brave and great men, but now I honor it for itself. They are mistaken who sneer at its ceremonies as a mere mechanical force; they have a powerful and salutary effect on the mind. Those who have witnessed the services in this Benedictine church, and deny what I say, must either be singularly stupid and insensible by nature, or rendered so by prejudice.

Saturday. I recall what I said of the beauty of the Sicilian women — so far, at least, as concerns those of high rank. This is a holyday. They are all abroad, in carriages and on foot. One passed me in the church of the Capuchin convent, with the black eye, the warm rich cheek, and the bright glance that belong to southern climates. They are beautiful beyond all else.

Sunday. Took leave of the hospitable family of Consul Payson with much regret, and went off to the steamer Palermo, bound for Palermo. I found her completely surrounded by boats, wedged close together; friends were kissing their adieus, and boatmen cursing. The delicacy of sentiment expressed in the Italian national oath is admirable — they rival the Spaniards in that matter, — " Arcades ambo ; id est, blackguards both." At length visitors were warned off, the boats dispersed, scattering from a common centre, in all directions ; a man screamed the names of the passengers, by way of roll-call; and among the rest the illustrious one of Signore Park-a-man ; and we got under weigh. It was late at night. We passed the long array of bright lights from the fine buildings along the quay of Messina, — could just discern the mountains behind the town, indistinct in the darkness, like thunder-clouds, — left a long train of phosphoric light behind us, as we steered down between Scylla and Charybdis, and in half an hour were fairly out on the Sicilian Sea. The ghost of departed perils still lingers about the scene of Ulysses' submarine adventures ; an apology for a whirlpool on one side — still bearing the name of Scylla — and an insignificant shoal on the other. I thought as we passed, and the moon made a long stream of light on the water, that it would be an adventure worth encountering, to be cast away in that place, — but my unwonted classical humor was of very short duration ; for, going below, I found a cabin full of seasick wretches, which attractive spectacle banished all recollection of Virgil and Homer. I was doomed to lie all night a witness to their evolutions ; a situation not many degrees more desirable than being yourself a sufferer. . . .

Wednesday. I have just arranged an expedition to Girgenti, at the southern point of the island. Traveling in Sicily is no joke, especially at this season. I engaged a man named Luigi to furnish three mules, supplies of provisions, cooking apparatus, an attendant, and thus to pilot me round the island, paying himself all tavern reckonings and *buona manos*. For this I am to give him four dollars a day. I thus avoid all hazard of being imposed upon, or robbed, for I shall have scarce any money with me. Luigi is perfectly familiar with the island ; has, moreover, the reputation of an honest man, notwithstanding which I follow Mr. Marston's advice in making him sign a written agreement. I have laid it down as an inviolable rule to look on everybody here as a rascal of the first water, till he has shown himself by undeniable evidence to be an honest man.

Giuseppe has been with me as a servant of late. The chief fault with him was his continually stopping to kiss some of his acquaintances in the street. He seems to know everybody, understands perfectly how to cheat everybody, has astonishing promptness and readiness for all kinds of service. " It is 'trange, Mister Park-a-man," he modestly remarked the other day, "that I cannot go nowhere, but what all the people seem to like-a me, and be good friends with me." He is vain as a turkey-cock — dresses infinitely better than I ever did. He is a great coward, trembling continually with fear of robbers in all our rides. The Sicilian robbers, by the way, are a great humbug. When I engaged Giuseppe I

offered him half a dollar a day for wages. " No,
Mist'r Park-a-man, I no take-a wages at all.
When you go away, you make-a me a present,
just as much as you like; then I feel more better." So I told him I would make-a him a present of half a dollar a day; which I did, a mode
of remuneration more suited to Giuseppe's self-
importance.

Thursday, Jan. 18th. All this morning Luigi
Rannesi was in a fever-heat of preparation. I
told him to be ready at two; he came to me at
twelve announcing that all was ready; that he
had engaged mules at Marineo, and that the
carriage was at the door to take us there. I was
not prepared for such promptitude. After some
delay, I got ready too, and we set out. Luigi, a
diminutive Sicilian with a thin brown face and
an air of alertness about every inch of him, began
to jabber Italian with such volubility that I could
not understand a word. He must needs exhibit
every article of the provisions he had got ready
for the journey, extolling the qualities of each, —
and they deserved all his praises, — and always
ended by pounding himself on the breast, rolling
up his eyes, and exclaiming, " Do you think
Luigi loves money? No! Luigi loves honor!"
and then launching forth into interminable eulo-
gies of the country we were going to see, and the
adventures we should meet there. We stopped
at night at Marineo, where Luigi provided a
most sumptuous dinner; talked and gesticulated,
half frenzied because he found I could not understand half he said; then seized my hand, which
he dutifully kissed, and left me to my medita-

tions. He reappeared, however, bringing a decanter of wine, and a large book of antiquities which he had brought for me to read. All this was at his own expense. The terms of his bargain bound him to nothing else than to keep me alive on the road.

(Castel Termini.) Luigi is a great antiquarian. He rakes up ancient money at every village as he goes along. His antiquarian skill is a passport to introduce him anywhere; to the nobles and princes, who are not always, however, such dignified personages as would appear from their titles. I went with him to-night to the house of a judge, who produced a bottle of rosolio and showed me a grotto in his garden which he had stuck all over with specimens of the Sicily minerals. I then went with him to a "conversazione," where some dozen people were playing cards. They looked at the "signore Americano," as the judge introduced me to them, with great curiosity, and at last left their game and clustered round me, very curious to know something of the place I came from. I talked to them for some time in a most original style of Italian; but getting tired of being lionized in such a manner, I bade them good-night and went back to the albergo.

I went to visit the famous sulphur works not far from these places. In the shaft I entered the rock was solid sulphur — scarce any mixture of foreign ingredients. As we rode away, a noble prospect of volcanic mountains lay off on our right. Soon after the mule-track became a good road. A carriage from Caltanisetta passed us,

belonging to some English travelers who had
made a wide détour for the sake of a road. We
saw at last the battlements and church spires of
Girgenti, crowning a high hill before us, and had
occasional glimpses of the sea through the valleys.
Approaching the hill, we found a deep and shadowed valley intervening. Luigi left the road and
descended into it by a wretched mule-track.
Flocks of goats passed on the road above us,
mules and asses loaded with their panniers came
down from the city. One of his fits of enthusiasm had taken possession of Luigi. He began
to lash his mule and drive him along over sand
and rocks at such a rate that I thought him mad,
till he told me that it was necessary to get to
Girgenti before the Englishmen. "Corragio!
my brave mule! Corragio, signore," he shouted,
"we shall be the victors!" At that he drove
full speed up the steep hill toward the gate.
Nothing would stop him. He leaped over ditches,
scrambled through mud and stones, shouting
"Corragio" at the top of his lungs. At last
an insuperable gully brought him up short. He
clapped his hand to his forehead, exclaiming,
"Santissima Maria!" in a tone of wrath and
despair, then recovered his spirits and dashed off
in another direction. We succeeded. When we
got to the top the carriage was quarter of a mile
off, and Luigi shouted "Vittoria!" as he rode
into the gate, as much elated as if he had accomplished some great achievement. It was a festa
day. All the people in the crowded streets and
in the little square wore white caps. They were
a hardy and athletic race — their faces, their

short strong necks, their broad and prominent chests, were all burnt to a dark ruddy brown.

(Girgenti.) Luigi brings me pockets full of ancient money and seems greatly astonished at my indifference. As for himself he is rabid. He dodges into every house and shop, inquiring for "antica moneta," stops contadini at work with the same question; he has scraped together an enormous bagful for which he pays scarce anything, perfectly familiar as he is with its true value, and with the "costumi del paese," as he says, the customs of the country. His enthusiasm embraces every object, far and wide. He raves of love on the road — tells how he eloped with his wife — sings love songs, then falls into the martial vein, shouts "Corragio," defies the wind, rain, and torrents. He enters into all my plans with the most fervid zeal, leaving me nothing to do. Every night he comes upstairs bringing all kinds of dresses and utensils of the people for me to look at. Sometimes he comes in with a handful of old coins, telling me with a chuckle that he had bought them for "pochissimo," kissing them repeatedly in the exultation of a good bargain. I have lived most sumptuously ever since I have been with him. He puts the whole inn into a ferment, rakes the town to find the best of everything, and waits on table with an eulogium of every dish. "Ah! signore," he repeats, "do you think Luigi loves money? No, Luigi loves honor." He has something to give to every beggar he meets. In short, the fellow is a jewel, and shall be my particular friend henceforward.

At the English consul's I met a blind traveler, a Mr. Holeman, who has been over Siberia, New Holland, and other remote regions, for the most part alone, and written seven volumes of his travels. Traveling, he told me, was a passion with him. He could not sit at home. I walked home with him through the streets, admiring his indomitable energy. I saw him the next morning sitting on his mule, with the guide he had hired, — his strong frame, his manly English face, his gray beard and mustaches, and his sightless eyeballs gave him a noble appearance in the crowd of wondering Sicilians about him.

From Girgenti our course lay westward to a village called Mont' Allegro. . . .

Luigi came up in the evening to hold " un discorso " with me, according to his custom. He was in his usual state of excitement. He takes a glass of wine in his hand, " Viva l' onore, signorino mio ! " rolling up his eyes and flourishing his hands, " viva Bacco ; viva Dio ; viva il consolo Americano ! " and so on, the finale being a seizure and kissing of my hand ; after which he inquires if I shall want him, looks about to see that all is right, kisses my hand again, and goes off.

One of Luigi's dignified acquaintances in this place was the Marchese Giacomo, a nobleman of great wealth and a determined virtuoso. Luigi called on him with an offering of coins, and returned with an invitation to his " signore " to visit the Marchese and see his pictures. He had a most admirable picture-gallery — among the rest was an original of Guido. He kindly in-

vited me to dine with him, but Luigi's care had
supplied me a plentiful meal already. So much
for one specimen of a Sicilian nobleman. I saw
one or two more of nearly the same stamp at a
conversazione. The next morning I found Luigi
at the albergo, sitting over a bottle of wine with
a large, fat, sleepy-looking man, in rather a
dingy coat, whom on my entering he slapped on
the shoulder, " Ecco, signore, mio amico il ba-
rone; un brav' uomo," etc., running on with a long
string of praises of his friend the baron, at which
this extraordinary specimen of a noble kept
shaking his large head in modest denial. . . .

The way was enlivened by the edifying sin-
gularities of the muleteer Michele, who walked
along talking without intermission for an hour
together, though no one listened or replied. He
interrupted his discourse only to belabor his
mule and curse him in Sicilian. When we came
to a steep place, he would take a firm hold of
the beast's tail with one hand, while he bela-
bored him with a rope's end that he held in the
other, and thus they would scramble up together. Where the mud was more than a foot
deep Michele would place both hands on the
mule's rump and vault, with a sort of grunt,
upon his back; wriggle himself about for a while
to find a comfortable seat, and then burst forth
with some holy canticle in praise of a saint.

Just after leaving the ruins of Selinuntum
we were struggling along in the mud of a lane
between rows of cork-trees and aloes, when Michele suddenly set up a yowling like a tom-cat,
— stopped in the midst of a note to expostulate

with his mule, — and then proceeded in a more dismal tone than before. Luigi clapped his hands and shouted, "Bravo! compare Michele, bellisima!" at which the gratified Michele redoubled his exertions, and squalled at the top of his throat, putting his hand to the side of his mouth to increase the volume of sound. A young contadino who was wading along on an ass at a little distance behind was seized with a fit of emulation, and set up a counter howl to one of the airs peculiar to the contadini. I cried bravo to this new vocalist, while Luigi cried bella and bellissima to the exertions of Michele. Michele jogged along on his mule, the tassel of his woolen cap flapping; while Luigi twisted himself in his saddle to see how I relished the entertainment, remarking with a grin, "Canta Michele," Michele is singing.

Marsala, as everybody knows, is famous for its wine. For travelers there is little to see. . . .

CHAPTER X

I HAVE seen my last of Sicily. I bade adieu to Luigi, who insisted on my receiving a number of valuable ancient coins, and would have given me an hundred if I had let him have his own way — took leave of the Marstons and Gardiners — had my baggage carried on board the Palermo by three facchini, and followed it myself.

The next morning the famous Bay of Naples looked wretched and dismal enough under the influences of an easterly storm, through which Vesuvius was just visible. I went to the Hotel de Rome, an excellent house, with a restaurant beneath where you get and pay for precisely what you want, an arrangement far better than a table d'hôte.

I spent the first day at the Royal Museum, where I could not determine which I liked best, the Hercules Farnese or the Venus of Praxiteles.

I met, at the house of Mr. Rogers, Mr. Theodore Parker and Mr. Farnam from Philadelphia. I had already met Mr. Parker at the Hotel de Rome. Yesterday we went up Vesuvius together. . . . We got some of the famous *Lacrimæ*

Christi wine at a house half way down. We reached Naples at three, where the outskirts of the town were deserted, with the exception of a few miserable old men and women sitting in the doorways. It was Sunday, the great day of the carnival. King Ferdinand, however, sets his face against the carnival, which for several years has been a mere nothing at Naples. This year, in consideration of the distress of tradesmen, he has consented, much against his inclination, to make a fool of himself. This was the day appointed for a grand masked procession, in which the king and his ministers were to pelt his subjects with sugar-plums, and be pelted in return. There was a great crowd as we entered the square upon the Toledo — the main street of Naples. While we were slowly driving through it, the head of the procession appeared. First came a dragon about fifty feet long, with his back just visible above the throng of heads, as if he was swimming in the water. He was drawn by a long train of horses. Five or six masked noblemen were on his back pelting the crowd and the people in the galleries of the houses on each side. Then came a sort of car, full of bears, cats, and monkeys, all flinging sugar-plums. The horses of this vehicle were appropriately ridden by jackasses. Then came a long train of carriages, which we joined. The crowd was enormous. The Toledo was one wide river of heads, the procession slowly moving down on one side and returning on the other. Along the middle, a line of dragoons sat motionless, with drawn swords, on their horses. Mrs. P. was hit on

the nose by a formidable sugar-plum flung by a
vigorous hand from one of the balconies. She
was in great trouble, but there was no such thing
as retreat. We got our full share. Mr. Farnam's
dignity was disturbed. Mr. Parker had a glass
of his spectacles broken. I alone escaped unin-
jured. At length the royal carriage appeared.
Ferdinand — a gigantic man, taller and heavier
than any of his subjects — was flinging sugar-
plums with hearty good-will, like all the rest.
As they passed our carriage the royal family
greeted us with a broadside, which completed
Mrs. Parker's discomposure. They threw genuine sugar-plums — the others were quite uneat-
able. The king wore a black silk dress which
covered him from head to foot. His face was
protected by a wire mask. He carried a brass
machine in his hand to fling sugar-plums with.
His uncle, his mother, his wife, and all his chief
noblemen soon appeared, all protected by masks.

The procession passed several times up and
down the Toledo, with occasional stoppages. One
of these happened when the king's carriage was
not far before us, while directly over against it, on
the other side of the street, was a triumphal car
full of noblemen. Instantly there began a battle.
Ferdinand and the princes sent volley after volley against their opponents, who returned it with
interest. The crowd set up a roar, and made a
rush for the spoils. There was a genuine battle
for the sugar-plums that fell between the two
carriages, pushing, scrambling, shouting, yelling,
confusion worse confounded, till the dignified
combatants thought proper to separate. . . .

The remoter and more obscure parts of this great city are quite as interesting. Here you may see an endless variety of costumes, of the women, almost all beautiful and neat. There is something particularly attractive about these women, who are seldom, however, handsome, properly speaking, but there is the devil in their bright faces and full rounded forms. Each town in the environs has its peculiar costume.

On Saturday I left Naples for Rome in the diligence, with Mr. and Mrs. Parker. . . .

At length we got a glimpse of St. Peter's. On every side of us were remains of temples, aqueducts, and tombs; Mr. Parker became inspired, and spouted Cicero and Virgil. Three young Romans followed us for a mile, running along in their rags, with their dingy peaked hats in their hands, constantly exclaiming in a wailing tone, "*Eccelenz, eccelenz! povero miserabile, molto di fame!*" — Your excellency, your excellency, I am a poor miserable devil, very hungry.

Monday. To-day is one of the great days. Mr. P. with his lady and myself went in a carriage to see the "show." The streets were crowded with maskers of all descriptions, in carriages and on foot. A blast of trumpets from the end of the Corso was the signal for all the carriages to draw up to one side and the crowd to divide, to make way for a column of the Pope's soldiers. First came the sappers, with beards and mustaches that fell over their chests, shaggy bearskin caps and leather aprons. Each carried a broadaxe over his shoulder, and his musket slung at his back. They were savage and martial-looking fellows. A long train of soldiers followed, with a body of cavalry bringing up the rear. So much for the Pope's summary measures for preserving order. After this the carnival began in earnest.

It was not the solemn sugar-plum foolery of Naples, but foolery entered into with right heartiness and good-will. There were devils of every description, from the imp of two feet high to a six foot monster with horns and hoofs and tail, and a female friend on each arm. There were harlequins with wooden swords, or with bladders tied to poles, which they beat over the heads of all they met; Pulcinellas, and an endless variety of nondescripts. Some of the carriages were triumphal cars gayly ornamented, full of maskers, men and girls, in spangled dresses. Instead of sugar-plums, they flung flowers at one another. Some of the women wore wire masks or little vizards, which left the lower part of the face bare; many, however, had no covering at all to their faces. Few had any regular beauty of features, but there was an expression of heart and spirit, and a loftiness, beside, which did not shame their birth. They flung their flowers at you with the freest and most graceful action imaginable. To battle with flowers against a laughing and conscious face — showering your ammunition thick as the carriage slowly passes the balcony — then straining your eyes to catch the last glance of the black-eyed witch and the last wave of her hand as the crowd closes around her, — all this is no contemptible amusement.

The inferior class of women walked in the

street, very prettily dressed in a laced jacket and a white frock that came an inch below the knee. Some were disguised as boys, some wore fierce mustaches, which set off well enough their spirited faces. Hundreds of men were shouting round the carriages with flowers for sale. Thus it went on for hours, till the report of a cannon gave the signal for clearing the Corso for the horse-race. . . .

So much for my classic " first impressions " of Rome! Yesterday was the 22d of February — the birthday of Washington. The Americans here must needs get up a dinner, with speeches, toasts, etc. It was like a visit home. There they sat, slight, rather pale and thin men, not like beef-fed and ruddy Englishmen ; very quiet and apparently timid ; speaking low to the waiters instead of roaring in the imperative tone of John Bull. There was not a shadow of that boisterous and haughty confidence of manner that you see among Englishmen — in fact most of them seemed a little green. A General Dix presided and made a speech about the repudiation ; the consul, Mr. Green, made another excellent speech, so did Dr. Howe. Mr. Conrade of Virginia gave us a most characteristic specimen of American eloquence, and toasted " Washington and Cincinnatus! Patrick Henry and Cicero ! "

There are numbers of American artists here, some of them fine fellows. In fact, it is some consolation, after looking at the thin faces, narrow shoulders, and awkward attitudes of the " Yankees," to remember that in genius, enterprise, and courage — nay, in bodily strength — they are a full match for the sneering Englishmen. Would that they bore themselves more boldly and confidently. But a time will come when they may meet Europeans on an equal footing.

Feb. 27th. A weary week of lionizing. I would not give a damn for all the churches and ruins in Rome — at least, such are my sentiments at present. There is unbounded sublimity in the Coliseum by moonlight, — that cannot be denied, — St. Peter's, too, is a miracle in its way; but I would give them all for one ride on horseback among the Apennines.[1]

A Virginian named St. Ives, lately converted to Catholicism, has been trying to convert me, along with some of the Jesuits here. He has abandoned the attempt in disgust, telling me that I have not logic enough in me to be convinced of anything, to which I replied by cursing logic and logicians.

I have now been three or four weeks in Rome, have been presented to his Holiness the Pope, have visited churches, convents, cemeteries, catacombs, common sewers, including the Cloaca Maxima, and ten thousand works of art. This will I say of Rome, — that a place on every account more interesting, and which has a more vivifying and quickening influence on the faculties, could not be found on the face of the earth, or, at least, I should not wish to go to it if it could.[1] . . .

Rome, Friday. Yesterday I went to the Capuchins for permission to stay there, which was refused peremptorily; but the Passionists told me to come again at night, and they would tell

[1] *Life of Francis Parkman*, p. 192.

me if I could be admitted. I came as directed, and was shown a room in the middle of the building, which contains hundreds of chambers connected by long and complicated passages, hung with pictures of saints and crucifixes. The monk told me that when the bell rang I must leave my hat, come out, and join the others, and then, displaying some lives of the saints and other holy works on the table, he left me to my meditations. The room has a hideous bleeding image of Christ, a vessel of holy water, and a number of holy pictures — a bed, a chair and a table. Also, hung against the wall was a " Notice to persons withdrawn from the world for spiritual exercises, to the end that they may derive all possible profit from their holy seclusion." The " Notice " prohibited going out of the chamber without necessity; prohibited also speaking at any time, or making any noise whatever, writing also, and looking out of the window. It enjoined the saying of three Ave Marias, at least, at night, also to make your own bed, etc.

The devil! thought I, here is an adventure. The secret of my getting in so easily was explained. There were about thirty Italians retired from the world, preparing for the General Confession, — and even while I was coming to this conclusion the bell clanged along the passage, and I went out to join the rest. After climbing several dark stairs, and descending others, pulling off their skull-caps to the great images of Christ on the landing places, they got into a little chapel, and after kneeling to the altar, seated themselves. The shutters were closed,

and the curtains drawn immediately after; there
was a prayer with the responses, and then a sermon of an hour and a half long, in which the
monk kept felicitating himself and his hearers
that they were of the genuine church — little
thinking that there was a black sheep among his
flock. The sermon over, we filed off to our
rooms. In five minutes the bell rang again for
supper, then we marched off to a conversazione
in another part of the building, where the in-
junction of silence was taken off. I told the directing priest that I was a Protestant. He
seemed a little startled at first, then insinuated
a hope that I might be reclaimed from my
damnable heresy, and said that an American
had been there before, who had been converted
— meaning my acquaintance St. Ives. He then
opened a little battery of arguments upon me,
after which he left me saying that a lay brother
would make the rounds to wake us before sunrise.

The lay brother came in fact, but not before
I had been waked by a howling procession of
the Passionists themselves, who passed along
about midnight. There was a mass, another
prayer, and another endless sermon, soon after
which we were summoned to coffee. I observed
several of the Italians looking hard at me as I
drank a glass of water instead of coffee, on account of my cursed neuralgia. Doubtless they
were thinking within themselves, How that pious
man is mortifying the flesh!

There was an hour's repose allowed, after
which came another sermon in the chapel. This
over, a bell rang for dinner, which was at eleven

in the morning. The hall was on the lower floor
— very long, high, and dark — with panels of
oak, and ugly pictures on the walls — narrow
oaken tables set all round the sides of the place.
The monks were all there, in their black robes,
with the emblem of their order on the breast.
They had their scowling faces, as well they
might, for their discipline is tremendously strict.
Before each was placed an earthen bottle of
wine and a piece of bread, on the bare board.
Each drew a cup, a knife, fork, and wooden
spoon from a drawer under the table; the attendant lay brothers placed a bowl of singular-
looking soup before each, and they eat in lugu-
brious silence. The superior of the order sat at
the upper end of the hall — a large and powerful man, who looked sterner, if possible, than his
inferiors. We, who sat at another table, were
differently served — with rice, eggs, fish, and
fruit. No one spoke, but from a pulpit above
a monk read at the top of his lungs from a book
of religious precepts in that peculiar drawling
tone which the Catholics employ in their exercises. There was, apparently, little fructifica-
tion in the minds of his hearers. The monks eat
and scowled; the laymen eat and smiled at
each other, exchanging looks of meaning, though
not a word passed between them. There were
among them men of every age and of various
conditions, from the field laborer to the gentleman of good birth. The meal concluded with a
prayer and the growling responses of the Passionists, who then filed off through the galleries
to their dens, looking like the living originals of

the black pictures that hang along the white-washed walls.

A monk has just been here, trying to convert me, but was not so good a hand at argument, or sophistry, as the Jesuits. I told him that he could do nothing with me, but he persisted, clapping his hand on my knee and exclaiming, "Ah, *figlio*, you will be a good Catholic, no doubt." There was a queer sort of joviality about him. He kept offering me his snuff-box, and when he thought he had made a good hit in argument, he would wink at me, with a most comical expression, as if to say, "you see you can't come round me with your heresy." He gave over at the ringing of a bell which summoned us to new readings and lecturings in the chapel, after which we were turned out into the garden of the convent, where we lounged along walks shaded with olives and oleanders. Padre Lucca, the directing priest, talked over matters of faith to me. He was an exception to the rest of the establishment — plump and well-fed, with a double chin like a bull-frog, and a most contented and good-humored countenance.

After supper to-night some of the Italians in the conversazione expressed great sympathy for my miserable state of heresy : one of them, with true charity, according to his light, said that he would pray to the Virgin, who could do all things, to show me the truth. The whole community assembled to vespers. The dark and crowded chapel fairly shook with the din of more than a hundred manly voices chanting the service.

There is nothing gloomy and morose in the religion of these Italians here, no camp-meeting long faces. They talk and laugh gayly in the intervals allowed them for conversation; but when the occasion calls it forth, they speak of religion with an earnestness, as well as a cheerfulness, that shows that it has a hold on their hearts.

Saturday. This morning, among the rest, they went through the Exercise of the Via Crucis, which consists in moving in a body around the chapel, where are suspended pictures, fourteen in number, representing different scenes in the passion of Christ. Before each of these they stop, the priest reads the appropriate prayer and expressions of contrition from the book, repeats a Pater Noster, etc., and so they make a circuit of the whole. I saw the same ceremony, on a larger scale, in the Coliseum, without knowing what it was.

A thin, hollow-eyed father tried to start my heresy this morning, but was horrified at the enormity of my disbelief; and when I told him that I belonged to a Unitarian family, he rolled up his bloodshot eyes in their black sockets, and stretched his skinny neck out of his cowl, like a turtle basking on a stone in summer. He gave me a little brass medal of the Virgin with a kind of prayer written on it. This medal he begged me to wear round my neck, and to repeat two or three Aves now and then. It was by this means, he said, that Ratisbon the Jew was converted, not long since; who, though he wore the medal and repeated the Aves merely to get rid of the importunities of a Catholic friend,

yet nevertheless was favored with a miraculous
vision of the Virgin, whereupon he fell on his
knees and was joined to the number of the Faithful. I told the monk that I would wear the medal
if he wished me to, but should not repeat the
Aves; so I have it now round my neck, greatly
to his satisfaction. [This medal Parkman kept
all his life.] Miracles, say all the Catholics here,
happen frequently nowadays. The other day a
man was raised to life who had just died in con-
sumption, and now is walking the streets in complete health !

These Italians have come to the seclusion of
this convent in order that their minds may not
be distracted by contact with the world, and that
the religious sentiments may grow up unimpeded
and receive all possible nutriment from the constant exercises in which they are engaged. It is
partly, also, with the intention of preparing them
for the General Confession. It is only for a few
days in the year that any are here. Their "exercises" are characteristic of the Church. The
forms of prayer are all written down; they read,
repeat, and sing. Very little time is allowed them
for private examinations and meditations, and
even in these they are directed by a printed card
hung in each of the rooms, and containing a list
of the subjects on which they ought to examine
themselves, together with a form of contrition to
be repeated by them. The sermons and readings
are full of pictures of Christ's sufferings, exhorta-
tions to virtue, etc., but contain not a syllable of
doctrine. One of the first in the printed list of
questions which the self-examiner is to ask him-

self is, "Have I ever dared to inquire into the mysteries of the Faith?"

Sunday. This is Palm Sunday, the first day of the famous Settimana Santa, — the Holy Week. I determined to get out of the convent and see what was going on. The day and night previous I had worn the medal, but had no vision of the Virgin, — at least of Santissima Maria. Padre Lucca was unfeignedly sorry to have me go with unimpaired prospects of damnation. He said he still had hopes of me; and taking the kindest leave of me, gave me a book of Catholic devotions, which I shall certainly keep in remembrance of a very excellent man. He looked at the book I had been reading the night before, and expressed his approbation, — it was a life of Blessed Paul of the Cross, detailing among other matters how the apostle hated women with a holy and religious hatred, justly regarding them as types of the devil, and fountains of unbounded evil to the sons of men; and how, when women were near, he never raised his eyes from the ground, but continually repeated Pater Nosters that the malign influence might be averted.

When I got into the fresh air I felt rather glad to be free of the gloomy galleries and cells, which, nevertheless, contain so much to be admired.[1] . . .

I heard it computed that there are forty thousand strangers in Rome, which must, however, be a great exaggeration. The English are the most numerous, esteemed, and beloved as usual.

[1] Cf. "A Convent at Rome," *Harper's New Monthly Magazine*, August, 1890.

One of them, standing in St. Peter's, before the ceremony yesterday, civilly exclaimed, "How long does this damned Pope expect us to stand here waiting for him!" A priest who spoke English reminded him that, since he had come to Rome, it was hoped that he would conform to the usages, or at least refrain from insulting the feelings of those around. The Englishman answered by an insolent stare; then turning his back, he said, "The English *own* Rome!"

FRANK TO HIS MOTHER.

Rome, April 5, '44.

DEAR MOTHER, — . . . We are in the midst of the fooleries of Holy Week. To-night the Pope took a mop, and washed the high altar, in the presence of some ten thousand people. . . . I have been spending a few days in a convent of the monks called Passionists. . . . I find that though I am very well indeed in other respects, there has not been any great change in the difficulty that brought me out here. . . . I have resolved to go to Paris and see Dr. Louis, the head of his profession in the world, and see if he can do anything for me. . . . I have been a perfect anchorite here, have given up wine, etc., and live at present on 40 cents a day for provisions — so if I do not thrash the enemy at last, it will not be my fault. . . . Here are four thousand English in Rome and they are tolerably hated by the Italians, while we sixty or seventy Americans seem, I am happy to say, liked and esteemed everywhere. . . .

Yours,　　　FRANK.

CHAPTER XI

The next day I left Rome for Florence, in the diligence — and left it with much regret, and a hope to return. A young American named Marquand went with me. . . .

I went to the studio of Powers the sculptor, a noble-looking fellow and a wonderful artist. I have seen Florence — that is, I have had a glance at everything there, but one might stay with pleasure for months. Its peculiar architecture and its romantic situation make it striking enough at first sight, but the interest increases, instead of diminishing. It is impossible to have seen enough of its splendid picture galleries, gardens, and museums.

On Wednesday I left Florence, unsatisfied, but unable to stay longer. After all, I shall not see Granada — at least for some years, thanks to the cursed injury that brought me to Europe; for as I find no great improvement, I judge it best to see what a French doctor can do for me, instead of running about Spain.

At ten in the evening we left Parma. At five in the morning we were at Piacenza. Here we stopped an hour or two. Here again the striking difference between the towns of northern and southern Italy was manifested. The people looked as grave and solemn as the brick fronts of the palaces and churches. . . .

We crossed the Po, by a wretched bridge of boats, and entered Lombardy and the domains of Austria. The black eagle of Austria was painted above the guard-house, on the farther bank, where a dozen sullen-looking soldiers loitered about. There was a barrack of them near the custom-house, where we must stop an hour and a half to be searched, and to pay the fellows for doing it. After that we rode all day through a beautiful and fertile country, passing through Lodi, the scene of Bonaparte's victory, till at night we entered Milan, saturated with dust.

As for the city, it is well enough. The people are different in appearance, in manners, in language, and in habits, from the southern Italians. The women are all out sunning themselves; whole flights of them came out of the Cathedral, with little black veils flung over their heads, and mass books in their hands. Their faces and figures are round and rich — of the fiery black eye of Rome I have seen nothing; their eyes are blue and soft, and have rather a drowsy meek expression, and they *look* excessively modest.

This morning, when the whole city was quiet, the shops shut in honor of Sunday, the people issuing from the Cathedral, gentlemen walking listlessly about, and porters and contadini sitting idle at the edge of the sidewalks. There was a group of gentlemen taking their coffee under awnings in front of each of the caffès on the piazza before the Cathedral. This vagabond way of breakfasting and seeing the world at the same time is very agreeable. There is no place where you can be more independent than in one of these cities; when you are hungry there is always a restaurant and a dinner at a moment's notice, when you are thirsty there is always a caffè at hand. If you are sleepy, your room awaits you, a dozen sneaking waiters are ready at your bidding, and glide about like shadows to do what you may require, in hope of your shilling when you go away. But give me Ethan Crawford, or even Tom, in place of the whole race of waiters and garçons. I would ask their pardon for putting them in the same sentence, if they were here.

A funeral procession filed into the Cathedral, each priest, layman, woman, and child with an enormous wax candle in hand. The noble chapel, at the left extremity of the transept, was hung with black for the occasion — the coffin was placed in the midst, and the ceremonies were performed. The priests seemed not fairly awake. One fat bull-frog of a fellow would growl out of his throat his portion of the holy psalmody, interrupting himself in some interesting conversation with his neighbor, and resuming it again as soon as the religious office was performed. Another would gape and yawn in the midst of his musical performances, another would walk about looking at the people, or the coffin, or the kneeling women, singing meanwhile with the most supreme indifference and content on his fat countenance. I could imagine the subject of their conversation, as they walked out in a double file, leaving the coffin to the care of the proper officials, after they had grunted a concluding anthem over it. " Well, we 've fixed this fellow's soul for him. It was a nasty job ; but it 's over now. Come! won't you take something to drink?" [The foregoing quotation and some others that I shall make to indicate the ginger and spice of his character, must be read with the recollection that they are the hasty jottings of a young man who was writing in his private notebook, never expecting them to be seen. If we were to misinterpret these sallies unfairly even for a moment, we should do injustice to the reasonableness of his character. Had he spoken them, his smile would have dispelled any misunderstanding.]

I used to like priests, and take my hat off and make a low bow, half in sport and half in earnest, whenever I met them, but I have got to despise the fellows. Yet I have met admirable men among them ; and have always been treated by them all with the utmost civility and attention.

I write on the Lake of Como, with three women, a boy, and four men looking over my shoulder, but they cannot read English.

I have seen nothing, at home or abroad, more beautiful than this lake. It reminds me of Lake George — the same extent, the same figure, the same crystal purity of waters, the same wild and beautiful mountains on either side. But the comparison will not go farther. Here are a hundred palaces and villages scattered along the water's edge and up the declivities. . . . All here is like a finished picture; even the wildest rocks seem softened in the air of Italy. Give me Lake George, and the smell of the pine and fir!

(Andeer.) I stopped here, and will stay here several days. Nothing could surpass the utter savageness of the scenery that you find by tracing up some of the little streams that pour down on all sides to join the Rhine — not a trace of human hand — it is as wild as the back-forests at home. The mountains, too, wear the same aspect.

. . . Here was a change, with a vengeance, from the Italian beauties of the Lake of Como! I sat on the rock, fancying myself again in the American woods with an Indian companion, but as I rose to go away the hellish beating of my heart warned me that no more such expeditions were in store for me — for the present, at least; but if I do not sleep by the camp-fire again, it shall be no fault of mine. . . .

(Zurich.) The Germans lighted their pipes with their flint and steel, and, stretching out their legs and unbuttoning their coats, disposed themselves to take their ease. Here was none of the painful dignity which an Englishman thinks it incumbent upon him to assume throughout his travels — no kneepans aching with the strain of tight strapped pantaloons, no neck half severed by the remorseless edge of a starched dickey. . . .

The journey to Paris occupies two days. Yesterday morning, looking from the window, I saw an ocean of housetops stretching literally to the very horizon. We entered the gate, but rode for nearly an hour through the streets before we reached the diligence office. Then I went to the Tuileries, the Palais Royal, the Boulevard des Italiens, and the Place Vendôme. "Let envious Englishmen sneer as they will," I thought, "this *is* the 'Athens of Modern Europe.'"

I had called on my uncle [Mr. Samuel Parkman], and found him not at home. He called on me with the same fortune, but left a note directing me to be at a celebrated café at a certain time, where he was to be distinguished by a white handkerchief in his hand. I found him there, and went with him to a ball at the Champs Elysées.

Boulogne, May 16th. I have been a fortnight in Paris, and seen it as well as it can be seen in a fortnight. Under peculiarly favorable circumstances, too; for it was the great season of balls and gayeties, and I had a guide, moreover, who knows Paris from top to bottom, within and without. . . .

When I got to London, I thought I had been there before. There, in flesh and blood, was the whole host of characters that figure in Pickwick. Every species of cockney was abroad in the dark and dingy looking streets, all walking with their heads stuck forward, their noses turned up, their chin pointing down, their knee-joints shaking, as they shuffled along with a gait perfectly ludicrous, but indescribable. The hackney coachmen and cabmen, with their peculiar phraseology, the walking advertisements in the shape of a boy completely hidden between two placards, and a hundred others seemed so many incarnations

of Dickens' characters. A strange contrast to
Paris ! The cities are no more alike than the
" dining room " of London and the elegant restaurant of Paris, the one being a quiet dingy
establishment where each guest is put into a box
and supplied with porter, beef, potatoes, and
plum-pudding. Red-faced old gentlemen of three
hundred weight mix their " brandy go " and read
the " Times." In Paris the tables are set in elegant galleries and saloons, and among the trees
and flowers of a garden, and here resort coats cut
by the first tailors and bonnets of the latest mode,
whose occupants regale their delicate tastes on
the lightest and most delicious viands. The waiters spring from table to table as noiselessly as
shadows, prompt at the slightest sign ; a lady,
elegantly attired, sits within an arbor to preside
over the whole. Dine at these places, then go to
a London " dining room " — swill porter and de-
vour roast beef !

I went immediately to Catlin's Indian Gallery.
It is in the Egyptian Hall, Piccadilly. There was
a crowd around the door ; servants in livery
waiting ; men with handbills of the exhibition
for sale ; cabmen, boys, and pickpockets. I was
rejoicing in Mr. Catlin's success, when the true
point of attraction caught my eye, in the shape
of a full-length portrait of Major Tom Thumb,
the celebrated American dwarf, who it seems
occupies the Indian Gallery for the present. I
paid my shilling and went in. The little wretch
was singing Yankee Doodle with a voice like a
smothered mouse, and prancing about on a table,
à la Jeffrey Hudson, with a wooden sword in his

hand; a great crowd of cockneys and gentlemen
and ladies were contemplating his evolutions.
But for the Indian Gallery, its glory had departed; it had evidently ceased to be a lion.
The portraits of the chiefs, dusty and faded, hung
round the walls, and above were a few hunting
shirts and a bundle or two of arrows; but the
rich and invaluable collection I had seen in Boston had disappeared, and no one thought of looking at the poor remains of that great collection
that were hung about the walls. Catlin had done
right. He would not suffer the fruits of his
six years' labor and danger to rot in the dampness to gratify a few miserable cockneys, so has
packed up the best part of his trophies. . . .

St. Paul's, which the English ridiculously compare to St. Peter's, is without exception the dir-
tiest and gloomiest church I have been in yet.
I went up to the ball at the top of the cupola,
whence the prospect is certainly a most wonderful one. . . .

Walk out in the evening, and keep a yard or
two behind some wretched clerk, who with nose
elevated in the air, elbows stuck out at right
angles, and the pewter knob of his cane playing
upon his under lip, is straddling his bow legs
over the sidewalk with a most majestic air. Get
behind him, and you see his dignity greatly disturbed. First he glances over one of his narrow
shoulders, then over the other, then he edges off
to the other side of the walk, and turns his va-
cant lobster eyes full upon you, then he passes
his hand over his coat-tail, and finally he draws
forth from his pocket the object of all this solici-

tude in the shape of a venerable and ragged cotton handkerchief, which he holds in his hand to keep it out of harm's way. I have been thus taken for a pickpocket more than a dozen times to-night, not the less so for being respectably dressed, for these gentry are the most dashy men on the Strand.

There is an interesting mixture of vulgarity and helplessness in the swarm of ugly faces you see in the streets — meagre, feeble, ill-proportioned, or not proportioned at all, the blockheads must needs put on a game air and affect the "man of the world" in their small way. I have not met one handsome woman yet, though I have certainly walked more than fifty miles since I have been here, and have kept my eyes open. To be sure, the weather has been raw and chill enough to keep beauty at home. Elsewhere Engglishmen are tall, strong, and manly; here, the crowd that swarms through the streets are like the outcasts of a hospital. . . .

I spent seven or eight days in London. On the eighth day I went up the river to Richmond in a steamboat, with a true cockney pleasure party on board, whose evolutions were very entertaining. . . .

I got into the cars one night — having sent my trunks to Liverpool — and found myself in the morning at Darlington, nearly three hundred miles distant. Thence I took stage for Carlisle, famous in Border story.

I went away at four in the morning for Abbotsford. We were in the region where one thinks of nothing but of Scott, and of the themes which he has rendered so familiar to the whole world. The Cheviot was on our right — the Teviot hills before us. The wind came down from them raw and cold, and the whole sky was obscured with stormy clouds. I thought as we left the town of the burden of one of his ballads : "The sun shines fair on Carlisle wall." It was little applicable now. The ancient fortification looked sullen and cheerless as tottering battlements and black crumbling walls, beneath a sky as dark and cold as themselves, could make it. I was prepared for storms and a gloomy day, but soon the clouds parted and the sun broke out clear over the landscape. The dark heathery sides of Teviot — the numberless bright rapid streams that came from the different glens, and the woods of ash, larch, and birch that followed their course, and grew on the steeper declivities of the hills — never could have appeared to more advantage. Esk and Liddel, Yarrow, the Teviot, Minto Crag, Ettrick Forest, Branksome Castle, — these and more likewise we passed before we reached the Tweed and saw Abbotsford on its banks among the forests planted by Scott himself. I left my luggage at the inn at Galashiels, telling the landlord that I was going away, and might return at night, or might not. I visited Abbotsford, Melrose, and Dryburgh — and consider the day better spent than the whole four months I was in Sicily and Italy. I slept at Melrose, and returned to Galashiels in the morning.

I like the Scotch — I like the country and everything in it. The Liverpool packet will not wait, or I should stay long here, and take a

trout from every "burnie" in the Cheviot. The
scenery has been grossly belied by Irving and
others. It is wild and beautiful. I have seen
none more so. There is wood enough along the
margins of the streams (which are as transparent
as our own); the tops of the hills alone are bare.
The country abounds in game, pheasants, moor-
cock, curlew, and rabbits. . . .

I walked up Arthur's Seat, passing the spot
where Jeanie Deans had her interview with her
sister's seducer, and, when I arrived at the top,
looking [sic] down on the site of her father's
cottage. Under the crags here is the place where
Scott and James Ballantyne used to sit when
boys and read and make romances together.
Edinburgh, half wrapped in smoke, lies many
hundred feet below, seen beyond the ragged pro-
jecting edge of Salisbury Crag, the castle rising
obscurely in the extreme distance. . . .

Frank was obliged to hurry off to Liverpool,
where he went aboard the packet Acadia, and
after an uneventful voyage, during which he
amused himself with a little satire upon some
fellow passengers, notably my lord bishop of
Newfoundland, returned safely home.

CHAPTER XII

A MAKE-BELIEVE LAW STUDENT

FRANK landed about June 20th, took his degree
of A. B., and attended a senior class supper, at
which we do not know whether he used the
temperance ticket for $2.12½, or the wine ticket
for $4.62½. Off he went again in the beginning
of July with a little green notebook about as
large as a *porte-monnaie* in his pocket, which
he brought back filled with notes, descriptions,
memoranda, reflections. Conscious of his bach-
elorhood in arts, of a philosophic superiority to
youth and folly, and dignified by a sense of a
horizon stretching from Palermo to Edinburgh,
he begins in fragmentary, critical mood : —

The traveler in Europe. Art, nature, history
combine. In America art has done her best to
destroy nature — association, nothing. Her former state. Her present matter of fact. . . .

July 4, '44. The celebration at Concord. The
admirable good humor of the people in the cars
during some very vexatious delays was remarkable. Some young men sang songs and amused

themselves with jokes, among whom my former
schoolmate was conspicuous. In spite of the cold-
ness attributed to the Am. character, he seems
to play the *rowdy* with all his heart, and as if
he considered it the height of glory.

The cheerfulness, the spirit of accommodation
and politeness was extraordinary. Perfect order,
in the most difficult evolutions of the day. An
hundred soldiers would not in Europe have assured such quiet and unanimity. Some young
men exhibited a good deal of humor and of
knowledge, in their observations, and I remembered that this is *our lowest class.* This orderly,
enthusiastic, and intelligent body is the nearest
approach to the peasantry of Europe. If we have
not the courtly polish of the European upper cir-
cles, the absence of their stupid and brutal peasantry is a fair offset. . . .

Students of H. [Harvard] do not on all occasions appear much better than their less favored
countrymen, either in point of gentlemanly and
distingué appearance or in conversation. . . .

The discussion on Fourierism, etc., of the she-
philosophers of W. Roxbury. Their speculations,
and the whole atmosphere of that heart of *new
philosophy*, were very striking and amusing after
seeing the manners of Paris and London, — the
entertainments and pleasures and the workings
of passions which they in their retirement seem
scarce to dream of. . . .

England has her hedges and her smooth green
hills, robed [?] with a spirit of power and worth,
strengthened and sanctioned by ages ; but give
me the rocky hillside, the shaggy cedar and scrub-

oak, the wide reach of uncultivated landscape, the
fiery glare of the sun . . . its wild and ruddy
light. All is new, all is rough, no charm of the
familiar. Fierce savages have roamed like beasts
amid its rugged scenery; there was a day of struggle, and they have passed away, and a race of
indomitable men have succeeded them. . . .

Nahant, July 17th. The company on board the
steamboat — difference in *silence* and intelligence
from a cackling party. The man with the model
of a beehive, Ohio. . . . The traveled fool, setting his name in the bar book as —— ——,
Cosmopolite. He finds some improvements here
"very creditable to the town," of which he is a
native. He imitates English dress and manners.
The dinner party was various and far from *distingué*.

Roland Green, Mansfield. His family have
relics of the Indians.

The disagreeable whining manner of some
vulgar Yankee girls.

"John Norton's Captivity," taken at a fort in
Adams, 1746.

Springfield. The independent Yankee whom
I spoke to about his failure to call me. In Job's
language he "stood right up to it," giving shot
for shot. No English creeping.

The landlord — no bowing.

Montague. — Grape shot dug up.

The landlord of Chester Factory, sitting cross-legged on his chair, took no notice of me as I came in, but on my asking if the landlord was in, he said, " Yes, here I be."

. . . An American landlord does not trouble himself to welcome his guests. He lets them enter his house, and sits by quite indifferent. He seems rather to consider himself as conferring an obligation in anything he may do for them.

Stockbridge. Maple and beech have followed the fir of the original growth. . . .

Dr. Partridge. The old man was in his laboratory, bedroom, etc., among his old tables, bookcases, etc., with shelves of medicines, and scales suspended hard by. He is about 94, and remembered Williams [Capt. Ephraim Williams] well, who he describes as a large, stout man, who used often to visit his father, and take him on his knee. He says he remembers the face as if he saw it yesterday, especially the swelling of the ruddy cheeks. His father, Colonel Partridge, was in the service, and despised Abercrombie as a coward. The Dr. remembers seeing a thousand of Abercrombie's Highlanders at Hatfield or some other town where they were billeted. Abercrombie was always trembling with fear of Indians, and sending out scouts about camp. When Howe fell, Partridge, the Dr. says, was at his side, and his lordship said, " The army has no leader, and is defeated." . . .

Gt. Barrington . . . Mt. Washington . . . Bash-a-Bish. . . .

The hearty, horse-swapping, thumping young Dutchman, who would be damned if he cared for anything if he could only swap off his old wagons for Jim Pray's colt. . . .

The crouching, cadaverous, lank old man with the opium for his rheumatic wife. . . . The Irish priest, with his jovial conversation and hints about a mitre. [Here follow various rumors concerning letters, journals, remembrances, traditions, concerning perhapses and may-be's, concerning Capt. Ephraim Williams and Rogers the Ranger, all clues carefully noted, followed by a " *Nil Desperandum.*"]

The two girls on the road from N. Adams. One of them was a mixture of all the mean qualities of her sex with none of the nobler. She was full of the pettiest envy, spite, jealousy, and malice, singularly impudent and indelicate.

" Should have given ye a pie to-day, but ain't got no *timber* to make 'em."

Then follow memoranda of books, maps, histories, memoirs, travels, letters, papers, pamphlets, notes from a French MS., etc., ending with a reminder to be at Cambridge on the third Wednesday of August.

But before the middle of September, with another neat little leather-tongued notebook, he went off to Concord. On the flyleaf is the note " Read Dryden's prose " and also a copy of a plan of old Fort Mackinaw made by

Lieutenant Whiting. This notebook served the purpose of a spleen-valve, for in the midst of historical notes and references are interspersed very caustic descriptions of acquaintances and companions. It would be unjust to think that these satirical sketches indicate the usual pitch of his judgments. A lad of twenty-one or two, with a proud resolution hidden in his breast, with strong ambition and high purposes, and perhaps not unmindful of certain maidenly opinions, entertained at Keene and Salem, as to what the world and young men should be, may well be forgiven if he measures his fellows by exacting standards, — standards to which he endeavors to conform his own conduct. Perhaps it was the memory of a girl at Keene that provoked this little irritation.

Sunday, Sept. 21. Some men are fools, utter and inexpressible fools. I went over to Dr. Z's last night to call on Miss ——. Heaven knows I am quite indifferent to her charms, and called merely out of politeness, not caring to have her think I slighted her. But the Dr. in the contemptible suspicion that he is full of, chose to interpret otherwise. William X was there, whom I allowed to converse with Miss Y while I talked with the Dr.'s lady. The Dr. watched me, though I was not aware of it at the time, till happening to rise to take a bottle of cologne, out of a mere whim, and applying some of it to my handker-

chief, the idiot made a remark, in a meaning
tone, about "long walks" in the evening. He
soon after asked me to take a glass of wine, saying that it would make me *feel better.* He whispered in my ear that X would go soon — and I
better stay. What could I do or say? I longed
to tell him the true state of my feelings, and
above all what I thought of his suspicious imper-
tinence. I left the house vexed beyond measure
at being *pitied* as a jealous lover, when one object of my visit to Miss —— that evening was to
prove to her and the rest how free I was from
the influence of her attractions. Is it not hard
for a man of sense to penetrate all the depths of
a blockhead's folly? and to know what inter-
pretation such a fellow will put on his conduct?
I sent him a letter which I think will trouble not
a little his jealous and suspicious temper. . . .

L——'s freaks; his disgusting habits at table;
windows broken and he will not mend them;
goes to B——'s room, looks into his drawers,
"Hulloo, you 've got some gingerbread!" invites
himself to spend the evening there; stays till
morning, and sleeps standing against the wall,
like a horse!

Neither was our young gentleman very broad-
minded: —

May 30, 1845. A great meeting of the Fou-
rierites in Tremont Chapel. Most of them were
rather a mean set of fellows — several foreign-
ers — plenty of women, none pretty — there was
most cordial shaking of hands and mutual con-

gratulations before the meeting began. A dirty
old man four feet high, filthy with tobacco, came
and sat down by me and was very enthusiastic.
He thought Mr. Ripley, who made the opening
speech, "one of the greatest men our country can produce." Ripley was followed by a
stout old man; he spoke with his hands in his
pockets, and gave nothing but statistics, in a
very dry uninteresting manner. It surprised me
to see these old fellows, who looked like anything but enthusiasts, attached to the cause.
H—— ——, the editor from N. Y., spoke in
a very weak indecisive manner, seemingly afraid
of himself and his audience. . . . Brisbane and
Dana followed in a pair of windy speeches, and
Channing was beginning a ditto when I came
away. They say that there is a system of laws
by which the world is to be governed "harmo-
niously," and that they have discovered those
laws. F. —— was there looking much more
like a lunatic or a beast than a man.

The young man had standards of his own; to
his thinking there were certain things a man
should endeavor to do, certain behaviors to
which a gentleman must conform; and as he
was endowed with a masterful quality of mind
and an impatience of bad work, Frank had a
youthful tendency to abrupt and severe judgments; of which, be it said, there is not a trace
in his history.

At Cambridge, soon after the summoning bell
of the third Wednesday, he began a new note-

book, not of the holiday kind incased in green leather, but a large square blue-covered notebook intended for the base uses of grinds. This little book proves his great zeal in acquiring knowledge of European history. Long notes from Gibbon on polytheism, policy, population, roads, trade, and other great matters, so heavy to read, so light to forget. On Gibbon's heels follow Robertson and the Feudal System, then Gibbon again, who had not been finished but intermitted; after him de Mably and Sismondi, then Gibbon back again, like a great whale coming up to breathe, all about kings, popes, declines of this and growths of that; then, on loose and separated pages as befitted a lesser dignity, hints of Poliziano and Savonarola. Then come Sully, Wraxall, Michelet, glimpses of the humanities, and so on through close pages of abstracts and memoranda, until Notebook, No. 2, is reached, which to the reader's relief of mind is dated six months later, where Frank makes a headlong plunge into the Holy Roman Empire, and all for the sake of a background for Indian and *coureur de bois*. Macaulay, von Ranke, Guizot, Dunham, Millot, Pfeffel, Giannone (unless perchance these latter two be makers and not writers of history), primogeniture, Salic law, patriotism, vavasours, decretals, Venice, heresy, and despotism, all come up to be taxed according to the decree of the young Cæsar, who had resolved to put a new province under his subjection. No doubt even such a hearty appetite, whetted by ambition, helped by a strong memory, could not digest the great stretch of recorded time from Augustus to the sailing of Jacques Cartier from Havre de Grace, but he learned enough to know what he must follow up more closely and what he might pass by. Professor Wendell relates how he once met Parkman in the Louvre, in front of a picture of the murder of the duc de Guise, and Parkman immediately recounted with finished detail all the story. The immediate service of the Roman Empire, of the feudal system, of mediæval Europe was, not to stand either as scenery or background, but to fill the vast spaces behind, — where carpenters, machinists, stage-managers toil and sweat, — all to cast the right lights upon the stage on which Pontiac was to play his brilliant part.

When the Law School opened, Frank took a room in Divinity Hall, and using Blackstone as a stalking horse betook himself to the immediate object of his thoughts. Here is a list of some of the books he took from the college library while in college and at the Law School: Scott, Shakespeare, Coleridge, Goldsmith, Dr. Johnson, Irving, Chateaubriand, Carlyle, Machiavelli in Italian, and, first interspersed but soon dominating general reading, books of American history, " Long's Expedition," " Indian Wars," "New Hampshire Historical Collection," "Lewis and Clark," " Travels in Canada," " American Annals," " Rogers's Journal," " Carver's Travels," " Bouquet's Expedition," " Tracts on the War," " Charlevoix," Colden's " Five Nations," " Mœurs des Sauvages," and scores more, many or all contributing their tale of notes to fill little books.

But study did not play too tyrannical a part in his life; he gave friendship and social pleasure their dues.

PARKMAN TO GEORGE S. HALE, KEENE, N. H.

CAMBRIDGE, Monday, Oct. 6, [1844].

DEAR GEORGE, — . . . When shall I hear of you and of your intentions with regard to your profession? Have you decided on the black gown? Believe me it will turn out the best spec. I am down at Divinity, devoting one hour *per diem* to law, the rest to my own notions. It is a little dismal here without the *fellers*, and no Cary [George Blankern Cary, a classmate] to laugh at — life a dull, unchanging monotony, varied by a constitutional walk, or an evening expedition to see Macready. . . .

We have here in the Law School a sprinkling of fine fellows from north, south, east, and west — some in the quiet studying line, some in the *all Hell* style, and some a judicious combination

of both. Dr. Walker pronounces a "very good
spirit" to prevail among the undergraduates, so
that there is no chance of a rebellion or any
other recreation to entertain us lookers-on. . . .
Please remember me to your father, mother, and
sister.   Yrs. very truly,
                              FRANK PARKMAN.

HALE TO PARKMAN, CAMBRIDGE
                              KEENE, Oct. 28, 1844.

DEAR FRANK, — . . . In common with you I
have paid a little attention to Blackstone, and
hope to finish the second volume this week, but
not in such a way as to feel confident that I am
gaining much certain knowledge. Will you tell
me when you write how you study at C, at what
[and what] your lectures amount to, how fast
you read, etc. [embarrassing questions to a young
gentleman whose attention was already fixed on a
"Ranger's Adventure" and a "Scalp-Hunter"].
. . . You ask about the black gown — It trem-
bles in the balance. Would I could see my way
clear — I should certainly feel more at ease. To
tell the truth sub rosa, I am not in love with any
one of the learned professions. Oh glorious literary ease, "sweet *otium* cum scientia"! — "*glorious humbug*" "*sweet nonsense*," says Frank
Parkman and perhaps rightly. In the mean-
time we both shout Vive l'amitié — and cherish
faithfully the remembrance of youthful efforts
which made the . . . [Chit Chat Club] worthy of
fame to our vanity, as it certainly was a bond of
union to its members.

Please tell Ned Dwight he owes me a letter,

and remember that you also are now my debtor.
Meanwhile and ever, I am most truly
          Yr. friend and classmate,
                    GEORGE S. HALE.

SAME TO SAME.

KEENE, N. H., Nov. 17, 1844.

DEAR FRANK, — . . . I was very glad to hear
from you so soon. Quick replies are the life of
a friendly correspondence. . . . I think the balance is rather inclining to sackcloth and the
black gown, but I do not wish to decide at present. Miss Hall was very glad to hear from you
and will welcome you to Keene with pleasure
whenever your memory or fancy may lead you
away from your present literary ease. Do not
forget the maxim I laid down upon quick replies.
I assure you that your letters can never wear out
the hearty welcome they always get from me.
          Most sincerely your friend,
                    GEORGE S. HALE.

Keene was not the only place where Frank
was in favor.

SALEM, Noon, Wednesday, Jan. 15th, '45.

MY DEAR FRANK, — You will scarcely expect me to pop in again on you so soon, but I
wish to nudge your memory, which seems to be
very short lived in regard to your Fair friends
in this City of Peace; our next Assembly is to-
morrow night, — i. e. Thursday, Jan. 16th, '45, —
and my grandmother begs me to assure you that
your chamber is ready for your occupation on

said night, and your knife and fork will be placed
for as many meals as you will honor her ; for be
it known to you, she considers the " Rev. Dr. P.'s
son as a young man of remarkably quick parts
and very correct," to say nothing of his being
my friend. . . . So if the recollection of the last
Assembly is agreeable enough to tempt you, and
nothing better offers nearer home, you must come
down to-morrow. Besides, we must chat over and
arrange the Keene expedition. . . .

If you will dine *en famille* with us to-morrow,
I should be happy to measure appetites with
you. . . .

Farewell — my estomac cries " cupboard," and
half-past one — our primitive dinner hour — is
at hand.   Kind remembrances,

JOE PEABODY.

Dancing and flirting, if that light word may
be applied to Salem in the forties, were not the
only indications of youth and lightheartedness
to be found in the life of Francis Parkman,
Junior, ostensible votary of Blackstone and
Kent.

PARKMAN TO HALE, KEENE, N. H.

CAMBRIDGE, Nov. 24, '44.

DEAR GEORGE, — . . . We wanted you the
other night. Joe got up one of his old-fashioned
suppers on a scale of double magnificence, inviting thereunto every specimen of the class of
'44 that lingered within an accessible distance.
There was old S. and Snaggy, N. D., Ned W.

(who by the way is off for Chili !), P., etc., etc.
The spree was worthy of the entertainment.
None got drunk, but all got jolly ; and Joe's
champagne disappeared first ; then his Madeira ;
and his whiskey punch would have followed suit
if its copious supplies had not prevented. At
first all was quiet and dignified, not unworthy
of graduates ; but at length the steam found vent
in three cheers for '44, and after that we did not
cease singing and roaring till one o'clock. . . . I
succeeded in actually singing in the chorus to
Yankee Doodle without perceptibly annoying
the rest. . . . The whole ended with smashing a
dozen bottles . . . and a war dance with scalp
yells in the middle of the Common, in the course
of which several nightcapped heads appeared at
the opened windows of the astonished neighbors.[1]

PARKMAN TO GEORGE B. CARY.

CAMBRIDGE, Dec. 15, '44.

DEAR GEORGE, — Here I am, down in Divinity Hall enjoying to my heart's content that
otium cum dignitate which you so affectionately
admire ; while you poor devil are jolted in English coaches. . . . Do you not envy me in my literary ease ? — a sea-coal fire — a dressing-gown
— slippers — a favorite author; all set off by
an occasional bottle of champagne, or a bowl of
stewed oysters at Washburn's ? This is the cream
of existence. To lay abed in the morning, till
the sun has half melted away the trees and cas-
tles on the window-panes, and Nigger Lewis's
fire is almost burnt out, listening meanwhile to

[1] *Life of Francis Parkman*, p. 23.

the steps of the starved Divinities as they rush
shivering and panting to their prayers and reci-
tations — then to get up to a fashionable breakfast at eleven — then go to lecture — find it a
little too late, and adjourn to Joe Peabody's
room for a novel, conversation, and a morning
glass of Madeira. . . . — After all a man was
made to be happy ; ambition is a humbug — a
dream of youth ; and exertion another ; . . . I
think the morbid tendency to unnecessary action
passes away as manhood comes on. . . .

At this time he injured sight and health by
getting up very early and studying by candle-
light, often without a fire.

Perhaps you may imagine me under some vi-
nous influence in writing this. Not at all ; yet if
I had written this a few nights ago, perhaps it
might have smacked more of inspiration. We
had a class spree ! Where if there was not much
wit, there was, as the Vicar of Wakefield says,
a great deal of laughing, not to mention singing,
roaring, and unseemly noises of a miscellaneous
character. . . . Our brothers, whilom of . . . [Chit
Chat Club] accused me in the beginning of the
term of an intention of authorship ! probably
taking the hint from the circumstance of my
never appearing till eleven o'clock, à la Scott ;
but I believe they no longer suspect me of so ill
advised an intention. It would run a little counter
to my present principles, though I do remember
the time when G. B. C. [Cary] meditated the
Baron of B——; and Snow felt sure (in his
cups) of being Captain General of Transatlantic

Literature, while your humble servant's less soaring ambition aspired to the manufacture of blood and thunder chronicles of Indian squabbles and massacres. . . . You will answer this, will you not ? I am very eager to hear from you.

Yours truly,   F. PARKMAN.[1]

Frank kept his purpose to himself, and concealed from even his intimate friends that " Capt. Jonathan Carver " had been at work on a tale entitled " The Ranger's Adventure," and after that on another entitled " The Scalp-Hunter."

[1] *Life of Francis Parkman*, pp. 19–22.

CHAPTER XIII

PREPARATION FOR PONTIAC

THE earlier progress of the relations between Frank and his first publisher may be deduced from the following letters : —

KNICKERBOCKER OFFICE, NEW YORK, Feb. 18, '45.
To Capt. JONATHAN CARVER :

Dear Sir, — I thank you most cordially for your excellent sketch, " The Scalp-Hunter," which you were so good as to send us. It is truly a thrilling story, and, to my mind, the closing scene is worthy of Cooper's pen. It is even better than " The Ranger's Adventure," which graces our March issue. It shall have a " place of honor " in our April number.

I need not say that we shall be but too happy to hear from you *at all times ;* and it gives me pleasure to say to you, that your impression of the character of the medium of communication with the public which you have chosen is by no means a mistaken one. If ever there was a periodical that could be proud of its class of readers, it is the " Knickerbocker." There is an affection in the public mind toward it, which I am sure is not surpassed by any kindred work at home or

abroad. Pardon this seeming egotism, my dear
sir. I love the "Old Knick.," having been for
eleven years its editor; and the feeling is widely
shared; for more than half our subscribers are
of that long standing. Our corps of contributors
— God bless them! — can't be exceeded; as one
may see, by looking at their names on the cover.

You will receive the "Knickerbocker" regu-
larly hereafter. Is "Capt. Jonathan Carver" a
nom de plume? I partly suspect so, since probability seems rather to favor the conclusion that a
gentleman tolerably familiar with his own name
would n't be very apt to make a mistake in spell-
ing it. I observe you subscribe yourself Captain
"Jo*h*nathan" Carver! May I hope to hear from
you.   Gratefully and truly yrs,

L. GAYLORD CLARK.

Capt. "Jo*h*nathan" Carver.

KNICKERBOCKER SANCTUM, Monday, March 10th, 45.
MY DEAR SIR, — . . . I must again cordially
thank you for the "Scalp-Hunter." I am an
"old stager" in matters of the sort; and it must
be something *really* "thrilling" to keep me
awake at night, after reading a proof sheet. . . .
I should be glad to hear from you as often as
may be agreeable to you; and as early as the
sixth of each month, if intended for the ensuing
Number.   Very truly, your obliged

L. GAYLORD CLARK.

Frank was, not unnaturally, taxed by his
friends with "concealment," or with what among
law students was probably known as *suppressio*

veri, the suppression of an important matter, which the intimacy of friendship claimed a title to hear. This charge, made by an affection that felt a little hurt to find itself ranked lower than it ranked itself, was not without justification.

By the way, what do you mean by charging me (for the fourth time, is it?) with a design to write a novel, or a poem, or an essay, or whatever it is? Allow me to tell you that though the joke may be good, it is certainly old. . . . If you catch me writing anything of the sort, you might call me a "darned fool" with great propriety as well as elegance.[1]

Frank, boy and man, was not oversensitive to criticism. His own judgment was the only tribunal of much consequence to him; moreover, he was already in full cry upon the scent of Pontiac, "laboring through an army of musty books and antiquarian collections," and what between European history, which he was reading hard, and a decent appearance of attending lectures on law, he was too much occupied to trouble himself with animadversions on what he deemed his own business. And, though Frank was a good son, then and always, he did not take his family into his confidence about his literary work any more than he did his comrades. This

[1] *Life of Francis Parkman*, p. 22.

was natural, as his father was out of sympathy with his interests, and wished him — as fathers do — to pursue a safe career, and win a high position at the Suffolk bar. But Frank was always dutiful, and their relations, if not intimate, were right-minded and affectionate.

This summer's trip was begun in July, but in the mean time, by dint of five o'clock in the morning application, Frank had sent off the copy for another tale to be published in the "Knickerbocker Magazine" for June, and also a poem, entitled, "The New Hampshire Ranger," to be published in August. This year's little notebook, crammed as usual with memoranda of MSS., maps, pamphlets, and addresses of possible antiquarians, shows that Frank stopped in New York long enough to make caustic notes on some young women, and quickly continued his journey to Philadelphia.

PHILADELPHIA, July 14, '45.

DEAR MOTHER, — Though I have been several days here, I have been compelled to remain quiet and passive by the furious heat ; it has now got up to 100° of the thermometer. There is positively no place tolerably comfortable but the bath, where I spend most of my time. Yesterday I was at a Quaker meeting, where, as it was too hot for the Spirit to move anybody, the whole congregation slept in perfect quiet for an hour and then walked off, without a word said. . . . The Philadelphians have shrunk away to the dimensions of Frenchmen, by the effects of the climate. People lounge about at corners and around pumps, rapidly cooking in the sun. . . . I go to Lancaster to-morrow, thence to Harrisburg, thence to Pittsburg, thence give a look at Ohio, and thence go to Detroit, from which I propose to return by Niagara and Albany. My love to Carrie [his sister] and the rest, and believe me,

Affectionately yours,   FRANK.

At Lancaster he interested himself in observing the Dutch farmers; at Harrisburg he divided his attention between the Dutch and the Susquehanna, and made expeditions in the neighborhood to scenes of old forays. The railroads met with his disapproval, so did some of his fellow passengers; "a drunken, swearing puppy in the cars first amused and then disgusted me." At Buffalo he took the steamer for Detroit in company with "a host of Norwegian emigrants, very diminutive, very ugly, very stupid and brutal in appearance, and very dirty. They appeared to me less intelligent and as ignorant as the Indians." At Detroit he studied all the places which he describes in the chapters relating to the siege of the fort by Pontiac. Thence he went down Lake Huron to Mackinaw, noting woodland and marsh, promontory, beach and island, Indian huts and

Canadian settlements. Here he met a lieutenant in the regular army, an antiquarian like himself ("of which title I am a little ashamed," he modestly says). He went about as usual, hunting up the oldest inhabitants, buttonholing all persons suspected of special knowledge, conversing with Indians, crawling into caves, climbing hills, measuring fortifications, pacing the sites of ancient forts, jotting down odd scraps of information ready for use thereafter. Nor did he forget to find room in his diary for biting comments: —

The dyspeptic man who insisted on helping himself to such morsels as suited him (with his own knife and fork). He had nursed himself till he had reached a state of egotistic selfishness. . . . Niagara, Aug. 17. The "Cataract" is a bloated, noisy house ; a set of well-dressed blackguards predominated at table. . . . I have looked at the great cataract, but do not feel in the temper to appreciate it, or embrace its grandeur. An old woman, who for the pure love of talking and an itching to speak to every one, several times addressed me with questions about she knew not what, filled me with sensations of particular contempt instead of amusing me, as they would have done had not my stomach been disordered. I sat down near the rapids. " What's all this but a little water and foam ? " thought I. " What a pack of damned fools ! " was my internal commentary on every group that passed, and some of them deserved it. But, thank Heaven, I have partially recovered my good humor, can sympathize with the species, and to some degree feel the sublimity of the great cataract.

How many of the visitors here deserve to look on it? I saw in the tower a motherly dame and her daughters, amid the foam and thunder and the tremendous pouring of the waters. "Oh, ma! (half whispered) he's looking at us! There, I've torn my sash. I must go home and pin it up," etc.

From Niagara he went to Oswego, Syracuse, to the little Onondaga River, where he inspected the council-house of the Indians, presented to the chiefs gifts of cigars and pipes, and for return extracted what information he could; thence to Oneida, to the valley of the Mohawk, and homeward by Albany and New York.

These little notebooks not only show where Frank went and what he did, but by indirection reveal his dutiful character; for, secluded on back pages, there are accounts of expenditure, kept in boyish-clerkly fashion and somewhat spasmodically. Frank had little natural taste for the counting-room virtues, but he wished to please his father, and so we find entries such as these: —

Funds at starting, Tuesday, July 8, 1845 $103.17
A bill of credit for $100 more.

July 8.	Cravat	$ .75
"	Shave	.06
"	Cider	.04
"	Ticket to N. Y.	2.
"	Supper on board	.50

9th	Ale	.06
"	Boots	.12½
	Porter	.11
"	Carriage to Astor H.	.50
	Baths	.25

and so on with minute precision till his return.

In this same little book, at the top of a page, in among notes of American history, of Indians, of frontiersmen, of journals, of gazettes, and all the heady current of furious historic chase, is written, abbreviated in order to squeeze in amid more important matter : — ·

M. W. F.   —   Greenleaf
Tues. T. S.   —   Story
10–11 o'clock
Story on Bailments Tuesday from 10–11
Blackstone on Wednesday 11–12 2ᵈ & 3ᵈ Sections especially.

A poor pennyworth of law to an intolerable deal of border war; this affords a fair measure of the division of his interest between law and history.

The next year he lived at home in Boston, partly because his third term at the Law School would be completed on January 16, and partly because he was not well; at times he lay in bed and listened to his little sister, Eliza, read a stumpy little volume of Blackstone, and on one day at least Frithiof's Saga. The girl was shy about reading poetry, and the admired big brother, perceiving her diffidence, turned and praised her; then and always his careless seeming but instinctive tenderness knit bonds that grew stronger and stronger all their lives.

In spite of Kent and Blackstone, Frank continued to give his almost exclusive interest to historical research, and we find traces of a widespread correspondence, — Ohio, Delaware, Italy, — questions and answers about Pontiac, Paxton Boys, Jesuits, etc. Some of these letters were to his cousin, J. Coolidge Shaw, a young man lately converted to Catholicism, then studying in Rome for the priesthood.

SHAW TO PARKMAN.

ROME, Nov. 16th, 1845.

MY DEAR FRANK, — I have inquired at the Gesù of Father Glover and Father de Villefort concerning your Canada affairs, but it was in 1762 that the Company of Jesus was suppressed in France, and though the missionaries in Canada were not meddled with, this of course destroyed the communication between them and the mother country. [Here follows advice as to getting historical information, and the names of several Jesuit Fathers.] If these cannot give you what you seek, I fear it cannot be found.

Do you think you shall stick to the Law, or cut it in a year or two to give yourself completely to history? I am glad you have taken this turn, for we want literary men, and a fair historian is a great desideratum. . . . It was history made Hunter a Catholic; and I think if you continue it, it will make you one; . . . and we may live to see the poor Pope stripped of what little earthly power yet remains to him, and as completely a beggar as St. Peter or our Saviour himself; but we shall see him still the Pope, and his people still look to him as father. *Negas?* Well, we shall see. . . . Remember me with all love to Uncle Francis. . . . Tell him we are now studying the treatise *De Trinitate*, which I think, if he read it, would convince him that our Lord is not over well pleased at being stripped of his Divinity and only honored as a man when he ought to be worshiped as a God.

Hope to have the pleasure of reading your work when it is out, and that its success will give you a right to make it your fixed pursuit. . . .

Truly and affectionately yrs,
J. C. SHAW.

With theology and formal religion Frank had little sympathy; but random comments in his diaries show that all his life he had a "reverent gratitude for Christianity" and a strong sentiment for what he deemed a real and masculine religion. Probably the epithet, "reverent agnostic," which near the end of life he accepted in a conversation with his sister, of right belonged to him in youth. Manliness was an essential characteristic of everything that found favor in his eyes, and he believed the agnostic position the most manly, for with that belief, so he thought, a man stood on his own feet and faced the universe, asking no prop except his own stout heart. But metaphysics never interested him, and at this time history crowded out every other thought from his mind.

Frank now perceived that he had reached a point in his studies at which he must take a new course. On his summer excursions he had got much information concerning the Yankee frontiersman, he had read all the books he could find that dealt with his subject, he had quizzed farmer, antiquarian, and wayfarer for tradition, gossip, hearsay ; he must now study the Indians, not the tamed savages living by the Kennebec, or the Onondaga, but the aboriginal savages, in their homes. He knew that personal knowledge of their life and customs was essential to his work, and now that he had performed the filial duty of taking his lawyer's degree, he felt that it was high time to go westward to the land of the Sioux and the Snakes. Accordingly he gladly accepted a suggestion from Mr. Quincy A. Shaw, Coolidge's brother, — he, too, bred upon Cooper and Catlin, — to join him and to take a journey towards Oregon and California.

Already that year, immediately on the completion of his third term in the Law School, Frank had made a trip to Philadelphia and Baltimore, on which he had acquired certain valuable experiences carefully jotted down in his notebook: "N. B. Always take a driver's card. . . . N. B. Employ a porter in preference to a carriage for baggage. . . . Always ask for a porter's card — see your baggage ticketed in person and get the number of the car that contains it." From this trip he got home about the middle of February, and on March 28th started off again, this time on his memorable expedition upon the Oregon Trail. The careful little record of accounts, in which bills for copying MSS. begin to appear — item $1.50, item $5.00, item $25.00 — show that he went to New York, Philadelphia, Cincinnati, and so to St. Louis.

FRANK TO HIS MOTHER.

CINCINNATI, April 9th, 1846.

DEAR MOTHER, — . . . To-day I reached Cincinnati, after a two days' passage down the Ohio. The boat was good enough though filled with a swarm of half-civilized reprobates, gambling, swearing, etc., among themselves. . . . The great annoyance on board these boats is the absurd haste of everybody to gulp down their meals. Ten minutes suffices for dinner, and it requires great skill and assiduity to secure a competent allowance in that space of time. As I don't much fancy this sort of proceeding, I generally manage to carry off from the table enough to alleviate the pangs of hunger without choking myself. The case is much the same here in the best hotel in Cincinnati. When you sit down, you must begin without delay — grab whatever is within your reach, and keep hold of the plate by main force till you have helped yourself. Eat up as many potatoes, onions, or turnips as you can lay hands on ; and take your meat afterwards, whenever you have a chance to get it. It is only by economizing time in this fashion that you can avoid starvation — such a set of beasts are these western men. . . . In three or four days I shall be at St. Louis, stopping a short time at Louisville, Kentucky. My eyes are decidedly improved, and my health excellent. In going about Cincinnati this morning, I found a most ridiculous piece of architecture, in utter defiance of taste or common sense ; and learned that it was built by Mrs. Trollope during her stay here. . . . I am, dear mother,

Very affectionately yrs,   F. P.

This letter must have crossed two from his sister Caroline.

CAROLINE TO FRANK.

April 4, 1846.

MY DEAR FRANK, — . . . I don't believe you can form any idea of your importance in our family. We wish for you just as much to-day as we did a week ago, when you left us. I was really truly sorry that I had not a better command of myself when you went away, for it is too bad to give way to the feelings and make a leave-taking for such a pleasant journey so gloomy. If I could have gone over the good-by again, it should have been with smiles rather than tears, for I would not be so selfish as to think of myself, when there is so much pleasure in prospect for you. . . . With true love,

CARRIE.

CAROLINE TO FRANK.

April 7, BOSTON, 1846.

. . . I spent Sunday with Aunt Mary, who misses your visits and the prospect of them very much. I mean to spend a day or two with her every week. Mrs. Swan wished me to give her love to you, and says that she cannot realize that such a quiet little boy as you were should ever be such a " Will-o-the-Wisp." . . . I forgot to tell you in our last letter how extremely disappointed Perry [his classmate, H. J. Perry] was on coming to see you on the afternoon you had gone. . . . They all send their love, especially Elly [his little brother], who misses you very much, as we all do. . . .

With much love, CARRIE.

Frank was making notes all the time. He had stopped to see the site of Fort Duquesne, the remains of Fort Pitt, the spot of Braddock's defeat, and various scenes of border war; nor did he pretermit his practice of making comments on the people he met. " The English reserve or *offishness* seems to be no part of the western character — I observe this trait in myself — to-day, for instance, when a young fellow expressed satisfaction that he should accompany me to St. Louis, I felt rather inclined to shake him off, though he had made himself agreeable enough." This trait of Parkman's remained with him through life ; it may receive sympathy or blame, according to temperament, or perhaps according to the mood of the moment, but those who, like this young fellow, wished to come within a line beyond which Parkman proposed that they should stay, were sometimes wounded in their vanity.

He reached St. Louis about the 13th of April, and was soon joined by Shaw.

CHAPTER XIV

OFF ON THE OREGON TRAIL [1]

In the early part of 1846 Oregon was still the whole country west of the Rocky Mountains, stretching from Mexico (as it was then still undispossessed by the United States), on the south, as far north as the parallel 50° 40′, and was jointly occupied by Great Britain and the United States, until later in that year the treaty fixed the boundary between them at the 49th parallel. The trail was the somewhat uncertain track followed by emigrants and traders.

This expedition, which Shaw wished to extend to California but could not as Frank had not the time to give, took them into the vast region east of the Rocky Mountains which is now cut up into the States of Nebraska, Colorado, and Wyoming.

Parkman and Shaw left St. Louis on the 28th of April, 1846, on board a river steamboat in a somewhat disorderly company of traders, adventurers, gamblers, negroes, Indians, and emi-

[1] See *The Oregon Trail.*

grants. They landed on the western frontier of
Missouri near Kansas City, which they reached
the next day. There they made their headquarters while purchasing horses, mules, and various
articles necessary for the journey. Near by, encamped on the prairie, were a multitude of emigrants. Some of them were sober men, interested in the doctrine of regeneration, others were
rogues from the lowest layer of society, prompted
by a forlorn hope of bettering their condition,
or by mere restlessness, or perhaps by a wish to
shake off the restraints of law and society.
Parkman and Shaw did not like such company,
and therefore they joined forces with a small
party of Englishmen for the sake of mutual
protection.

Their first experiences of the journey westward
were a mild foretaste of what was to come. No
sooner were the animals put in harness than the
shaft-mule reared and plunged, burst ropes and
straps, and nearly flung the cart into the Missouri. The beast was uncontrollable, and another had to be procured. This done, their cart
started, but had barely gone a few miles before
it stuck fast in a muddy gully, where it remained
for more than an hour. Their outfit was suffi-
cient but not elaborate. Their guide was dressed
in broad felt hat, moccasins, and deerskin trousers; he rode a Wyandot pony and carried his

rifle in front, resting on the pommel of the saddle, bullet-pouch and powder-horn at his side, and knife in belt. Parkman and Shaw wore flannel shirts, buckskin breeches, and moccasins; each had a blanket rolled up behind, holsters with heavy pistols, and the trail-rope coiled and fastened to the front of the saddle. Each had a gun, and a horse beside the one he rode. The cart carried the provisions, tent, ammunition, blankets, and presents for Indians. The muleteer, Deslauriers, was a Canadian.

Neither fatigue, exposure, nor hard labor could ever impair his cheerfulness and gayety, or his politeness to his *bourgeois* [employer]; and when night came he would sit down by the fire, smoke his pipe, and tell stories with the utmost contentment. The prairie was his element.

The guide, Henry Chatillon, was of a much higher type; he came of a family of French Canadians, though he was born in Missouri. He was a tall, powerful, fine-looking fellow.

The prairies had been his school; he could neither read nor write, but he had a natural refinement and delicacy of mind, such as is rare even in women. His manly face was a mirror of uprightness, simplicity, and kindness of heart; he had, moreover, a keen perception of character, and a tact that would preserve him from flagrant error in any society. He had not the

restless energy of an Anglo-American. He was
content to take things as he found them; and
his chief fault arose from an excess of easy gen-
erosity not conducive to thriving in the world.
Yet it was commonly remarked of him that,
whatever he might choose to do with what
belonged to himself, the property of others was
always safe in his hands. His bravery was as
much celebrated in the mountains as his skill in
hunting; but it is characteristic of him that, in
a country where the rifle is the chief arbiter between man and man, he was very seldom involved in quarrels. Once or twice, indeed, his
quiet good-nature had been mistaken and pre-
sumed upon, but the consequences of the error
were such that no one was ever known to repeat
it. No better evidence of the intrepidity of his
temper could be asked than the common report
that he had killed more than thirty grizzly bears.
I have never, in the city or in the wilderness,
met a better man than my true-hearted friend,
Henry Chatillon.

After a few days of varied discomforts, chief
of which were insects and thunderstorms, they
came to the Big Blue River, which they crossed
on a raft, and then they struck the regular trail
of the Oregon emigrants. Soon they came upon
a party of them.

These were the first emigrants that we had
overtaken, although we had found abundant and
melancholy traces of their progress throughout
the course of the journey. Sometimes we passed

the grave of one who had sickened and died on
the way. The earth was usually torn up, and
covered thickly with wolf-tracks. Some had escaped this violation. One morning a piece of
plank, standing upright on the summit of a
grassy hill, attracted our notice, and riding up
to it, we found the following words very roughly
traced upon it, apparently with a red-hot iron : —

MARY ELLIS
Died May 7th, 1845.
Aged two months.

Such tokens were of common occurrence.

Here a small emigrant train was invited by
the Englishmen to join company with them,
much to the disgust of Parkman and Shaw, as
the emigrant wagons drawn by oxen must necessarily hinder their progress. The emigrants
themselves, however, were good fellows, and all
journeyed on in amity ; in one respect the addition was an advantage, for every night two men
mounted guard, and with a greater number each
man's turn came round less frequently. Parkman rather enjoyed his watches in spite of loss
of sleep and rest.

A few days' journey brought them to the top
of some sand-hills, from which they could see
the valley of the Platte.

We all drew rein, and sat joyfully looking
down upon the prospect. It was right welcome,
— strange, too, and striking to the imagination ;

and yet it had not one picturesque or beautiful feature; nor had it any of the features of
grandeur, other than its vast extent, its solitude, and its wildness. For league after league a
plain as level as a lake was outspread beneath
us; here and there the Platte, divided into a
dozen thread-like sluices, was traversing it, and
an occasional clump of wood, rising in the midst
like a shadowy island, relieved the monotony of
the waste. No living thing was moving throughout the vast landscape, except the lizards that
darted over the sand and through the rank grass
and prickly pears at our feet. [From here their
course lay westward through a long, narrow,
sandy plain, flanked by two lines of sand-hills,
and stretching nearly to the foot of the Rocky
Mountains. Before and behind them the plain
spread level to the horizon.] Sometimes it glared
in the sun, an expanse of hot bare sand; sometimes it was veiled by long coarse grass. Skulls
and whitening bones of buffalo were scattered
everywhere; the ground was tracked by myriads
of them. . . . The naked landscape is, of itself,
dreary and monotonous enough; and yet the
wild beasts and wild men that frequent the valley of the Platte make it a scene of interest and
excitement to the traveler. Of those who have
journeyed there, scarcely one, perhaps, fails to
look back with fond regret to his horse and his
rifle. [Here they made acquaintance with the
Pawnee Indians, an idle, thieving tribe. Many
stories of their depredations were current, and
the travelers kept careful watch. The weather
was most fitful.] This very morning, for in-

stance, was close and sultry, the sun rising with
a faint oppressive heat; when suddenly darkness
gathered in the west, and a furious blast of sleet
and hail drove full in our faces, icy cold, and
urged with such demoniac vehemence that it felt
like a storm of needles. It was curious to see
the horses; they faced about in extreme dis-
pleasure, holding their tails like whipped dogs,
and shivering as the angry gusts, howling louder
than a concert of wolves, swept over us. Wright's
[the Englishmen's muleteer] long train of mules
came sweeping round before the storm, like a
flight of snow-birds driven by a winter tempest.
. . . The thing was too good to last long; and
the instant the puffs of wind subsided we pitched
our tents, and remained in camp for the rest of
a gloomy and lowering day.

[The even tenor of the journey was soon broken
by the presence of buffalo. Their tracks had
been frequent for some days, and a few stray
bulls had been shot, but before this no herd had
been seen.] One day somebody cried, "Buffalo,
buffalo!" It was but a grim old bull, roaming
the prairie by himself in misanthropic seclusion;
but there might be more behind the hills. Dread-
ing the monotony and languor of the camp, Shaw
and I saddled our horses, buckled our holsters
in their places, and set out with Henry Chatillon
in search of the game. Henry, not intending to
take part in the chase, but merely conducting
us, carried his rifle with him, while we left ours
behind as incumbrances. We rode for some five
or six miles, and saw no living thing but wolves,
snakes, and prairie-dogs. . . . The ground was

none of the best for a race, and grew worse as we proceeded; indeed, it soon became desperately bad, consisting of abrupt hills and deep hollows, cut by frequent ravines not easy to pass. At length, a mile in advance, we saw a band of bulls. Some were scattered grazing over a green declivity, while the rest were crowded together in the wide hollow below. Making a circuit, to keep out of sight, we rode towards them, until we ascended a hill within a furlong of them, beyond which nothing intervened that could possibly screen us from their view. We dismounted behind the ridge, just out of sight, drew our saddle-girths, examined our pistols, and mounting again, rode over the hill and descended at a canter towards them, bending close to our horses' necks. Instantly they took the alarm; those on the hill descended, those below gathered into a mass, and the whole got into motion, shouldering each other along at a clumsy gallop. We followed, spurring our horses to full speed; and as the herd rushed, crowding and trampling in terror through an opening in the hills, we were close at their heels, half suffocated by the clouds of dust. But as we drew near, their alarm and speed increased; our horses, being new to the work, showed signs of the utmost fear, bounding violently aside as we approached, and refusing to enter among the herd. The buffalo now broke into several small bodies, scampering over the hills in different directions, and I lost sight of Shaw; neither of us knew where the other had gone. Old Pontiac [Parkman's horse] ran like a frantic elephant uphill and down hill, his ponderous hoofs striking the prairies like sledge-hammers. He showed a curious mixture of eagerness and terror, straining to overtake the panic-stricken herd, but constantly recoiling in dismay as we drew near. The fugitives, indeed, offered no very attractive spectacle, with their shaggy manes and the tattered remnants of their last winter's hair covering their backs in irregular shreds and patches, and flying off in the wind as they ran. At length I urged my horse close behind a bull, and after trying in vain by blows and spurring to bring him alongside, I fired from this disadvantageous position. At the report Pontiac swerved so much that I was again thrown a little behind the game. The bullet, entering too much in the rear, failed to disable the bull, for a buffalo requires to be shot at particular points or he will certainly escape. The herd ran up a hill, and I followed in pursuit. As Pontiac rushed headlong down on the other side, I saw Shaw and Henry descending the hollow on the right at a leisurely gallop; and in front the buffalo were just disappearing behind the crest of the next hill, their short tails erect, and their hoofs twinkling through a cloud of dust.

At that moment I heard Shaw and Henry shouting to me ; but the muscles of a stronger arm than mine could not have checked at once the furious course of Pontiac, whose mouth was as insensible as leather. Added to this, I rode him that morning with a snaffle, having the day before, for the benefit of my other horse, unbuckled from my bridle the curb which I commonly used. A stronger

and hardier brute never trod the prairie; but the
novel sight of the buffalo filled him with terror,
and when at full speed he was almost incontrol-
lable. Gaining the top of the ridge, I saw nothing
of the buffalo; they had all vanished amid the
intricacies of the hills and hollows. Reloading
my pistols in the best way I could, I galloped on
until I saw them again scuttling along at the base
of the hill, their panic somewhat abated. Down
went old Pontiac among them, scattering them
to the right and left; and then we had another
long chase. About a dozen bulls were before us
scouring over the hills, rushing down the declivities with tremendous weight and impetuosity,
and then laboring with a weary gallop upward.
Still Pontiac, in spite of spurring and beating,
would not close with them. One bull at length
fell a little behind the rest, and by dint of much
effort I urged my horse within six or eight yards
of his side. His back was darkened with sweat;
he was panting heavily, while his tongue lolled
out a foot from his jaws. Gradually I came up
abreast of him, urging Pontiac with leg and rein
nearer to his side, when suddenly he did what
buffalo in such circumstances will always do, —
he slackened his gallop, and turning towards us,
with an aspect of mingled rage and distress, lowered his huge, shaggy head for a charge. Pontiac,
with a snort, leaped aside in terror, nearly throw-
ing me to the ground, as I was wholly unprepared
for such an evolution. I raised my pistol in a
passion to strike him in the head, but thinking better of it, fired the bullet after the bull,
who had resumed his flight; then drew rein, and

determined to join my companions. It was high time. The breath blew hard from Pontiac's nostrils, and the sweat rolled in big drops down his sides; I felt myself as if drenched in warm water. . . . I looked about for some indications to show me where I was, and what course I ought to pursue. I might as well have looked for landmarks in the midst of the ocean. How many miles I had run, or in what direction, I had no idea; and around me the prairie was rolling in steep swells and pitches, without a single distinctive feature to guide me. I had a little compass hung at my neck; and ignorant that the Platte at this point diverged considerably from its easterly course, I thought that by keeping to the northward I should certainly reach it. So I turned and rode about two hours in that direction. The prairie changed as I advanced, softening away into easier undulations, but nothing like the Platte appeared, nor any sign of a human being: the same wild, endless expanse lay around me still; and to all appearance I was as far from my object as ever. I began now to think myself in danger of being lost, and, reining in my horse, summoned the scanty share of woodcraft that I possessed (if that term be applicable on the prairie) to extricate me. It occurred to me that the buffalo might prove my best guides. I soon found one of the paths made by them in their passage to the river; it ran nearly at right angles to my course; but turning my horse's head in the direction it indicated, his freer gait and erected ears assured me that I was right. . . . Being now free from anxiety, I was at leisure to observe minutely the objects around me; and here for the first time I noticed insects wholly different from any of the varieties found farther eastward. Gaudy butterflies fluttered about my horse's head; strangely formed beetles, glittering with metallic lustre, were crawling upon plants that I had never seen before; multitudes of lizards, too, were darting like lightning over the sand.

He followed the buffalo path until at last he came in sight of the river, and then with the aid of Pontiac he found the emigrant trail, and seeing that his party had not passed he turned to meet them.

Having been slightly ill on leaving camp in the morning, six or seven hours of rough riding had fatigued me extremely. I soon stopped, therefore, flung my saddle on the ground, and with my head resting on it, and my horse's trail-rope tied loosely to my arm, lay waiting the arrival of the party, speculating meanwhile on the extent of the injuries Pontiac had received.

Soon afterwards Shaw and the mule-team came up, and the party resumed their way.

CHAPTER XV

THE OGILLALLAH

On June 8th the party forded the South Fork of the Platte. Here they parted from their companions. The Englishmen affected authority to decide when and where they should encamp, and were domineering in their bearing; so Parkman and Shaw, careless of the security afforded by numbers, took a somewhat abrupt leave, and, having less baggage, soon left the others behind. They pushed on along the North Fork of the Platte without adventures, beyond meeting a Dakota village wandering along in rude procession under the command of Old Smoke, and crossed what is now the boundary between Nebraska and Wyoming. They forded Laramie Creek, the southern of two streams that unite just east of Fort Laramie to form the North Fork of the Platte, and, a short distance beyond, arrived at the fort. This post was occupied, not by a garrison of United States troops, as the name might suggest, for in fact the nearest soldiers were seven hundred miles to the east, but by servants

of the American Fur Company, who bought
skins and furs of the trappers and Indians. The
scene was like that in a French fort on the frontier a hundred years before. The fort itself,
built of bricks dried in the sun, was oblong in
shape. Its walls were about fifteen feet high,
and were fortified at two of the corners by
blockhouses built of clay. Within, the area was
divided by a partition; on one side was a court
surrounded by storerooms, offices, and bed-
rooms; on the other side was an inclosure where
the horses and mules were shut in at night. The
inhabitants were a motley crew. There were
the servants of the company, men of French Canadian blood, in breeding and education not
much above their friends the Indians, who loafed
about with solemn faces in white buffalo robes,
or dozed in the sunshine. There were gayly
painted squaws in large numbers, a troop of
mongrel children tumbling about, and half-breed
trappers, who had either just come back from
a trapping expedition or were about to start.
Parkman and Shaw were hospitably received.
The chamber, ordinarily occupied by the *bourgeois* [the "boss"] of the post, who was absent,
was put at their disposal. Its furniture was a
bare bedstead, two chairs, a chest of drawers,
and a pail; buffalo robes were stretched on the
floor for beds, as the bedstead was only an orna-

ment. On the wall, side by side, hung a crucifix
and a fresh scalp. The food consisted of dried
buffalo meat, "an excellent thing for strengthening the teeth," and cakes of bread. Here they
stayed several days, observing the ways and customs of their hosts and of the Indians. Old
Smoke's village had encamped near by, and they
used to go there and spend most of their evenings.

Parkman was very glad to observe the Indian
at home, but he desired with greater eagerness
to study him on the warpath; for this an opportunity seemed to be at hand. The son of an
Ogillallah chief, The Whirlwind, had been killed
by the Snake Indians; and in revenge The
Whirlwind had roused all the Dakota villages
within three hundred miles to take part in a
campaign against the Snakes. The Ogillallah Indians belong to the Dakota or Sioux tribe, and
their kith and kin, having also grievances of
their own against the Snakes, acknowledged their
duty to punish the injury, and many villages,
making altogether five thousand persons or more,
were already on the march to the appointed
meeting ground on the river Platte. There they
were to celebrate the solemn rites which in Indian usage precede a campaign, and then the warriors, one thousand strong, were to start on the
warpath. "I was greatly rejoiced to hear of it. I

had come into the country chiefly with a view of
observing the Indian character. To accomplish
my purpose it was necessary to live in the midst
of them, and become, as it were, one of them. I
proposed to join a village, and make myself an
inmate of one of their lodges." The first plan
had been to join Old Smoke's village, but Henry
Chatillon, the guide, was very anxious to go to
The Whirlwind's village to see his squaw, who
belonged to that village, and was there very ill,
so Parkman changed his plan to accord with
Chatillon's desire. Parkman was not well he
says : —

I had been slightly ill for several weeks, but
on the third night after reaching Fort Laramie
a violent pain awoke me, and I found myself
attacked by the same disorder that occasioned
such heavy losses to the army on the Rio Grande
[Mexican war]. In a day and a half I was reduced to extreme weakness, so that I could not
walk without pain and effort. Having no medical adviser, nor any choice of diet, I resolved to
throw myself upon Providence for recovery,
using, without regard to the disorder, any portion of strength that might remain to me. So
on the twentieth of June we set out from
Fort Laramie to meet The Whirlwind's village.
Though aided by the high-bowed "mountain-
saddle," I could scarcely keep my seat on horseback.

They halted at a spot on Laramie Creek which

The Whirlwind must necessarily pass on his way
to the meeting place, and there pitched their
camp to await his coming. Days went by, but
the dilatory Whirlwind did not come.

If our camp was not altogether safe [a troop
of hostile Indians had passed within rifle-shot, but
had missed them on account of a heavy mist], still
it was comfortable enough; at least it was so to
Shaw, for I was tormented with illness and vexed
by the delay in the accomplishment of my designs.
When a respite in my disorder gave me some
returning strength, I rode out well armed upon
the prairie, or bathed with Shaw in the stream,
or waged a petty warfare with the inhabitants
of a neighboring prairie-dog village. Around our
fire at night we employed ourselves in inveighing
against the fickleness and inconstancy of Indians,
and execrating The Whirlwind and all his crew.

Parkman's impatience could brook the delay
no longer, so he rode back to the fort, which was
about eighteen miles distant, to learn what news
he could of the war. At the fort, to his surprise,
he found The Whirlwind, whom the traders, in
their zeal to prevent any detriment to trade, were
urging to abandon the warpath. The Whirlwind
was fickle, and it seemed likely that the traders
would persuade him. Parkman returned to his
camp in great vexation, for his philanthropy, as
he said, was no match for his curiosity to see the
Indian on the warpath; but he tried with poor

success to console himself with the thought that he avoided a very fair chance of being plundered, and perhaps stabbed or shot into the bargain. In a few days, however, they were cheered by the arrival of a young chief from The Whirlwind's village, who stated that The Whirlwind had not been persuaded to abandon the warpath, and was on his way to the meeting place, and would arrive at the spot where Parkman was encamped in two days; and so it came to pass. Parties of Indians arrived by twos and threes, and then the main village in disorderly array straggled to the camping ground, and pitched their lodges, above one hundred and fifty in number. Here they lingered for several days; Parkman made friends with the warriors and learned their several histories.

After tarrying at this place long enough to allow a proper period for vacillation, The Whirlwind made up his mind not to repair to the meeting place of the war-party, but to cross the Black Hills and proceed to the hunting grounds beyond, so that his people might secure enough buffalo meat for the coming season, and fresh skins for their lodges. When that should have been done, The Whirlwind proposed to send a band of warriors against the enemy. Parkman and Shaw held a council together whether to go to the meeting place in the hope of finding other bands of Dakota there, or to abide with The Whirlwind's village and share its fortunes. They chose the latter course, and started on July first with the Indians, but before they had ridden many miles a message came from a fur trader, Bisonette, whom they had met at the fort, saying that he was going to the meeting place and urging them to go, too; so they changed their minds, parted company with The Whirlwind, who was westward bound, and turned their horses' heads to the north. On the third day they reached the appointed place, but found neither Indians nor Bisonette. They dismounted and relieved their indignation with tobacco and criticism of the whole aboriginal race in America.

For myself, I was vexed beyond measure; as I well knew that a slight aggravation of my disorder would render this false step irrevocable, and make it impossible to accomplish effectually the object which had led me an arduous journey of between three and four thousand miles. . . . After supper that evening, as we sat round the fire, I proposed to Shaw to wait one day longer, in hopes of Bisonette's arrival, and if he should not come, to send the [muleteer] with the cart and baggage back to Fort Laramie, while we ourselves followed The Whirlwind's village, and attempted to overtake it as it passed the mountains. Shaw, not having the same motive for hunting Indians that I had, was averse to the plan; I therefore resolved to go alone. This design I adopted very

unwillingly, for I knew that in the present state
of my health the attempt would be painful and
hazardous. I hoped that Bisonette would appear
in the course of the following day, and bring us
some information by which to direct our course.

But Bisonette did not come, though Shaw took
a day's ride to find him, and the next morning
Parkman made ready to start. He had exchanged
Pontiac for a fleet little mare, Pauline, and all
his baggage was tied by leather thongs to her
saddle. In front of the black, high-bowed moun-
tain-saddle were fastened holsters with heavy
pistols. A pair of saddle-bags, a blanket tightly
rolled, a small parcel of Indian presents tied up
in buffalo skin, a leather bag of flour, and a
smaller one of tea, were all secured behind, and
a long trail-rope was wound round her neck.
Raymond had a strong black mule equipped in
a similar manner. They crammed their powder-
horns to the throat and mounted. Raymond was
a French Canadian trapper hired as guide the
week before. " I will meet you at Fort Laramie
on the first of August," said Parkman to Shaw.
So they parted; Parkman and Raymond rode
off in the direction taken by The Whirlwind's
village, and Shaw after some misadventures returned, under the compulsion of ivy-poison, to
the fort.

CHAPTER XVI

A ROUGH JOURNEY

PARKMAN'S way led across wide plains and rough
ridges of hills, all cracked and split with fissure
and ravine, and dazzling white under the burning sun; no trees cheered the waste, except a
stray pine here and there. But at sunset they
came upon a line of thick bushes which clothed
the banks of a little stream; here they dismounted, made their fire, and, wrapped in their
blankets, fell fast asleep, in complete disregard
of howling wolves. In the early morning the
animals were grazing and Raymond had gone
for a shot at an antelope, when on a sudden
Pauline broke her hobbles and galloped off, and
the mule bounded after her as best he could on
his hobbled legs. Raymond, still near enough to
hear Parkman's call, ran in pursuit, and soon all
three were out of sight, leaving Parkman, too
weak to join in the chase, to his meditations.

It seemed scarcely possible that the animals
could be recovered. If they were not, my situation was one of serious difficulty. Shaw, when I

left him, had decided to move that morning, but whither he had not determined. To look for him would be a vain attempt. Fort Laramie was forty miles distant, and I could not walk a mile without great effort. Not then having learned the philosophy of yielding to disproportionate obstacles, I resolved, come what would, to continue the pursuit of the Indians. Only one plan occurred to me: this was, to send Raymond to the fort with an order for more horses, while I remained on the spot, awaiting his return, which might take place within three days. But to remain stationary and alone for three days in a country full of dangerous Indians was not the most flattering of prospects. Resolving these matters, I grew hungry; and as our stock of provisions, except four or five pounds of flour, was by this time exhausted, I left the camp to see what game I could find.

A further danger was that Raymond might catch the animals and not return. But Raymond was faithful; after a chase of ten miles and more, he caught the fugitives, and Parkman was able to start again upon his westward course in the afternoon, but they were not destined to make much progress that day. A tremendous storm deluged them. After a time a blue rift appeared in the clouds, and, growing larger, made room for a rainbow; the sun shone warm on the plain, and revealed a belt of woods in front, which proffered a good place for camp.

Raymond kindled a fire with great difficulty. The animals turned eagerly to feed on the soft rich grass, while I, wrapping myself in my blanket, lay down and gazed on the evening landscape. The mountains, whose stern features had frowned upon us so gloomily, seemed lighted up with a benignant smile, and the green, waving undulations of the plain were gladdened with warm sunshine. Wet, ill, and wearied as I was, my heart grew lighter at the view, and I drew from it an augury of good.

The next day they struck Laramie Creek, and following the stream found marks of the Indians at the point where they had forded the river. Delighted to find the trail, Parkman and Raymond dined on haunch of antelope, and in high spirits made ready to follow ; but as Parkman was saddling the exhausted Pauline, she staggered and fell. With an effort she regained her feet, and was able to carry her master at a slow pace. The trail was clear at one spot where anthills held the dint of trailing lodge-poles, at another it disappeared on flinty ground ; then it became visible again where the leaves of the prickly pear showed bruises. Towards evening they lost the trail completely, but far away, a little to their right, in a black valley at the foot of Mount Laramie, which rose in purple darkness above its fellow peaks, they could see volumes of smoke curling upward. At first they were

inclined to ride thither, but reflection dissuaded
them, and they afterward had reason to believe
that the smoke was raised as a decoy by hostile
Crows. That night they lay beside Laramie
Creek, and at daybreak Parkman plunged in,
and for the moment felt the tingling of health;
but the sensation was momentary; as soon as he
was in the saddle, he says, " I hung as usual in
my seat, scarcely able to hold myself erect."

From where they were they could see a pass
in the mountain wall, which gave cause to think
that the Indians had gone through it.

We reached the gap, which was like a deep
notch cut into the mountain ridge, and here we
soon found an ant-hill furrowed with the mark
of a lodge-pole. This was quite enough; there
could be no doubt now. As we rode on, the opening growing narrower, the Indians had been compelled to march in closer order, and the traces
became numerous and distinct. The gap termi-
nated in a rocky gateway, leading into a rough
and steep defile, between two precipitous mountains. Here grass and weeds were bruised to fragments by the throng that had passed through.
We moved slowly over the rocks, up the passage,
and in this toilsome manner advanced for an hour
or two, bare precipices, hundreds of feet high,
shooting up on either hand. Raymond, with his
hardy mule, was a few rods before me when we
came to the foot of an ascent steeper than the
rest, and which I trusted might be the highest

point of the defile. Pauline strained upward for
a few yards, moaning and stumbling, and then
came to a dead stop, unable to proceed farther.
I dismounted, and attempted to lead her; but
my own exhausted strength soon gave out, so I
loosened the trail-rope from her neck, and tying
it round my arm, crawled up on my hands and
knees. I gained the top, totally spent, the sweat-
drops trickling from my forehead. Pauline stood
like a statue by my side, her shadow falling upon
the scorching rock; and in this shade, for there
was no other, I lay for some time, scarcely able
to move a limb. All around, the black crags,
sharp as needles at the top, stood baking in the
sun, without tree or bush or blade of grass to
cover their nakedness. The whole scene seemed
parched with a pitiless, insufferable heat. [After
a pause Parkman was able to mount again, and
they descended the defile on the farther side;
here they were cheered by a clump of trees, a
fringe of grass, and a little icy brook. At the
foot of the mountains lay a plain, a half dozen
miles across and bad riding, and beyond the
plain there were thick woods and more mountains; through these a rocky passage wound
among gigantic cliffs and led into a second
plain. Here they stopped to eat.] When we
had finished our meal Raymond struck fire, and
lighting his pipe, sat down at the foot of a tree
to smoke. For some time I observed him puffing
away with a face of unusual solemnity. Then
slowly taking the pipe from his lips, he looked
up and remarked that we had better not go any
farther. " Why not? " asked I. He said that the

country was become very dangerous, that we were entering the range of the Snakes, Arapahoes, and Gros-ventre Blackfeet, and that if any of their wandering parties should meet us, it would cost us our lives; but he added, with blunt fidelity, that he would go anywhere I wished. I told him to bring up the animals, and mounting them we proceeded again. I confess that, as we moved forward, the prospect seemed but a doubtful one. I would have given the world for my ordinary elasticity of body and mind, and for a horse of such strength and spirit as the journey required. Closer and closer the rocks gathered round us, growing taller and steeper, and pressing more and more upon our path. We entered at length a defile which, in its way, I never have seen rivaled. The mountain was cracked from top to bottom, and we were creeping along the bottom of the fissure, in dampness and gloom, with the clink of hoofs on the loose shingly rocks, and the hoarse murmuring of a petulant brook which kept us company. . . . Looking up, we could see a narrow ribbon of bright blue sky between the dark edges of the opposing cliffs. This did not last long. The passage soon widened, and sunbeams found their way down, flashing upon the black waters. The defile would spread to many rods in width; then we would be moving again in darkness. The passage seemed about four miles long, and before we reached the end of it the unshod hoofs of our animals were broken, and their legs cut by the sharp stones. Issuing from the mountain, we found another plain. All around it stood a

circle of precipices that seemed the impersona-
tion of Silence and Solitude.

From this amphitheatre there was but one
outlet, over a low hill, and beyond that the
prairie spread wide and desolate. Here they
dismounted for the night and dined on their
last bit of antelope steak. Parkman was about
to shoot a rabbit, in order to replenish their
larder, but Raymond out of not unnecessary
caution stopped him, for fear lest the report
might attract visitors.

That night for the first time we considered
that the danger to which we were exposed was
of a somewhat serious character; and to those
who are unacquainted with Indians it may seem
strange that our chief apprehensions arose from
the supposed proximity of the people whom we
intended to visit. Had any straggling party of
these faithful friends caught sight of us from
the hilltop, they would probably have returned
in the night to plunder us of our horses, and
perhaps of our scalps. But the prairie is unfavorable to nervousness; and I presume that
neither Raymond nor I thought twice of the
matter that evening. [The next day they lost
the trail again on a broad flat plain, with nothing in front but a long line of hills. Raymond
became discouraged.] "Now," said he, "we had
better turn round." But as Raymond's *bourgeois*
thought otherwise, we descended the hill and began to cross the plain. We had come so far that

neither Pauline's limbs nor my own could carry me back to Fort Laramie. I considered that the lines of expediency and inclination tallied exactly, and that the most prudent course was to keep forward.

On they went, and drearily climbed the far-off hills; from the top Parkman discerned a few dark spots moving, which he took to be buffalo, but Raymond shouted "Horses!" and galloped on, lashing his mule to its best pace, and in a few minutes, standing in a circle, they saw the lodges of the Ogillallah. "Never, says Parkman, "did the heart of wanderer more gladden at the sight of home than did mine at the sight of that Indian camp."

There, after the customary ceremony of shaking hands with everybody, the first business was to choose a host, and after inquiry Parkman decided to partake of Big Crow's hospitality.

So Raymond and I rode up to the entrance of Big Crow's lodge. A squaw came out immediately and took our horses. I put aside the leather flap that covered the low opening, and, stooping, entered the Big Crow's dwelling. There I could see the chief in the dim light, seated at one side, on a pile of buffalo robes. He greeted me with a guttural "How, cola!" I requested Reynal [a Canadian acquaintance hunting with the Indians] to tell him that Raymond and I were come to live with him. The Big Crow gave another low exclamation. The announcement may seem intrusive, but, in fact, every Indian in the village would have deemed himself honored that white men should give such preference to his hospitality. The squaw spread a buffalo robe for us in the guest's place at the head of the lodge. Our saddles were brought in, and scarcely were we seated upon them before the place was thronged with Indians, crowding in to see us. The Big Crow produced his pipe and filled it with the mixture of tobacco and *shongsasha*, or red willow bark. Round and round it passed, and a lively conversation went forward. Meanwhile a squaw placed before the two guests a wooden bowl of boiled buffalo-meat; but unhappily this was not the only banquet destined to be inflicted on us. One after another, boys and young squaws thrust their heads in at the opening, to invite us to various feasts in different parts of the village. For half an hour and more we were actively engaged in passing from lodge to lodge, tasting in each of the bowl of meat set before us, and inhaling a whiff or two from our entertainer's pipe.

The Whirlwind was not there; he had not come, rumor said, from fear of going so far into the enemy's country, for the village was now encamped on the Snake hunting ground; the main body of the community had disregarded his authority, and were on their way to hunt the buffalo.

The next day brought with it a return of hospitality.

I intended that day to give the Indians a feast, by way of conveying a favorable impression of my character and dignity; and a white dog is the dish which the customs of the Dakota prescribe for all occasions of formality and importance. I consulted Reynal: he soon discovered that an old woman in the next lodge was owner of the white dog [a big dog on which Parkman had cast his eye]. I took a gaudy cotton handkerchief, and, laying it on the ground, arranged some vermilion, beads, and other trinkets upon it. Then the old squaw was summoned. I pointed to the dog and to the handkerchief. She gave a scream of delight, snatched up the prize, and vanished with it into her lodge. For a few more trifles, I engaged the services of two other squaws, each of whom took the white dog by one of his paws, and led him away behind the lodges. Having killed him they threw him into a fire to singe; then chopped him up and put him into two large kettles to boil. Meanwhile I told Raymond to fry in buffalo-fat what little flour we had left, and also to make a kettle of tea as an additional luxury. The Big Crow's squaw was briskly at work sweeping out the lodge for the approaching festivity. I confided to my host himself the task of inviting the guests, thinking that I might thereby shift from my own shoulders the odium of neglect and oversight. When feasting is in question one hour of the day serves an Indian as well as another. My entertainment came off at about eleven o'clock. At that hour Reynal and Raymond walked across the area of the village, to the admiration of the inhabitants, carrying the two kettles of dog meat slung on a pole between them. These they placed in the centre of the lodge, and then went back for the bread and the tea. Meanwhile I had put on a pair of brilliant moccasins, and substituted for my old buckskin frock a coat which I had brought with me in view of such public occasions. I also made careful use of the razor, an operation which no man will neglect who desires to gain the good opinion of Indians. Thus attired, I seated myself between Reynal and Raymond at the head of the lodge. Only a few minutes elapsed before all the guests had come in and were seated on the ground, wedged together in a close circle. Each brought with him a wooden bowl to hold his share of the repast. When all were assembled, two of the officials, called "soldiers" by the white men, came forward with ladles made of the horn of the Rocky Mountain sheep, and began to distribute the feast, assigning a double share to the old men and chiefs. The dog vanished with astonishing celerity, and each guest turned his dish bottom upward to show that all was gone. Then the bread was distributed in its turn, and finally the tea. As the "soldiers" poured it out into the same wooden bowls that had served for the substantial part of the meal, I thought it had a particularly curious and uninviting color. "Oh," said Reynal, "there was not tea enough, so I stirred some soot in the kettle, to make it look strong!" Fortunately an Indian's palate is not very discriminating. The tea was well sweetened, and that was all they cared for. Now, the feast being over, the time for speechmaking was come. The Big Crow produced a flat piece of wood, on which he cut up tobacco and *shongsasha*, and mixed them in due proportions. The pipes were filled and passed from hand to hand around the company. Then I began my speech, each sentence being interpreted by Reynal as I went on, and echoed by the whole audience with the usual exclamations of assent and approval. As nearly as I can recollect, it was as follows : " I had come," I told them, " from a country so far distant that at the rate they travel, they could not reach it in a year." — " How ! How ! " — " There the Meneaska (white men) were more numerous than the blades of grass on the prairie. The squaws were far more beautiful than any they had ever seen, and all the men were brave warriors." — " How ! How ! How ! " — I was assailed by twinges of conscience as I uttered these last words. But I recovered myself and began again. " While I was living in the Meneaska lodges, I had heard of the Ogillallah, how great and brave a nation they were, how they loved the whites, and how well they could hunt the buffalo and strike their enemies. I resolved to come and see if all that I heard was true." — " How ! How ! How ! " — " As I had come on horseback through the mountains, I had been able to bring them only a few presents." — " How ! " — " But I had enough tobacco to give them all a small piece. They might smoke it, and see how much better it was than the tobacco which they got from the traders." — " How ! How ! How ! " — " I had plenty of powder, lead, knives, and tobacco at Fort Laramie. These I was anxious to give them, and if any of them should come to the fort before I went away, I would make them handsome presents!" — "How! How! How! How!" Raymond then cut up and distributed among them two or three pounds of tobacco, and old Mene-Seela [the principal chief] began to make a reply. It was long, but the following was the pith of it. "He had always loved the whites. They were the wisest people on earth. He believed they could do anything, and he was always glad when any of them came to live in the Ogillallah lodges. It was true I had not made them many presents, but the reason of it was plain. It was clear that I liked them, or I never should have come so far to find their village!" Other speeches were made. A short silence followed, and then the old man (Mene-Seela) struck up a discordant chant, which I was told was a song of thanks for the entertainment I had given them. "Now," said he, "let us go, and give the white men a chance to breathe." So the company all dispersed into the open air, and for some time the old chief was walking round the village, singing his song in praise of the feast, after the custom of the nation.

CHAPTER XVII

LIFE IN AN INDIAN VILLAGE

AFTER some indecision, for the village was without a leader, — even The Whirlwind when he was present had no authority, — the Indians set forward again for the hunting fields. The line of march was always highly picturesque, painted warriors riding gayly, iron-tipped lances glittering in the sun, packhorses heavily laden with bundles and babies, or dragging lodge poles, ponies ridden by grinning young squaws, old men on foot wrapped in white buffalo robes, slim boys and girls, barking dogs, all apparently led by the genius of confusion. It was always as good as a play to Parkman, though he was hardly in fit state of body to enjoy a pageant.

At our encampment that afternoon I was attacked anew by my old disorder. In half an hour the strength that I had been gaining for a week past had vanished again, and I became like a man in a dream. But at sunset I lay down in the Big Crow's lodge and slept, totally unconscious till the morning. The first thing that awakened me was a hoarse flapping over my head, and a sudden light that poured in upon me. The camp was breaking up, and the squaws were moving the covering from the lodge. I arose and shook off my blanket with the feeling of perfect health; but scarcely had I gained my feet when a sense of my helpless condition was once more forced upon me, and I found myself scarcely able to stand. Raymond had brought up Pauline and the mule, and I stooped to raise my saddle from the ground. My strength was unequal to the task. "You must saddle her," said I to Raymond as I sat down again on a pile of buffalo robes. He did so, and with a painful effort I mounted. As we were passing over a great plain surrounded by long broken ridges, I rode slowly in advance of the Indians, with thoughts that wandered far from the time and the place. Suddenly the sky darkened, and thunder began to mutter. Clouds were rising over the hills, as dark as the first forebodings of an approaching calamity; and in a moment all around was wrapped in shadow. I looked behind. The Indians had stopped to prepare for the approaching storm, and the dense mass of savages stretched far to the right and left. Since the first attack of my disorder the effects of rain upon me had usually been injurious in the extreme. I had no strength to spare, having at that moment scarcely enough to keep my seat on horseback. Then, for the first time, it pressed upon me as a strong probability that I might never leave those deserts. "Well," thought I to myself, "the prairie makes quick and sharp work. Better to die here, in the saddle to the last, than to stifle in the hot air of a sick chamber ; and a thousand times better than to drag out life, as many have done, in the helpless inaction of lingering disease." So, drawing the buffalo robe on which I sat over my head, I waited till the storm should come. It broke at last with a sudden burst of fury, and passing away as rapidly as it came, left the sky clear again. My reflections served me no other purpose than to look back upon as a piece of curious experience; for the rain did not produce the ill effects that I had expected.

The Indians, being in enemy's country, were anxious to lose no time, and pushed on westward ; in a day or two their scouts reported herds of buffalo marching slowly over the hills in the distance. The lodges were pitched, and things got ready for the hunt. Early in the morning the huntsmen were off.

I had taken no food, and not being at all ambitious of further abstinence, I went into my host's lodge, which his squaws had set up with wonderful dispatch, and sat down in the centre, as a gentle hint that I was hungry. A wooden bowl was soon set before me, filled with the nutritious preparation of dried meat called *pemmican* by the northern voyagers and *wasna* by the Dakota. Taking a handful to break my fast upon, I left the lodge just in time to see the last band of hunters disappear over the ridge of the neighboring hill. I mounted Pauline and gal-

loped in pursuit, riding rather by the balance
than by any muscular strength that remained to
me. . . . I left camp that morning with a philosophic resolution. Neither I nor my horse were
at that time fit for such sport, and I had determined to remain a quiet spectator ; but amid the
rush of horses and buffalo, the uproar and the
dust, I found it impossible to sit still; and as
four or five buffalo ran past me in a line, I lashed
Pauline in pursuit. We went plunging through
the water and the quicksands, and clambering
the bank, chased them through the wild sage
bushes that covered the rising ground beyond.
But neither her native spirit nor the blows of
the knotted bull-hide could supply the place of
poor Pauline's exhausted strength. We could
not gain an inch upon the fugitives.

After a shot, which hit but did not maim the
cow he was chasing, Parkman turned back and
rode slowly to camp.

In this place they remained five days, the
braves hunting every day and killing great numbers of buffaloes. The hides were skinned,
scraped, and rubbed, the meat was cut up and
hung to dry in the sun. Parkman, and also
Pauline, were too tired to take further part in
the hunting, so he strolled over the prairie for
an occasional shot at an antelope, and watched
his hosts and their squaws at their various occupations. His repose at night was not all that
weary limbs might wish. In the next lodge

gambling would be going on, fast and furious;
ornaments, horses, garments, and weapons were
staked upon the chances of the game to the ac-
companiment of yells, chants, and the thumping
of an Indian drum. In Parkman's own lodge
Big Crow would rouse himself every night at
twelve o'clock and sing a doleful dirge to ap-
pease the spirits; and the children, who were allowed to eat too much during the day and were
petted and generally spoiled, had a habit of
crawling about the lodge over Parkman and
every other object, and sometimes they cuddled
under his blanket. He was obliged to keep a
short stick at hand and punch their heads some
five times during the night.

On the twenty-fifth the camp broke up, and
the return journey was begun. . . . The lodges
were pitched early, and the chiefs sat in a circle
smoking and chaffing one another.

When the first pipe was smoked óut, I rose
and withdrew to the lodge of my host. Here I
was stooping, in the act of taking off my powder-
horn and bullet-pouch, when suddenly, and close
at hand, pealing loud and shrill, and in right
good earnest, came the terrific yell of the war-
whoop. Kongra-Tonga's [Black Crow] squaw
snatched up her youngest child and ran out of
the lodge. I followed, and found the whole village in confusion, resounding with cries and
yells. The circle of old men in the centre had

vanished. The warriors, with glittering eyes, came darting, weapons in hand, out of the low openings of the lodges, and running with wild yells towards the farther end of the village. Advancing a few rods in that direction, I saw a crowd in furious agitation. Just then I distinguished the voice of Reynal [a French Canadian living with the Indians] shouting to me from a distance; he was calling to me to come over and join him [on the farther side of a little stream]. This was clearly the wisest course, unless we wished to involve ourselves in the fray; so I turned to go, but just then a pair of eyes, gleaming like a snake's, and an aged familiar countenance was thrust from the opening of a neighboring lodge, and out bolted old Mene-Seela, full of fight, clutching his bow and arrows in one hand and his knife in the other. . . . The women with loud screams were hurrying with their children in their arms to place them out of danger, and I observed some hastening to prevent mischief by carrying away all the weapons they could lay hands on. On a rising ground close to the camp stood a line of old women singing a medicine-song to allay the tumult. As I approached the side of the brook, I heard gunshots behind me, and turning back saw the crowd had separated into two long lines of naked warriors confronting each other at a respectful distance, and yelling and jumping about to dodge the shots of their adversaries, while they discharged bullets and arrows against each other. At the same time certain sharp, humming sounds in the air over my head, like the flight of beetles on a summer evening, warned me that the danger was not wholly confined to the immediate scene of the fray. So, wading through the brook, I joined Reynal and Raymond, and we sat down on the grass, in the posture of an armed neutrality, to watch the result. Happily it may be for ourselves, though contrary to our expectation, the disturbance was quelled almost as soon as it began. When I looked again, the combatants were once more mingled together in a mass. Though yells sounded occasionally from the throng, the firing had entirely ceased, and I observed five or six persons moving busily about, as if acting the part of peacemakers. One of the village heralds or criers proclaimed in a loud voice something which my two companions were too much engrossed in their own observations to translate for me. The crowd began to disperse, though many a deep-set black eye still glittered with an unnatural lustre, as the warriors slowly withdrew to their lodges. This fortunate suppression of the disturbance was owing to a few of the old men, less pugnacious than Mene-Seela, who boldly ran in between the combatants, and, aided by some of the " soldiers," or Indian police, succeeded in effecting their object.

It was contrary to etiquette to inquire into the cause of the brawl, and Parkman only learned it some time afterwards. Mad Wolf had presented Tall Bear with a horse, expecting, according to the well-understood custom, to receive another gift of equal value in return. Tall Bear, how-

ever, made no reciprocal gift, whereupon Mad
Wolf strode up to Tall Bear's lodge, untied the
horse he had given, and started to lead it home;
Tall Bear leapt from his lodge and stabbed the
horse dead. Mad Wolf, quick as a flash, drew
an arrow to the head against Tall Bear's breast,
but the other stood impassive as a statue, and
Mad Wolf lowered his bow. Partisans rallied
to each, and the fray began, but no one was
killed, thanks to the vigorous intervention of the
old chiefs and of the "soldiers," a species of con-
stabulary appointed in council and charged with
the duty of preserving the peace.

The next step in the Indian preparation for
winter was to cut lodge poles. For these, which
could only be cut from tall straight saplings, it
was necessary to go to the Black Hills. So they
traveled eastward for two days and arrived at
the foot of the gloomy ridges; here, after traversing a long ravine between precipitous cliffs
and masses of rock, they came upon the desired
groves. The Indians cut their poles, while Parkman cultivated the friendship of Mene-Seela,
and persuaded Black Crow, the White Eagle,
and the Panther, his more intimate comrades,
to spin yarns of their adventures. Most of the
Indians Parkman did not trust, and did not like.

They were thorough savages. Neither their
manners nor their ideas were in the slightest

degree modified by contact with civilization. They knew nothing of the power and real character of the white men, and their children would scream in terror when they [first] saw me. Their religion, superstitions, and prejudices were those handed down to them from immemorial time. They fought with the weapons that their fathers fought with, and wore the same garments of skins. They were living representatives of the " stone age ; " for though their lances and arrows were tipped with iron procured from the traders, they still used the rude stone mallet of the primeval world. . . . For the most part, a civilized white man can discover very few points of sympathy between his own nature and that of an Indian. With every disposition to do justice to their good qualities, he must be conscious that an impassable gulf lies between him and his red brethren. No, so alien to himself do they appear that, after breathing the air of the prairie for a few months or weeks, he begins to look upon them as a troublesome and dangerous species of wild beast. Yet, in the countenance of the Panther (. . . who, unless his face greatly belied him, was free from the jealousy, suspicion, and malignant cunning of his people), I gladly read that there were at least some points of sympathy between him and me.

As they approached Fort Laramie Parkman became eager to make haste, for August 1st, the day on which he had promised to meet Shaw, had already come; so, when the buttes, near which he had encamped while waiting for the unpunctual Whirlwind, lifted their rough cones above the horizon, he rode away from his savage hosts in company with Raymond and one Indian who was bound for the fort. Several of the Indians proffered him their horses as parting presents, for the sake of receiving Pauline in return, but their offers were promptly declined; Parkman shook hands with Reynal, but in deference to aboriginal custom, took no leave of the Indians, and with mixed feelings of regret and pleasure parted with them forever. That night they encamped near their old site.

" First, however, our wide-mouthed friend [the Indian] had taken the precaution of carefully examining the neighborhood. He reported that eight men, counting them on his fingers, had been encamped there not long before, — Bisonette, Paul Dorion, Antoine Le Rouge, Richardson, and four others whose names he could not tell. All this proved strictly correct. By what instinct he had arrived at such accurate conclusions, I am utterly at a loss to divine.

Parkman's impatience got them up long before sunrise, and they reached the fort well before noon; there they found Shaw, Chatillon, and Deslauriers the muleteer, and had a banquet on biscuit, coffee, and salt pork, which they ate and drank with all the ostentation of plates, knives, forks, and cups, sitting on stools before a wooden structure politely called a table. Shaw then produced his library,— Shakespeare, Byron, and the Old Testament.

I chose the worst of the three, and for the greater part of that day I lay on the buffalo robes, fairly reveling in the creations of that resplendent genius which has achieved no more signal triumph than that of half beguiling us to forget the unmanly character of its possessor.

The young men bade good-by to their companions, especially to Chatillon, with much regret, left the fort, and turned their faces eastward. They had made great friends with Chatillon, and thereafter friendly letters and gifts passed between them. Once they made the mistake of offering payment for rich gifts from him, and hurt his feelings. Chatillon prospered in a worldly sense, and years afterwards Parkman saw him at St. Louis, an owner of houses, dressed in the discomforts of white shirt, urban coat, and trousers.

The returning journey was made without much ill luck. From Westport they went by boat to St. Louis, which they reached in the beginning of October, and the young men made haste to give their friends news of themselves.

St. Louis, Oct. 7th, '46.

My dear Mother, — . . . Everybody here speaks of the intense heat of the past summer. We, Q. and I, may congratulate ourselves on having escaped it, besides gaining a great deal of sport, and a cartload of practical experience. I feel about ten years older than I did five months ago. To-day, for the first time, I have mounted the white shirt, tight dress coat, etc. . . . My temperament is bilious, and a meat diet, I suppose, acts unfavorably on it; and hence the particularly uncomfortable state to which I was reduced when in the Indian country; but in spite of this, they tell me here that I look better than when I set out for the mountains.

. . . I shall go by stage, as the rivers are low, to Chicago, thence by railroad to Detroit, and thence to Buffalo. Ask Carrie to write, as I want very much to hear from her. You will hear from me often, and meanwhile believe me, dear mother, respectfully, your affectionate   FRANK.

On his return he felt that he had qualified himself by practical experience to write the history of the Indian and French wars, and grateful that so loose a rein had been given to his inclination, he was ready to do his duty towards his father and the law.

CHAPTER XVIII

UNDER DR. ELLIOTT'S CARE

FRANK had come back with a great store of information and experience; he had garnered the grain and was ready to begin to grind. But violent exertion, exposure, bad food, wet clothes, and all evil attendants of physical hardship, began to exact their scot, and the chief burden of their exaction fell on his weakest member, his eyes. No sooner had he got home than he was obliged to be off again to New York to put himself under the care of Dr. Elliott, a famous oculist, whose skill had already wrought a cure for his sister Caroline, who had suffered with her eyes. From this time his physical life assumes the grim and strained attitude of one long wrestle with ill health. At first there was hope that two months would suffice to make the weak eyes strong and undo the hurt that the Oregon journey had done; but though his eyes sometimes got better and sometimes got worse, the two months lengthened out, and at the end of the second year his eyes were worse, much worse. In this wrestling-match with fate there were recesses, pauses, breathing spaces, but from this fatal year his body was but a ragged fort in which the spirit was incessantly beleaguered. In his brief autobiographical letters he has told the story in a soldier's way; it reads like the journal of a fighting regiment. Those pages tell of hardships; these are intended to chronicle the happier intervals between bouts of pain, to record recollections and the careless gossip of letters which show the tender love of his family, the proud affection of his friends, and to relate the gradual progress of his work.

CAROLINE TO FRANK.

Boston, Dec. 17th, 1846.

It is a great while since I have written to you, for I do not get time to do half what I want to. . . . The historical lectures take a great deal of time, and if I read half of the books he [the teacher] recommends I should be able to do nothing else. They are very interesting and edifying. How glad I am that your eyes are improving so much and what a comfort to be able to read so long. Don't you occasionally turn your thoughts homeward and remember that the two months are almost gone? I fear that when they are gone, the Dr. will think that it would be better to stay a little longer. I wish you were at home to go with me to Aunt Shaw's party next Tuesday. . . . I must say the party has no great attractions for me . . . if you were here I should like it much better. . . . I hope I shall have a letter from you soon, but don't write unless you can without the least difficulty. Mother and all send their love. . . . Good-by, my dear brother.

Jan. 11, 1847.

Let me in the first place wish you a happy New Year, though ten days of it has gone, but there is enough left beside. We had a most remarkable day here as to weather: it was oppressively warm with winter clothes. . . . Did you make many calls? There were some families here who received their friends, but I should not care about its becoming a general custom; there seems no satisfaction in such visits, and it must be a real hard day's work for gentlemen. . . . We heard from Aunt Mary yesterday. She is at Providence now, as I suppose you know, but is not much better than she has been since the summer. . . . She writes in pretty good spirits though, and wants to know particularly about you, and sends her love. We are going this evening to see the " Viennoises Danseuses " (I am quite willing to write it, but would n't think of pronouncing it). Father saw them in Dublin, and was so delighted with them that he is willing to be seen at the theatre in such a cause, custom notwithstanding. I think it will be quite an inducement in itself to go, just for the sake of seeing him sitting in one of the boxes!

Tuesday, Feb. 23d, 1847.

. . . I believe that father told you in his last
letter that Dr. Elliott gave "encouraging accounts" of you when he was here; but he mis-
understood me, for I was the only one of the
family that the Dr. saw, and all that he said
was that yours was a difficult case, that he had
no doubt of his curing you finally, but that after
you had been with him a few weeks he found there
were peculiarities of the system that at first he
could not discover. He said that your nervous
system was a good deal deranged, which made it
difficult to affect you by medicine, or something
to that purpose; if I have not represented it as
it was told, do not think he made out a better
statement just to please us, for all he said to
encourage was that it was a curable case, and
that he should do all he could to enable you to
come home as soon as possible, as father desired. . . . Last week I had a miniature party,
and wish you had been here, for it was very
pleasant. . . . They came to tea, and it was a
very sociable little soirée. We had music of the
first order, for they are a very musical set, and
Matilda Abbot sings remarkably well. . . .

Now Frank, my dear, I have heard that you
have written some account of your journey in the
"Knickerbocker," and how brotherly it would
be if you would send us the number which contains it, for I suppose you have it, or at least
you might have told us that it was to be seen
there, for you know how much interested I
should be in everything you write, and all that
you do. Only think how long it is since you

have lived at home, almost a year. Sometimes I feel that you know so much more, and that we are so different in mind and in our feelings about some things that we might not be so near to each other as is my sincerest wish ; but this feeling, perhaps, is quite unnecessary, and I hope that our love will be just as strong as if I did not feel there was any difference. I never could have told you this, it is so much easier to write one's secret feelings than to speak them, but I am glad to let you know them. . . . Write to us soon, and I hope you will have better accounts to give. Mother sends her love, and with much love from your sister   CARRIE.

Tuesday, March 2d, 1847.

Your letter reached us yesterday, and I cannot tell you how badly we feel on account of your health. It is a hard trial, I am sure, not to be able at least to use your mind while you are shut out from reading. I do hope that this state will not continue long. . . . I hope that next summer you will feel inclined to *loafe round* at Phillips beach with us. For we have the prospect of the same pleasant family that we had last year, and you would be able to have quite a variety in your occupations too, . . . and there are beautiful rides and walks all around there, and perhaps we might renew our horseback expeditions, which are very popular there, especially the ride to Nahant over the beach, and when you get there you would find many of your friends, Mary Eliot among others. Is n't that a pleasant prospect? It would be so plea-

sant to have you there with us, you don't know
how we used to long for you last summer. . . .
I go to history in a few minutes, so I am in a
hurry. . . . Mother and all the rest send their
love and wish you were with us that we might
do something for you. I hope it will not be long
before we can see you. Maria Eldredge is going
to N. Y. in a few weeks to stay. I should like to
go with her to stay with you. Suppose I should
not be admitted to Delmonico's, though. . . .

Friday, March 19th, 1847.

We were very glad to hear from you yesterday, and I hope you will feel the good effects of
the new system, but if it is much more severe
than that which the Dr. generally uses, I *should*
think you would be in torture. . . . I cannot
tell you how delighted Elly [his brother John
Eliot] was with the book you sent him, and you
could not have chosen a better time to send it.
. . . He is quite overcome by your thinking of
him and is going to write you a letter next week.
Father sends his love. Mother and the girls send
love also. . . .

Boston, May 14th, [1847].

. . . We were very glad to receive a letter
from you this morning, and hope you will feel
that your eyes are continuing to improve without any more drawbacks. . . . Mary gets on
very well with the copying; it is about finished
now. . . . I hope you will be able to read this
yourself, and out of compassion for your eyes I
will not inflict more, but believe me, dear Frank,
that nothing would make me happier than to

feel that I could do something to make your un-
occupied time pass pleasantly. . . . I hope we
shall hear very soon. With much love,

CARRIE.

In the course of nature a father, as the purse-
holder, has relations and correspondence with a
son which differ a little in tenor from those
which mother and sister have, and as the Parkman family did not differ in any marked particular from other families, we find traces of that
eternal dialogue between the purse-holder and
the purse-emptier, which commonly fills so much
larger a part in the correspondence between
father and son.

BOSTON, March 2, [1847].

MY DEAR SON, — We have read your letter
to Carrie with no little regret and disappointment. I am pained by what you write of your
general state of health as well as of your eyes.
And I hardly know what course it will be best
for you to pursue. . . .

You write in a short postscript that you are
in want of money. I am most happy, as you
well know, to supply it. But I confess, my dear
son, that I am somewhat surprised by the fre-
quency of your calls. Since I was in New York,
when I gave you fifty dollars in addition to
twenty or thirty you then had, I sent you seventy dollars, in anticipation, as I thought, of
your needs for the present. I take it for granted
that it was ample for the bills at Delmonico's,

etc., for the month just ended, and that those bills are paid. I request that instead of a short postscript thro' Caroline [mark the full complement of syllables] you would let me know more particularly of the amount of your expenses, and what is necessary for a month. All that is proper for your comfort and gratification shall always and most readily be supplied. But for the four months you have been in New York you have received $400, or at the rate of $1200 a year. . . . I wish you would write to me particularly if your eyes permit. Your mother sends her love, and we earnestly hope, my dear son, that you will find yourself better soon.

I am your affectionate father,

FRANCIS PARKMAN.

Then those honest friends, — great peacemakers, that knit up the raveled sleave of a father's care, — exact accounts, served their good offices.

Item	.	.	.	Bootblack	.	.	.10
"	.	.	.	Ale .	.	.	.12
"	.	.	.	Breakfast	.	.	.37
"	.	.	.	Umbrella	.	.	.75
"	.	.	.	Chocolate, etc.	.	.	.18
"	.	.	.	Ale .	.	.	.12
"	.	.	.	Breakfast	.	.	.25
"	.	.	.	Dinner	.	.	.75
"	.	.	.	Tea	.	.	.25
"	.	.	.	Waiter	.	.	.25
"	.	.	.	Carriage	.	.	.50
"	.	.	.	Books	.	•	1.50, etc.

In the next letter their service is recognized.

Monday, March 8, 1847.

MY DEAR SON, — Your statement of your
expenses at Delmonico's is altogether satisfactory. . . .

I am at present at a loss what to advise as to
your remaining from home. It seems to me very
desirable that you should have more of domestic
comfort than you can possibly have as you are.
. . . Think over the matter in your own mind,
and at your leisure give me your ideas. We are
all well.   Your affectionate father,

F. PARKMAN.

Frank, however, was obliged to stay away all
the spring and all the summer too.

In the mean time "The Oregon Trail" had
begun its slow publication in the "Knickerbocker Magazine." Frank had kept a full notebook of his expedition and adventures, and soon
after his return, from these notes and from his
admirable memory, had dictated the book to
his friend and comrade, Shaw. The first chapters appeared in February. Frank, in his modest, reserved, self-sufficient way, deigned to tell
neither his family nor his friends. His sister
found it out by chance, so did his friends. It was
put out into the world to stand on its own feet,
and like a waif win what success it might in the
estimation of the impartial, cold-hearted subscribers to the "Knickerbocker." If it deserved
success, Frank wished it to succeed; if not, why

let it go and keep company with mediocrity and failure, as it deserved.

The book was not as successful, not as popular with the public, as might well have been expected even by a young man much less cool and self-contained than Frank. It was more than twenty years since the "Last of the Mohicans" had been published, and it was reasonable to anticipate an eager reception for a fresh tale of the wild life of the West. The editor of the "Knickerbocker," however, justly appreciated its worth; so did others.

> DOBB, HIS CROSSING,
> Woden, his day, Aug. 30, ['47].

MY DEAR PARKMAN, — Your next "Trail" has the place of honor in the "Knickerbocker," — that is, the one for October. They are excellent papers. Washington Irving told me to-day that he read them with great pleasure — as I always do. I hope you find them as correctly printed as you could expect, under the circumstances. I read them carefully; but the manuscript is sometimes very obscured. How are your eyes? I long much to hear that they are getting well. . . .

Will you let me say how much I am, and truly, yours, L. GAYLORD CLARK.

REV. F. PARKMAN TO SAME.

> Monday Morning, Aug. 7th, ['47].

MY DEAR SON, — . . . Though I wrote to you something of a long letter on Friday, yet I cannot help "taking pen in hand," just to tell you of a little incident which, as it gave pleasure to your mother and me, will not, I think, be otherwise than agreeable to you.

Last week Elly came into town, and having a half day's leisure, strolled over to the Navy Yard at Charlestown. As he was looking round, as boys love to look, an officer met him and asked him his name; and finding it Parkman, he asked him, further, if he was any relation to the gentleman who wrote articles in the "Knickerbocker." Elly told him that he was his brother, which, as you know, was no more than true. The officer then said, "Come with me, and I will show you all there is to see; for I am glad to know a brother of the writer of those pieces. He writes well, and I read 'The Oregon Trail' with great pleasure." He then took Elly all over the yard, and when he had shown him fully all there was to be seen he invited him into his own room, and among many other things showed him the numbers of the "Knickerbocker" which he said had given him so much pleasure.

I confess, my dear Frank, I was much gratified by this; but I should not be studious to write it out at length, did I not feel that under your trials and inability to do as much as you desire, you are entitled to know that what you have done, and still can do, is fully appreciated. It is a consolation, when some of our plans are interrupted, to know that others have so well succeeded. And I congratulate you on having accomplished so much and so successfully amidst great discouragements. . . . Mother sends her love; and I am your affectionate father,

F. PARKMAN.

SAME TO SAME.

BOSTON, Friday, Sept. 3, [1847].

MY DEAR SON, — . . . I have received for you a diploma as Honorary Member of the New York Historical Society. I hear frequently of your "Oregon Trail," and of the success of your lucubrations. . . .

With sincere affection, I am yours,

F. PARKMAN.

By this time, finding that his eyes had not improved, Frank had gone to Brattleboro, Vermont, to try the water-cure, somewhat fashionable in those days. But the success of this experiment, though he repeated it several times, was slight, and he went back again to Dr. Elliott's care.

CHAPTER XIX

BEFORE the " Oregon Trail " had run its slow course in the " Knickerbocker Magazine," Parkman had been busying himself in putting into narrative the varied mass of information which he had been gathering during the previous six or seven years. It was not easy to make one straight-away story of it, there was such lack of unity in the subject. Pontiac was but the most conspicuous chief in a long line of border war that encircled the English settlements from Maine to Carolina. There was need of art, of grouping and arrangement, of dragging certain events and actors into the foreground, of pushing others back, of exalting here and abasing there; in short, of the infinite pains that only can overcome an unwieldly narrative. Parkman himself says in the preface that lack of eyesight, which forced him to long periods of darkness and meditation, during which he thought out the sequence of his story, was really of service to him. It is a generous instance of giving the devil his due. I

quote his autobiography [1] for an account of this
period of composition.

In the spring of 1848, the condition indicated
being then at its worst, the writer resolved to
attempt the composition of the history of the
conspiracy of Pontiac, of which the material had
been for some time collected and the ground prepared. The difficulty was so near to the impossible that the line of distinction often disappeared,
while medical prescience condemned the plan as
a short road to dire calamities. His motive, however, was in part a sanitary one, growing out of
a conviction that nothing could be more deadly
to his bodily and mental health than the entire
absence of a purpose and an object. The difficulties were threefold : an extreme weakness of
sight, disabling him even from writing his name,
except with eyes closed ; a condition of the brain
prohibiting fixed attention, except at occasional
brief intervals ; and an exhaustion and total de-
rangement of the nervous system, producing of
necessity a mood of mind most unfavorable to
effort. To be made with impunity, the attempt
must be made with the most watchful caution.

He caused a wooden frame to be constructed
of the size and shape of a sheet of letter paper.
Stout wires were fixed horizontally across it, half
an inch apart, and a movable back of thick pasteboard fitted behind them. The paper for writing
was placed between the pasteboard and the wires,
guided by which, and using a black lead crayon,
he could write not illegibly with closed eyes. He

[1] *Life of Parkman*, pp. 325–327.

was at the time absent from home, on Staten
Island, where, and in the neighboring city of
New York, he had friends who willingly offered
their aid. It is needless to say to which half of
humanity nearly all these kind assistants belonged. He chose for a beginning that part of
the work which offered fewest difficulties, and
with the subject of which he was most familiar,
namely, the Siege of Detroit. The books and
documents, already partially arranged, were procured from Boston, and read to him at such times
as he could listen to them; the length of each
reading never, without injury, much exceeding
half an hour, and periods of several days frequently occurring during which he could not listen at all. Notes were made by him with closed
eyes, and afterwards deciphered and read to him
till he had mastered them. For the first half
year the rate of composition averaged about six
lines a day. The portion of the book thus composed was afterwards partially rewritten. His
health improved under the process, and the re-
mainder of the volume — in other words, nearly
the whole of it — was composed in Boston, while
pacing in the twilight of a large garret [5 Bowdoin Square], the only exercise which the sensitive condition of his sight permitted him in
an unclouded day while the sun was above the
horizon. It was afterwards written down from
dictation by relatives under the same roof, to
whom he was also indebted for the preparatory
readings. His progress was much less tedious
than at the outset, and the history was complete
in about two years and a half.

This story was given to the world after his death ; in life Parkman concealed his disabilities from his acquaintances under a cool reserve. Once a friend, coming from a distance, entered the room where Parkman sat in the dark with curtains drawn and eyes bandaged ; surprised by sympathy, he betrayed his pity. The tone of Parkman's voice made him think for an instant that his own eyes had deceived him, and that he was in the presence of a perfectly well, untroubled man. Nevertheless, Parkman's intimates knew what odds he struggled with, and having in their minds the young man who had spent his time crying " words of manage to his bounding steed," leaping on and off while at full gallop, — one of them has said that on horseback, with his face grim and resolute, he looked like *Colleoni*, — they could not wholly forbear to express their sympathy.

Mr. Edmund Dwight was a classmate and dear friend.

EDMUND DWIGHT TO PARKMAN.

Boston, April 23d, '48.

MY DEAR FRANK, — I received your most welcome note three days ago. Thank you for it. . . . Your account of yourself is perhaps as good as could have been expected. I wish that it had been a great deal better, but still it is enough for us to build our hopes upon that all will yet be well. I believe I have told you how certain I consider your final success to be if your health is spared. So keep up your spirits, dear Frank. No one ever did so more thoroughly and bravely than you have done. Your reward is as certain as any future event can be. . . .

Pray let me hear from you soon, and believe me, dear Frank, faithfully and warmly, your friend.

Boston, April 30th, 1848.

I saw Quincy Shaw last night, who told me he heard indirectly that you were getting on pretty well, which is very good news so far as it goes. Charlie Norton will bring more minute intelligence, and I hope soon to get a word having your own authority for it. . . .

I have read " The Oregon Trail " for April and admire it exceedingly, though I think they would be still more interesting if read without a month's intermission between the chapters. . . . If you have not already made up your mind to collect and publish what has been portioned out to us, I hope you will for your friends' sake as well as your own. I will not give you the opinions which I hear expressed unless you prove intractable; if you do I have that which will bring you round. . . .

Boston, May 18, 1848.

I was heartily glad to receive a line from you on Sunday, giving so encouraging account of your condition and prospects. You know that if my good wishes could do you any good, you would have had the full benefit of them long ago. . . .

BOSTON, June 10, 1848.

I received your letter of the 9th upon my return from Springfield to-day. No words can tell
you, dear Frank, how deep my sympathy is for
you in all your terrible sufferings, nor how ardent my admiration for the noble fortitude with
which you bear them. Nor is my faith that in
this world you will find at last that happiness
which you are so faithfully earning less deep
than my sympathy and sorrow for your misfor-
tunes. The postscript of your letter adds a
ground of belief and opens a prospect of success.
It cannot, it will not be that you shall be disappointed and foiled at last. No, dear Frank, it
will all be well with you before long, and your
reward will be as great as the difficulties you
have overcome. The darkest cloud has a silver
lining, and that will soon be turned toward you,
and all these storm clouds pass away. I know
how truly religious you are amidst all this dread-
ful trial. Only recollect that "hope" is ranked
next to "faith" among the Christian virtues.
Heaven bless the Doctor who gives you such
good grounds for belief in the place of hope, and
with one skillful Dr. for your eyes and another
for your nerves all will be well before long. . . .
Farewell, my dear friend. Heaven be with you
and send you bright days quickly.

July 19, 1848.

I was very glad indeed to receive your letter two days ago confirming the impression I
had received when with you that you were growing better. The progress may be, or rather, I
suppose, must be, slow, and changes for the

worse will occur; still, so long as the direction is
the right one, there is a certainty of coming out
right at last. . . .

July 22d.

The returned volunteers parade the streets to-
day, and the city is full of gaping countrymen
to see the warriors. Do you still hold to your
old notions about the glory of a soldier and the
high qualities that are required to make a man
fight well? Because if you do I should like to
argue the point with you. A good officer is a
noble fellow, and so is any other good man in
active business. I'm getting a contempt for
men who only preach and theorize. If a man
does keep straight through the bad influences of
such a life it says a vast deal for him. Good-by.
Keep up your spirits, and believe me, dear Frank,
yours sincerely,

EDMUND DWIGHT, JR.

In some of the letters there are references to
politics which seem to imply that Dwight and
Parkman shared the views prevailing in well-to-
do Boston, — dislike of the ad valorem clauses
in the tariff, indignation with the South, disapproval of the Mexican war. But Parkman's
world had shrunk to the four walls of a darkened room, and his thoughts were too closely
concentred on his work to wander far afield.

He valued his friends, and always kept the
letters that bore witness to the affection they
felt for him.

Sunday, June 18, 1848.

MY DEAR FRANK, — I have long meant to write to you, and should have done so before now had I supposed my letter would have given you pleasure. But as Ned Dwight told me last week that you spoke in your last letter to him of not being so well, except as regards your eyes, I determined to write to you, if for no other reason than to assure you of my continued and sincere sympathy with you. You have, my dear friend, one great source of support and comfort in your sufferings, the consciousness that they have not been sent to you as the retribution for your past life, but that they have come in accordance with the inscrutable design of God, and will finally work out their own result by bringing you nearer to him. Let me quote from Miss Barrett two or three lines : —

> " With earnest prayers
> Fasten your soul so high that constantly
> The smile of your heroic cheer may float
> Above all floods of earthly agonies."

All this is, I know, very familiar to you, and for the last year or two you have given proof to every one who has known you that you carry your principles, which so few of us do, into daily action ; and in the midst of suffering you may have the encouragement of knowing that your example is one which we shall always cherish as inciting us to manliness and patience and faith.

. . . Good-by. Write to me if you can. With kindest remembrances from the whole family.

Boston, Sept. 4th, 1848.

I have just got and looked over the worthless number of the " Knickerbocker " for this month. Where is the " Oregon Trail " ? Have you quarreled with the editor, or he with you? Or was the manuscript lost ? Or is Clark, knowing that there are but three numbers more, keeping it back that he may have a number or two for his new volume, so as to retain his subscribers who subscribe for the sake of that alone? It is not good policy in an editor of a magazine to have one contributor who so far excels the rest. Pray write to me to tell me about the missing chapter and about yourself. I hope you still keep to your intention of publishing the " Trail " in a volume this autumn. The time is drawing near when it should be out. Do begin to print, and either make arrangements with some New York publisher, or let me make them with some publisher here. At any rate, let me do as much for you in looking over the proofs, or in any other way, as I can. . . .

New York, Febr'y 25th, 1849.

It seemed almost as if I were going to meet you, when yesterday morning I went down to Putnam's to see him about your book. . . . I found Putnam, and learned from him that the "Oregon and California Trail " would be out in about ten days — some time in next week. He said that so far as he knew there had not been the least difficulty in making out the corrections in the copy you had sent him, that he had received the last proof that morning, that the engravings were so nearly finished that he thought he could give me copies of them to send on to you to-morrow, and that he could have six copies bound and sent to you early. I selected a neat and handsome style in which to have them bound, and told Putnam's clerk to be careful to have the matter attended to. . . .

MILAN, April 18th, 1850.

I have owed you a letter for a long time. It has not been from any want of frequent remembrance that I have not written — if I did not know that you would believe in that, I should certainly have written before. Your last letter came to me at Alexandria. I was very glad to receive it, as it contained good accounts of yourself. I hope that you could have written in the same way all the winter. . . . During this last January I was traveling from Agra to Bombay, and during the journey, which was a solitary one, I often thought over and with constant pleasure the mornings of the January of the year before spent with you. I trust you will have a very long manuscript for me to read a year hence, when I am once more at home. . . .

Ever your very faithful friend,

CHARLES ELIOT NORTON.

E. George Squier, another friend, was an antiquarian interested in Central America, a man of scholarly tastes and archæological learning, full of energy and exuberant vigor.

PARKMAN TO SQUIER [dictated].

BOSTON, Oct. 15th, 1849.

MY DEAR SQUIER, — . . . As for me I am rather inclined to envy you less for your success and your prospects, enviable as they are, than for your power of activity. From a complete and ample experience of both, I can bear witness that no amount of physical pain is so intolerable as the position of being stranded and doomed to lie rotting for year after year. However, I have not yet abandoned any plan which I have ever formed, and I have no intention of abandoning any until I am made cold meat of. At present I am much better in health than when you last saw me, and do not suffer from that constant sense of oppression on the brain which then at times annoyed me almost beyond endurance. I find myself able to work a little, although my eyes are in a totally useless state and excessively sensitive. The eyes are nothing to the other infernal thing, which now seems inclined to let me alone, good riddance to it; so I continue to dig slowly along by the aid of other people's eyes, doing the work more thoroughly, no doubt, and digesting my materials better than if I used my own. I have just obtained the papers that were wanting to complete my collection for the illustrative work on the Indians which I told you about. The manuscripts amount to several thousand pages. I am inclined to think that the labor of collecting them might have been better bestowed, but I was a boy when I began it, and at all events the job will be done thoroughly. . . . If I can serve you in the way of writing or otherwise, I wish you would let me know, and I shall be very glad to do anything in my power. By some practice I have caught the knack of dictating and find it as easy as lying.

Believe me, with much regard, very truly yours,

[F. PARKMAN.]

In May, 1850, he married Miss Catherine Scollay Bigelow, a daughter of Dr. Jacob Bigelow, at that time a distinguished physician in Boston.

CHAPTER XX

PARKMAN'S married life was very happy, especially in these first years before the devil of lameness clutched him. He and his wife were rarely suited to each other; she was a spiritually-minded and an intellectual woman, religious, fond of poetry, dearly loved by those who knew her best. She was endowed by nature with a sweet, joyful disposition, with humor and flashes of wit, and with the high courage requisite to tend unfalteringly the pain and suffering of the man she loved. She, too, was calm outwardly and ardent underneath, and in self-abnegation and devotion bore her great sorrows. She put aside everything to minister to him, became his eyesight and his health, and lived his life in all ways possible. The death of her little son, Francis, broke her heart, and it never healed; after that she went about like one who belonged in another world. In the last year of her life she was called upon to bear her husband's worst illness; but the first years of married life were gay and happy. They were poor, with not much more than six hundred dollars a year to begin housekeeping : —

Sie hatten nichts und doch genug —

In the winter they lived part of the time at his father's house, and part at Dr. Bigelow's ; one summer they spent at Milton, the next at Brookline. Some letters to Mr. Norton, who was at that time in Europe, written soon after their marriage, reveal their interests and their happiness.

PARKMAN TO NORTON [dictated].

MILTON, June 15, [1850].

MY DEAR CHARLEY, — . . . I have a place near Milton Hill, small, snug, and comfortable, where I can offer entertainment for man and beast, of which I hope you and your steed will one day avail yourselves. We have woods about us dark enough for an owl to hide in, very fair society, not too near to bore us, and, what is quite as much to the purpose, a railroad to place us within arm's reach of town. This kind of life has one or two drawbacks, such as the necessity of paying bills, and the manifold responsibilities of a householder, an impending visit from the tax-gatherer, and petitions for the furtherance of charitable enterprises which, as I am informed, the son of my father will not fail to promote. . . .

I have a reader for an hour or two, and when it is not too bright play the amateur farmer, to the great benefit of my corporeal man. Kate

[Mrs. Parkman] is generally my amanuensis, as perhaps you may see by this handwriting. Pontiac is about three quarters through, and I hope will see the light within a year. I calculated at starting it would take four years to finish it, which, at the pace I was then writing, was about a straight calculation, for I was then handsomely used up, soul and body on the rack, and with no external means or appliances to help me on. You may judge whether my present condition is a more favorable one. I detest being spooney or an approximation to it, so I say nothing, but if you want to understand the thing, take a jump out of hell-fire to the opposite extreme, such a one, in short, as Satan made when he broke bounds and paid his visit to our first parents. . . .

With the greatest regard, very truly yours,

F. PARKMAN, JR.

SAME TO SAME [dictated].

MILTON, Sept. 22d, 1850.

MY DEAR CHARLEY, — It is a fortnight since your letter came to hand, and I have been too busy to answer it; rather a new condition of things for me, but the fact is all the time which I could prudently give to work has been taken up in carrying forward my book so as to be ready for publication next spring. I see that you are a true-hearted American, and have too much sense to be bitten by the John Bull mania, which is the prevailing disease of Boston in high places and in low. A disgusting malady it is, and I pray Heaven to deliver us from its influence.

We can afford to stand on our own feet and travel our own course without aid or guidance; and my maxim is, that it is about as well to go wrong on one's own hook as to go right by slavishly tagging at the heels of another. But in the present case the thing is reversed. It is we that are going right, and John Bull may go to the devil. Fine Yankee brag, — is n't it? In spite of Taylor's [President Taylor] death we have come out right at last. There is no danger, thank God, of the Union breaking up at present, in spite of all the efforts of Garrison and his coadjutors.

I wish with all my heart that you could be here, as you kindly wish, at the forthcoming of my book; but a copy shall be put by for you. I find it seriously no easy job to accomplish all the details of dates, citations, notes, etc., without the use of eyes. Prescott could see a little — confound him, he could even look over his proofs, but I am no better off than an owl in the sunlight. The ugliest job of the whole is getting up a map. I have a draught made in the first place on a very large scale. Then I direct how to fill it in with the names of forts, Indian villages, etc., all of which I have pretty clearly in my memory from the reading of countless journals, letters, etc., and former travels over the whole ground. Then I examine the map inch by inch, taking about half a minute for each examination, and also have it compared by competent eyes with ancient maps and draughts; then I have the big map reduced to a proper size. I have got to the end of the book and killed off Pontiac. The opening chapters, however, are not yet complete. I have just finished an introductory chapter on the Indian tribes, which my wife pronounces uncommonly stupid. Never mind, nobody need read it who don't want to, . . . I shall stereotype it myself and take the risk. . . .

I remain, my dear Charley, ever faithfully yours,

F. PARKMAN, JR.

Another extract from this correspondence shall be the last.

SAME TO SAME [dictated].

Nov. 10th, 1850.

. . . Just now we are on the eve of an election — a great row about the Fugitive Slave Law, and an infinity of nonsense talked and acted upon the subject. A great union party is forming in opposition to the abolitionists and the Southern fanatics. For my part, I would see every slave knocked on the head before I would see the Union go to pieces, and would include in the sacrifice as many abolitionists as could be conveniently brought together. . . .

All his life Parkman liked common sense. He was irritated by sentimentality, by fanaticism, by transcendentalism, by eccentricity of thought; and he was wont to relieve his mind by a little emphatic language, which he was pleased to enhance with a certain extravagance, half in jest, half in relief of his humors.

The "Conspiracy of Pontiac," was published in 1851, but it had been ready for more than a twelve-month. Mr. Jared Sparks read a portion of the manuscript in March, 1850. "It affords," he says, "a striking picture of the influence of war and religious bigotry upon savage and semi-barbarous minds." But the old pedagogical historian of the earlier American generation, missing in the young historian of a new school a proper predilection for moral lessons, so ready to hand, could not find it in his heart to stop there. Referring to the massacre by the Paxton Boys,[1] he writes: "The provocation and surrounding circumstances afford no ground of mitigation of so inhuman a crime. It is one of the great lessons of history, showing what passion is capable of doing when it defies reason and tramples on the sensibilities of nature, to say nothing of the high injunctions of Christianity. Although you relate events in the true spirit of calmness and justice, yet I am not sure but a word or two of indignation now and then, at such unnatural and inhuman developments of the inner man, would be expected of a historian, who enters deeply into the merits of his subjects." But Parkman preferred to state facts as he believed them to be, and to let his readers make their own philosophical deductions and

[1] *Conspiracy of Pontiac*, chap. xxiv.

ejaculate their own exclamations of indignation or content.

Negotiations for publication began in the summer, when the manuscript was submitted to Messrs. Harper & Brothers by a friend. Parkman would have preferred to have the book published in two volumes, in appearance similar to Prescott's " Conquest of Mexico," but the precise form was indifferent to him " provided the book appear in a decent and scholar-like dress." The title caused him some perplexity. He suggested the following name, " which, however, I don't greatly admire," — it certainly is open to criticism from a bookbinder who should wish to stamp the name on the back, — " A History of the War with Pontiac and the Indian Tribes of North America in their combined attack upon the British Colonies after the Conquest of Canada," or " A History of the Conspiracy of Pontiac and the Struggle of the North American Indians against the British Colonies after the Conquest of Canada ; " and again, " The War with Pontiac (or Pontiac's War), a History of the Outbreak of the Indian Tribes of America against the British Colonies after the Conquest of Canada." The difficulty for the outside of the book was the same as for the inside ; the far-spread border war resisted the attempt to crib and confine it within the circle of unity.

The prudent Harpers, scared perhaps by these titles, submitted the MS. to their reader, and wrote back : —

" Our Reader [the capital R served both to show how Rhadamanthine that gentleman was, and to soften the Rejection] has just returned to us Mr. Parkman's MS. His opinion, as regards the literary execution of the work, etc., is very favorable, — but he is apprehensive that the work, highly respectable as it is, will not meet with a very rapid or extensive sale," etc., etc.

" Our Reader " had said : —

The subject is handled with very considerable ability — in a manner highly creditable to the industry, intelligence, and literary skill of the author. The narrative is lively and often graceful, the rules of historical perspective are well observed, and the whole effect of the picture is pleasing and impressive. It will worthily fill a notch among the standard works of American history. At the same time, I do not anticipate for it a remarkably brilliant reception. This is forbidden both by the subject and the style. . . . It will require a good deal of effort to push it into general circulation among the people.

Therefore the Harpers, in the self-respecting phraseology of the old-fashioned counting-room, advised that Parkman should stereotype the work at his own cost, and then submit the plate proofs to various publishers, and find where he could get the best terms.

Parkman followed this advice and had the book stereotyped, having learned what terms to make by borrowing from the "confounded" Prescott the latter's contract with a printer for stereotyping the "Conquest of Mexico." The book was published by Messrs. Little & Brown.

"Our Reader" was sagacious; the book was not a popular success. But those who read it admired and enjoyed it. Mr. Jared Sparks may speak for the students of American history: —

CAMBRIDGE, June 4, 1850.

I have been intimately acquainted with ye progress of Mr. Parkman's historical studies several years. On ye subject of our Indian History, subsequent to ye French War, he has taken unwearied pains to collect materials, and has procured copies of many original manuscripts and papers both in this country and from ye public offices in London. I doubt if any writer has bestowed more thorough research, or has more completely investigated his subject. I have read one chapter of his work, wh. appeared to me to be written in a spirited style, and with good judgment and discrimination in ye selection of facts.

Other readers wrote their feelings, — perhaps none of them are entitled to speak for anybody but themselves. Mr. G. R. Russell, however, a relation, expressed a common opinion in a letter to Parkman: —

I have just finished reading your "History of the Conspiracy of Pontiac." I have read the work with great care, going over parts of it twice, not for purposes of criticism, but to enjoy the really beautiful descriptions, which place scenes before the reader as distinctly conspicuous as though he gazed at them wrought out on canvas by the hand of a master.

Particular reasons for enjoyment are unimportant matters of personal taste which the reader must determine for himself; but the young man, the middle-aged man, or the graybeard, is not to be envied who, even now, fifty years after its publication, cannot sit up half the night over the pages of "Pontiac" and read about the bloody scalpings, skirmishes, forays, and battles which arouse that central government of our being, the aboriginal savage in us. John Fiske says that the secret of Parkman's power is that his Indians are true to the life, — that Pontiac is a man of warm flesh and blood.

The book was also published in London by Richard Bentley at the time of the publication of the American edition. Mr. Bentley took a more hopeful view than the Reader for the Harpers, but that keen-scented gentleman, with his daintier sense of the reading public's appetites, was the more accurate. At the end of a year the English publisher's account carried a deficit of £53 0 2, and his ledger showed that of the five hundred copies printed, but one hundred and fifty-three had been sold.

Parkman, however, never fell before the temptation to dally over that which had been done, — stopping neither to regret this nor to wish that changed; he ever pressed onward to the things that were before. No sooner was "Pontiac" published than he strained in his leash to get after his great quarry, the English-French contest. But the devils of ill health leaped upon him. In the autumn of 1851 an effusion of water on the left knee lamed him; a partial recovery was followed by a relapse, which came to a crisis in 1853 and shut him up in the house for two years. An odd consequence was that all the irritability of his nervous system centred in his head, causing him great pain. When he tried to fix his attention, he felt as if he had an iron band clamped around his head, like an old instrument of torture; at other times his thoughts swooped through his brain like an infernal blast, with a horrid confusion of tossing pains. In the train of these furies followed sleepless nights. Work upon his history was impossible. Afterwards, when the rage of the crisis was spent, he betook himself to writing reviews of historical books, and in 1856 he published a novel, "Vassall Morton." Perhaps in writing the novel he wished to occupy time which he could not use in graver work, perhaps he desired to prove himself in a new field. The novel was not a success. To most readers to-day, merely seeking selfish amusement, the book does not appear to have deserved success. Parkman himself rated it at its worth, or probably at less than its worth; he never spoke of it, and did not include it in his collected works. Its real interest is in the self-revelation of the author; for Vassall Morton, the hero, is undoubtedly in great measure drawn from Parkman's own imagination of himself. The generation of that day, however, had its own appetite in novels, and people of taste here and there liked it.

George William Curtis, in "Putnam's Monthly," said that "Vassall Morton" was far the best of late American novels, but that it was sketchy, as if tossed off in intervals of severer study, and not equal to what was to be expected from Parkman's position in literature.

CHAPTER XXI

1858–1865

THE following years brought the great sorrows of his life; in 1857 his little boy died, the next year his wife died, leaving him with two little girls, Grace and Katharine, and as if to prove him, body and soul at once, another fierce attack of his malady fell upon him. Some friend sentimentally assumed that he had nothing more to live for, but his blunt answer intimated that Francis Parkman was not born to hoist the white flag.

This attack of illness was so bad that the doctor hardly expected him to live, but Parkman meant to make a fight for life, and went to Paris to consult the famous physician, Brown-Séquard. On the steamer he met Professor Child. The following letters show somewhat of his condition:

PROFESSOR F. J. CHILD TO PARKMAN.

GENOA, 21 January, [1859].

MY DEAR FRIEND, — . . . I must not ask about you because I know you cannot answer

me by pen and ink. You will believe that though
I have not written I have thought a great deal
of you. I wish that you may have found at least
some alleviation to your great sufferings in Paris,
— or if not there in the mountains, — and I wish
that we could meet every now and then, and go
back in the same ship. My dear fellow, you cannot even read much, and so you must believe
that there is a great deal in these last lines when
I say that I shall never forget your magnanimous
fortitude, that I felt an intense sympathy for
you that I could not express when we were together, and that I shall often pray God to help
you, as I have constant occasion to do for other
friends.

NICE, 23 February, [1859].

. . . I begin faintly to realize what I have
often supposed I thoroughly comprehended, —
but did not, — that happiness in this world is
par dessus le marché. I don't mean to talk like
a philosopher. Your experience, given with such
profound feeling and conviction in our first conversation on board ship, ought never to be lost
sight of by me. My dear fellow, I hope you get
some comfort from heaven, if none on earth.
Remember me kindly. I received your message.
God bless you ever.

Your affectionate friend,

F. CHILD.

This letter confirms what his closest friends
knew, that, where Parkman met a man like
Child, endowed by nature with ten talents for
tenderness, he laid aside the grim aspect of his

reserve and showed his sensitiveness to affection.

Parkman stayed in Paris for several months. He wrote home some scraps of information about his health, in answer to a loving appeal from his sisters, "Do not write the best of it to us, write the whole;" they were ready, as he knew, "to give their health to him," if only nature had allowed love to make the sacrifice.

PARKMAN TO HIS SISTER.

PARIS, Dec. 22, '58.

MY DEAR MOLLY, — I got y'r letter yesterday with Grace's remarkable designs. I was very glad to hear from home. . . . I am well lodged, Hôtel de France, 239 Rue St. Honoré — have felt much better since arriving. I find abundant occupation for the winter. I often see Anna Greene, and have been at Howland's and Mrs. Wharton's. For the rest, I shun Americans like the pest. I have not even given my address to my bankers, Hottinguer & Co., to whom please direct. I tell them to send my letters to Wm. Greene. I passed the Empress day before yesterday, in the Bois de Boulogne; I received a gracious bow in return of my salute. On the previous day, the heir of the Empress, about 3 years old, was walking with his gouvernante and servants in the garden of the Tuileries, while a line of Zouave sentinels kept the crowd at a safe distance. Paris is greatly changed since I was here 14 years ago. The

Emperor has made great improvements in many
parts and added vastly to the beauty of the city.
Tell Jack [his brother] I cannot advise him to
come, as the cigars are very bad. Give my love
to Grace [daughter], mother, Lizzie [sister], and
all.   Y'rs affect'ly,   F.

SAME TO SAME.

PARIS, Jan. 13, 1859.

MY DEAR MOLL, — I got y'r letter yesterday
and Lizzy's some time ago. By this time all
mine will have come. I wrote Dr. B. [Bigelow]
that I was floored with lameness. It still continues, but seems mending, so that I get about
— drive all day (chiefly on omnibuses! !), dine
at 6, and commonly spend the evening at the
cafés. I have seen Dr. Brown-Séquard, who fixed
Sumner's head. He says he can soon cure the
lameness, but that the head is quite another
matter. He says, however, that it will not kill
me, and at some remote period may possibly become better. He has 2 other cases of the kind
but says they are very rare. I am still unable to
walk more than 5 minutes at a time. . . .

I am greatly obliged to Uncle C. [Chardon]
for his remembrance, and hope the youngster
will do honor to the name. He should be
brought up to some respectable calling, and not
allowed to become a minister. . . . [He had a
high regard for many of the clergy, but liked to
chaff them as a body.] Love to Jack. Ditto
to Grace, to whom I would send a little doll, if
it would go into the letter. With love to mother and Lizzy,   Y'rs aff'ly,   F.

PARIS, Jan. 19, 1859.

MY DEAR LIZ, — My knees are somewhat
better, and I am about all day, sleep well, etc.
So much for my corporeal state. I mean to stay
here some time, as I am better off than elsewhere. . . . I see Anna Greene almost daily.
Greene is a capital fellow, and nothing of a par-
son. X wrote me a long letter in which she
advises me to leave Paris, as the contrast between outward gayety and inward sin must grate
dreadfully on my feelings! I used to think
her a woman of sense and understanding. What
the devil are your sex made of? Also that I
should leave my hotel and live at a boarding-
house kept by a female friend of hers, where I
should be surrounded by such kind people! I
shall stop off that sort of thing.

Y'rs affec'ly,   F.

PARIS, Feb. 30, 1859.

MY DEAR MOLLY, — I got y'r letter of Feb. 8
about a week ago. I am a little less lame. I get
on well enough. The omnibuses of Paris — of
which there are about 700 — are made with rail-
ings, etc., in such a way that with a little science I
can swing myself to the top with the arms alone,
and here I usually spend the better part of the
day smoking cigarettes and surveying the crowds
below. I have formed an extensive acquaintance
among omnibus cads and the like, whom I find
to be first-rate fellows in their way — also have

learned pretty thoroughly the streets of Paris, where much may be seen from the top of an omnibus. When hungry or thirsty, I descend to any restaurant, café, or "buffet" that happens to be near, whether of low or high degree, if only clean. In fine weather, an hour or two may always be spent pleasantly enough, between 2 and 5 o'clock, in the open air under the porches of the cafés on the Boulevards, where all Paris passes by.[1]

In one respect I have gained greatly from Brown-Séquard's treatment. The muscles, which ever since my first lameness have been very much reduced and weakened, are restored wholly to their natural size and strength, so that when the neuralgic pain subsides I shall be in a much better condition than before. . . .

Y'rs aff'ly,   F.

His health, however, made but little gain, and he went home after the winter was over. From this time he lived with his mother and sisters, at their house in town in the winter, at his house hard by Jamaica Pond in the summer. His daughters had gone to live with their aunt, Miss Bigelow, for he was unable to take the charge of them. This little country-place on Jamaica Pond was one of the great pleasures in his life. He had bought the cottage, with three acres of garden about it, after his father's death, in 1852, and there he lived, in warm weather, all his life.

[1] *Life of Francis Parkman*, pp. 101, 102.

It was on the border of Jamaica Pond that Parkman revealed a versatility of spirit which, in a man whose indomitable will was clinched upon a work of history, the dream of his boyhood, may well quicken the most sluggish admiration. Balked in his course, pulled off from his chosen work, another man would have felt justified in despair, at least in idleness; not so he. His wife had given him the suggestion, " Frank, with all your getting, get roses." Up he got and made a garden of roses. He had three acres, his man Michael, such enrichment of the soil as a horse, a cow, and a pig could supply, a few garden implements, and a wheeled chair, or in happy seasons a cane ; with these he grew his beautiful roses, " Madame Henriette, rosy pink, very large and beautiful," " Ætna, brilliant crimson tinted with purple," " Mariquita, white, lightly shaded, beautiful," " Maréchal Niel, beautiful, deep yellow, large, full, and of globular form, very sweet, the shoots well clothed with large shining leaves," " Euphrosyne, creamy buff, very sweet and good," and a thousand more. Success led to a head-gardener, spadesman, and hoeman, to greenhouse, hotbeds, hybrids, horticultural shows, medals, and all the pomp that Flora showers on her successful bedesmen. He loved what he calls " that gracious art which through all time has been the companion and symbol of peace ; an art joined in the closest ties with Nature, and her helper in the daily miracle by which she works beauty out of foulness and life out of corruption ; an art so tranquillizing and so benign ; so rich in consolations and pleasures." He turned to Nature like a lover, and with the industry and will of a man who meant to be " a jolly thriving wooer." His character was his art. In " The Book of Roses " he says : —

One point cannot be too often urged in respect to horticultural pursuits. Never attempt to do anything which you are not prepared to do thoroughly. A little done well is far more satisfactory than a great deal done carelessly and superficially. . . . The amateur who has made himself a thorough master of the cultivation of a single species or variety has, of necessity, acquired a knowledge and skill which, with very little pains, he may apply to numberless other forms of culture.

This is the way he went to work for a bed of roses. He took a plot some sixty feet long by forty wide, his gardener dug it, turned it, spaded it, and hoed it two feet and a half deep. Then a layer of manure was spread at a depth of eighteen inches; on top of that a spaded mixture of native yellow loam nicely intermingled with black surface soil was shoveled in; then, this time nine inches deep, a second layer of manure, and again on top of that a shoveling of the nicely intermingled dirt. On top of the bed he spread a third layer of manure, with a goodly supply of sandy road-scrapings. Each act was performed with sacerdotal exactness. The manure was not home-got, for he had " found no enriching material so good as the sweepings from the floor of a horseshoer, in which manure is mixed with the shavings of hoofs," — it was light and porous, and altogether deserving of commendation.

Sometimes in his wheeled chair he would propel himself from tuft to tuft, armed with trowel or sickle, but he liked best to superintend some delicate manœuvre, as of sowing the seeds of roses; there he sat, one hand on a wheel, to revolve himself along the edge of the bed, — carefully made of loam, old manure, leaf-mould, and sand, — and with the other hand scattered broadcast and thick over the expectant ground seeds born of some marriage of horticultural *convenance* contrived by himself. Thus he came to love stocks, stalks, runners, creepers, corollas, pistils, stamens; and, love of science mingling with his love of beauty, he gradually devoted himself almost exclusively to the hybridization of lilies and the cultivation of roses. Thus forced to leave library and desk, and the long lists of catalogued and ticketed manuscripts, he betook himself to the business of growing and selling

flowers. He was better at growing than at selling, and took a partner for a season.

JAMAICA PLAIN, Ap. 4, 1862.

MY DEAR MARY, — . . . I am daily here — in
Jamaica Plain — and am at last really busy, having formed a partnership with Spooner [a florist]
which will absorb all the working faculties I
have left. So you find me a man of business. I
am content with the move, and resolved to give
the thing a fair trial, and, by one end of the
horn or the other, work a way out of a condition of helplessness. At all events, this is my
best chance, and I will give it a trial. Spooner
wants me to go to England and France in the
fall, to look up new plants. The thing has difficulties and risks, not a few under any circumstances; but is attractive, and doubly so as it
gives me a prospect of meeting you. So I cherish
it, as probably an illusion, but still a very pleasing one. Turning tradesman has agreed with
me so far. Several bushels of historical MSS.
and fragments of abortive chapters have been
packed under lock and key, to bide their time.

Affec'ly y'rs,   F. P.

The firm did not make money, and dissolved
within a year. Parkman continued to labor in
his garden. He became member, and finally
president, of the Massachusetts Horticultural Society, and in due course won hundreds of prizes
at the flower shows. His experiments in hybridi-

zation of lilies were most careful, and (so Professor Goodale says) there are no better lessons
on this subject for the botanical student than
Parkman's own narrative of what he did. He
wished to combine two Japanese lilies, that they
should not "live unwooed and unrespected fade,"
the Lily Beautiful, with lancet leaves, and the
Lily Golden; the former was to be the bride.
Four or five varieties, in color from pure white
to deep red, were tended in pots under glass, for
the Lily Beautiful will not ripen its seed un-
coaxed in New England air. When the flowers
were on the point of opening, Parkman took a
forceps and removed all the anthers from the
expanding buds, — the pollen at that period was
still wholly unripe, and self-impregnation was
impossible. He then applied the pollen of the
Lily Golden to the pistils of the Lily Beautiful
as soon as they were in a condition to receive it.
Conception took place, the pods swelled, and
the seed ripened; though the pods looked full,
they held less seeds than chaff, and these seeds
were rough and wrinkled, not like the smooth
seeds of the Lily Beautiful when left to itself.
Fifty seedlings were got, their stems all mottled
like the father plant; "the infant bulbs were
pricked out into a cold frame" and left there
three or four years; then they were planted in a
bed for blooming. One bud at last opened, and

spread its flower nine and a half inches in diameter, resembling its father in fragrance and form, its mother in color ; the next year the bulb produced a flower whose extended petals measured twelve inches from tip to tip, and taken to England it produced other flowers fourteen inches across. This was the famous Lilium Parkmanni.[1] The other forty-nine hybrids all put forth flowers like their mother's.

In 1866 he published "The Book of Roses," in which he told the various processes of cultivation, training, and propagation, — both in open ground and in pots, — and gave accounts of the various families and groups, with descriptions of the best varieties. Among other fruits of this book was this letter : —

ESTEEMED SIR, — Allow one of your most ardent admirers to address you, for the purpose of obtaining from you a floral sentiment and your autograph. I am a great lover of flowers and the beauties of nature in general, and being well aware of the fact that you are a great floricultural historian, I take the liberty to address you. May I kindly ask if you will favor me with a quotation from your "Book of Roses" or else some sublime floral sentiment which may occur to your mind.

I am the fortunate possessor of floral sentiments from the pen of such celebrated botanists,

---

[1] Sold at last to an English florist for a thousand dollars.

floriculturists, and pomologists as . . . [the quick and the dead]. I assure you, sir, that such a contribution from you will be highly valued and appreciated, and long after you shall have gone to join that grand and immortal army of floral writers this contribution will be sacred to me. My object is only to possess letters or quotations dwelling on floriculture. If you cannot think of anything appropriate, will you kindly write for me those exquisite words of the late Solon Robinson, "A love of flowers is a love of the beautiful, and a love of the beautiful is a love of the good," from his "Facts for Farmers" (1864), p. 500.

Whether Mr. Parkman gave a floricultural or a pomological sentiment, or none, is not known.

Outdoor occupation did him good, but perhaps the tenderness of the flowers — comforters who comfort and ask neither thanks nor confidence in return — did him more good still. The whole garden was delightful, — the best of physicians, the best of friends. Sometimes in the richness of the blossoming time the colors were too heavily laid on by the horticultural hand;

> The fayre grassy grownd
> Mantled with green, and goodly beautifide
> With all the ornaments of Floraes pride,
> Wherewith her mother Art, as halfe in scorn
> Of niggard Nature, like a pompous bride
> Did decke her, and too lavishly adorne —

was too red and pink and yellow. The azaleas,

rhododendrons, magnolias, syringas, lilacs, and the big scarlet Parkman poppies were too bold for a less scientific eye, and overshadowed the columbine, foxglove, larkspur, violet, even the Japanese iris, whose seeds had been fetched from the Mikado's garden, and all the wee, modest flowers; but people would drive thither many miles to see the splendor of the blossoms.

The garden was of modest dimensions and sloped down sharply to the shore, so that the little walk from the house to the dock on the pond's edge ran past all the vegetable friends, trees, shrubs, and plants. There were a tall, wide-spreading beech, elms sixty feet high, a big chestnut, a tulip, a plane-tree, two white oaks, a sassafras, Scottish maples and scarlet maples, lindens, willows, pines, and hemlocks; and holding themselves a little aloof, as befitted their rarity and breeding, a Kentucky coffee-tree, a gingko, the magnolia acuminata, and the Parkman crab, first of its kind in New England, radiant with its bright-colored flowers.

Parkman always lived comfortably but simply, for though he had inherited a competence from his father, his books brought him in little, — even in his first days of fame he received hardly more, as he said, than the wages of a day-laborer, — and his researches were very expensive, and horticulture paid little. At the time of the partnership he was troubled by the thought that for the firm's benefit it might be his duty to sell the garden ; but he was not obliged to make that sacrifice. His purse gradually became somewhat heavier, so that in 1874 he was able to build a pleasant house in place of the original cottage.

I have not finished the list of Parkman's ills. He was forced to endure anew the poison of inaction when the Civil War broke out, and the " hand that should have grasped the sword " — an itching palm — could hold nothing but the trowel or the pen. He, with his heart and soul in the Union cause, and believing in the enforcement of right by might, was compelled to sit and hear the President's call for troops, to sit and read Governor Andrew's proclamation, to sit and see his friends and kinsmen ride away to the front, and in a wheeled chair or darkened room to receive the news of battle, of defeat, of victory. This was bitterer than any pain.

As he himself said : —

Who can ever forget the day when from spires and domes, windows and housetops, the stars and stripes were flung to the wind, in token that the land was roused at last from deadly torpor. They were the signals of a new life ; portentous of storm and battle, yet radiant with hope. Our flag was never so glorious. On that day it became the emblem of truth and right and justice. Through it a mighty people proclaimed a new faith — that peace, wealth, ease, material progress were not the sum and substance of all good. Loyalty to it became loyalty to humanity and God. The shackles of generations were thrown off. We were a people disenthralled, rising from abasement abject and insupportable.

There is not a chapter in his books which does not show that the bent of his spirit was to fight by day in the forest, and bivouac by night under the stars; and yet while a million men were under arms he was not able to take any part, even the very least. This was his purgatory; he sat with outward calm and inward wrath in his town house or on the banks of Jamaica Pond and wrote "The Book of Roses," and put together page by page "The Pioneers of New France." He was a stoic, and believed the stoic's creed, that the ills of life should be accepted at the hands of fate without petulance, without spleen, with no word, not merely not complaining, but not demanding sympathy, not telling even friendly ears. He believed in the virtue of silent fortitude. This rule he deliberately put aside for once. Before the close of the war he wrote the brief autobiographical letter published in Mr. Farnham's Life, which shows how much (in his uncertainty of life and of strength to labor) he wished the world to know that while his friends were dying for a great cause, he was not unworthy of their friendship, and that but for hostile fate he too would have accomplished no unworthy thing. This letter, indorsed "Not to be used during my life," was sent to Dr. George E. Ellis in 1868, with a note saying:—

MY DEAR FRIEND,—Running my eye over this paper, I am more than ever struck with its *egoism*, which makes it totally unfit for any eye but that of one in close personal relations with me. It resulted from a desire—natural, perhaps, but which may just as well be suppressed—to make known the extreme difficulties which have reduced to very small proportions what might otherwise have been a good measure of achievement. Having once begun it, I went on with it, though convinced that it was wholly unsuited to see the light. Physiologically considered, the case is rather curious. . . . If I had my life to live over again, I would follow exactly the same course again, only with less vehemence.

Very cordially,   F. PARKMAN.

He wrote a very similar, almost identical, letter in 1886 to Mr. Martin Brimmer, which is printed in the appendix. Both letters were kept secret till after Parkman's death, in accordance with his instructions.

CHAPTER XXII

HISTORY AND FAME

THE first volume of the great series on France and England in North America was not published till 1865. In the preface he writes : —

To those who have aided him with information and documents, the extreme slowness in the progress of the work will naturally have caused surprise. This slowness was unavoidable. During the past eighteen years, the state of his health has exacted throughout an extreme caution in regard to mental application, reducing it at best within narrow and precarious limits, and often precluding it. Indeed, for two periods, each of several years, any attempt at bookish occupation would have been merely suicidal. A condition of sight arising from kindred sources has also retarded the work, since it has never permitted reading or writing continuously for much more than five minutes, and often has not permitted them at all.

Thus, so far as concerns his history, the record of these laborious years, doing " day labor, light denied," is chiefly a chronicle of the spirit dominating continuous insurrections of the body. It is the story of a prize-fight — a bout, a respite, again a toeing of the line, again blows hard and heavy, and Parkman again and again coming back to the scratch, on guard, teeth set, and resolute " never to submit or yield." The cause of all these ills was the subject of great disagreement among physicians; Dr. George M. Gould, of Philadelphia, has written a very interesting monograph to prove that unsymmetric astigmatism and anisometropia were the prime devils in his body. *Sed non nobis — Procul, profani!* Enough of this, as he himself would have said.

At the time he published " The Pioneers of France in the New World " he had written parts of later volumes, near a third of " The Jesuits," a half of " La Salle; " also the material for " Frontenac " was partially arranged for composition, and most of the material for the whole series had been collected and was within reach. " The Pioneers " could not fail of flattering criticism from the newspapers; the episode of Menendez and Dominique de Gourgues, the story of Champlain, have all the spirit of the " Trois Mousquetaires " and all the accuracy of Agassiz. The " Tribune " ventured to say to New Yorkers that " in vigor and pointedness of description, Mr. Parkman may be counted superior to Irving; " and the " Nation " said, " This book will add his name to the list of those his-

torians who have done honor to American literature."

The other volumes followed with louder and
louder choruses of applause, — " The Jesuits in
North America " in 1867, " La Salle and the
Discovery of the Great West " in 1869, the
" Old Régime " in 1874, " Frontenac " in 1877,
" Montcalm and Wolfe " in 1884, for here he
broke the sequence of his story in order that he
might run no risk, but complete while yet time
served the last great scene of the play. Afterwards, in 1892, he published the " Half Century
of Conflict," and the long day's work was done.

The careless, pleasure-loving reader, who skips
prefaces and notes, might rashly conclude that
what is so delightful to read is not to be classed
with " profitable " books of research, — which
commonly have the charm of a law book and
read like a dictionary ; to such readers a page or
two must be addressed. In the preface to the
" Pioneers " Parkman says : —

Faithfulness to the truth of history involves
far more than a research, however patient and
scrupulous, into special facts. . . . The narrator
must seek to imbue himself with the life and
spirit of the time. He must study events in
their bearings near and remote ; in the character, habits, and manners of those who took
part in them. . . . With respect to that special research which, if inadequate, is still in the

most emphatic sense indispensable, it has been
the writer's aim to exhaust the existing material
of every subject treated. . . . With respect to
the general preparation, . . . he has long been
too fond of this theme to neglect any means
within his reach of making his conception of it
distinct and true.

For the second volume, " The Jesuits in North
America," there was a mass of materials, as
" nearly every prominent actor left his own record of events," and all the documents connected
with the Jesuits had to be studied and compared.
For " La Salle " he had to examine volumes of
manuscript drawn from the public archives of
France. For the " Old Régime " the story is very
much the same. For " Montcalm and Wolfe," besides books, pamphlets, *brochures*, memoirs, reports, documents, and all the multitudinous forms
of print, — brevier, long primer, small pica, not to
forget Borgis, nonpareille, Garmond, and Cicero,
and all the other outlandish types of foreign
lands, — six thousand folio pages of manuscript
had been copied from the Archives de la Marine
et des Colonies, the Archives de la Guerre, and
the Archives Nationales at Paris ; ten volumes
of copies had been made from the Public Record
Office and the British Museum in London ; and
on the heels of these he had to listen to the slow
deciphering of cramped writing, crabbed writing,
hasty, blotted, blurred writing, faded writing,

unpunctuated writing, — all sorts of writing, abbreviated by caprice and the waywardest fancy, naturally bad, worsened by time, by the corruptions of moth and dust, and all the foes of history. So, too, it was for the "Half Century of Conflict."

In the upper hall of the house of the Massachusetts Historical Society stands a large wooden press, — a bookcase with doors; over the top is carved Parkman's name. Within are his manuscripts, given by him to the Society. They not only tell of all the work he did, but they talk about him, and boast of the proud and affectionate interest he took in them. There the volumes of MSS. stand bound in their bindings, differing in degree according to size and dignity. There are the early-gathered "Pontiac Miscellanies" in big, red, shiny leather, with gilt lettered backs, standing eighteen inches high and near two inches thick, — neat copies of documents; one volume of them, of less elegant calligraphy, in Parkman's own hand, copied from records in the Maryland Historical Society in 1845. Next them come the letters of Pedro Menendez, the cruel Spaniard; and following him more great big red books, copied for Francis Parkman, Esq., by Ben: Perley Poore, Historical Agent of the Commonwealth of Massachusetts, as the frontispiece recounts in pied letters of great brilliancy. Very creditable calligraphy they are. Then follow volumes in rows, — volumes of "Correspondance Officiale," 1621–1679; volumes on Acadia, Isle Royale, Canada ; volumes of documents copied from the Public Record Office in London; volumes of Dinwiddie's letters, — these last in green leather, in self-satisfied distinction from their fellows. Then other volumes, English and French, of which none is more interesting than the "Voyage dans le Gulfe de Mexique," written by La Salle's brother, an old manuscript bought at a sale in London in 1857 for $48.50, as the fly-leaf says. It begins : —

MONSEIGNEUR, — Voicy la Relation du voyage que mon frère entreprit pour decouvrir dans le golfe du mexique, l'embouchure du fleuve de missisippy, une mort inopinée et tragique l'ayant empeché de le parachever et d'en rendre Conte à vôtre grandeur, j'espere quelle agreera que je suplée à son defaut.

In the days of Louis XIV even death was a poor excuse for not fulfilling the punctilios due the king.

Following these big books come little note-books of Parkman's own keeping, loose sheets, letters, journals, little parcels of papers neatly tied with ribbon, the MSS. of one or two of the histories, and a guerilla band of those enemies of peace and order, " Sundry documents."

His printed books, several thousands, were kept in his study on the third story of No. 50 Chestnut Street; so were the MSS. before they were given to the Historical Society. Up in that study he used to sit all the winter months, in the company of his books and manuscripts, while the fire from the open stove flickered salutations to the shelves opposite, and the books stared back at trophies got forty years before on the Oregon trail, — bow, arrows, shield, pipe of peace, hanging tamely on the wall; the little bronze cats on the mantelpiece played undismayed beside the couchant Barye lioness, embodiment of the eternal struggle, the triumph of the strong, the ruin of the weak; and Sir Jeffrey Amherst, out from his engraving after Reynolds's portrait, his head resting pensively on one hand, careless of baton and helmet, gazed ruminatingly at his fellow pictures, prints of the "Catterskills," of the ruins of Ticonderoga, of Lake George. From other walls Sir Walter Scott, a lion, and a cat looked gravely at Colonel Shaw, Colleoni, Dürer's Knight (a favorite), and at the facade of Notre Dame; but pictures had no great liberty of place, for the bookshelves spread themselves over most of the room.

Parkman used to sit in a simple easy-chair, his feet near the stove, while his sister, at a little table beside the window, wrote at his dictation.

But when his work was over, as the short winter twilights hurried away, his thoughts often must have wandered back over the forty years spent in the wilderness of physical ills, and with his jaw set firm, but with his kind heart unstrung, he must have remembered the old days of boyhood, of health, of promise, when Nature, too, was young and beautiful and savage, and perhaps he repeated the words of his youth: —

Thus to look back with a fond longing to inhospitable deserts, where men, beasts, and Nature herself, seem arrayed in arms, and where ease, security, and all that civilization reckons among the goods of life, are alike cut off, may appear to argue some strange perversity, and yet such has been the experience of many a sound and healthful mind. To him who has once tasted the reckless independence, the haughty self-reliance, the sense of irresponsible freedom, which the forest life engenders, civilization thenceforth seems flat and stale. Its pleasures are insipid, its pursuits wearisome, its conventionalities, duties, and mutual dependence, alike tedious and disgusting. . . . The wilderness, rough, harsh, and inexorable, has charms more potent in their seductive influence than all the lures of luxury and sloth. There is a chord in the hearts of most men, prompt to answer loudly or faintly, as the case may be, to such rude appeals. But there is influence of another sort, strongest with minds of the finest texture, yet sometimes holding a controlling power over those who neither acknowledge nor suspect its workings. There are so few imbruted by vice, so perverted by art and luxury, as to dwell in the closest presence of Nature, deaf to her voice of melody and power, untouched by the ennobling influences which mould and penetrate the heart that has not hardened itself against them. Into the spirit of such an one the mountain wind breathes its own freshness, and the midsummer tempest, as it rends the forest, pours its own fierce energy. . . . It is the grand and heroic in the hearts of men which finds its worthiest symbol and noblest aspiration amid these desert realms — in the mountain and in the interminable forest.[1]

So spake the lover at twenty-three, in the luxuriant exuberance of love and youth ; so thought the old man, thinking of his mistress whom he had not seen for forty years. Perhaps to his thin determined lips and firm-set jaw, up from his modest heart, came the ancient benediction, —

Blessed of the Lord be his land,
For the precious things of heaven, for the dew,
And for the chief things of the ancient mountains,
And for the precious things of the lasting hills,
And for the precious things of the earth and fulness
    thereof,
And for the good will of him that dwelt in the bush.

As I have said, his reputation increased as the series advanced, and on the publication of " Montcalm and Wolfe " he reached the height

[1] *Pontiac*, vol. ii. pp. 237–239.

of his fame; this book he and the world regarded as his best. He could then feel that,
even should he not fill in the intervening half
century between Frontenac and Montcalm, his
work had been in substance done, that his endurance had overcome its enemies. He enjoyed
applause, not so much that of the public — for
he had a smack of Coriolanus's opinion on the
" raskell many " — as that of men whose judgment was trained and instructed, and whose
speech was measured.

MR. HENRY ADAMS TO PARKMAN.

[WASHINGTON], 21 December, 1884.

MY DEAR PARKMAN, — Your two volumes on
Montcalm and Wolfe deserve much more careful study than I am competent to give them,
and so far as I can see, you have so thoroughly
exhausted your sources as to leave little or
nothing new to be said. The book puts you in
the front rank of living English historians, and
I regret only that the field is self-limited so that
you can cultivate it no further. Your book
is a model of thorough and impartial study and
clear statement. Of its style and narrative the
highest praise is that they are on a level with its
thoroughness of study. Taken as a whole, your
works are now dignified by proportions and com-
pleteness which can be hardly paralleled by the
" literary baggage " of any other historical writer
in the language known to me to-day. . . .

Ever truly y'rs,   HENRY ADAMS.

[New York], Dec. 14, 1885.

MY DEAR PARKMAN, — I have just finished your " Wolfe and Montcalm," and I cannot help doing what I have never done before — write to tell the author with what delight I read it. I do not think I have ever been so much enchained by a historical book, although I was passionately fond of history in my boyhood. Wolfe, too, was one of my earliest heroes, and although I have been familiar for over forty years with his story, I became almost tremulous with anxiety about the result of the night attack when reading your account of the final preparations, a few evenings ago.

What became of Montcalm's family? Has he any descendants now? What a pathetic tale his is!

. . . Thank you most sincerely for a great pleasure.   Yours very sincerely,
E. L. GODKIN.

A later letter, 1887, characteristically says: "I hope you are well and busy. *No one* else does nearly as much for American literature. This is 'gospel truth.'"

DOVER, [ENGLAND], August 24th, [1885].

MY DEAR PARKMAN, — This is only three lines, because I cannot hold my hand from telling you, as other people must have done to your final weariness, with what high appreciation and genuine gratitude I have been reading your

" Wolfe and Montcalm." (You see I am still so overturned by my emotion that I can't even write the name straight.) I have found the right time to read it only during the last fortnight, and it has fascinated me from the first page to the last. You know, of course, much better than any one else how good it is, but it may not be absolutely intolerable to you to learn how good still another reader thinks it. The manner in which you have treated the prodigious theme is worthy of the theme itself, and that says everything. It is truly a noble book, my dear Parkman, and you must let me congratulate you, with the heartiest friendliness, on having given it to the world. So be as proud as possible of being the author of it, and let your friends be almost as proud of possessing his acquaintance. Reading it here by the summer smooth channel with the gleaming French coast, from my windows, looking on some clear days only five miles distant, and the guns of old England pointed seaward, from the rambling, historic castle, perched above me upon the downs; reading it, I say, among these influences, it has stirred all sorts of feelings — none of them, however, incompatible with a great satisfaction that the American land should have the credit of a production so solid and so artistic. . . . Believe in the personal gratitude of yours, ever very faithfully,

H. JAMES.

MR. JAMES RUSSELL LOWELL TO PARKMAN.

31, LOWNDES SQUARE, [LONDON], S. W., 8th Decr., 1884.

DEAR PARKMAN, — I have just done reading your book, and write a line to thank you for what has been so great a pleasure. It went as delightfully as floating down one of the forest streams where your scene is laid. You have done nothing better, and you know how I liked the others.   Faithfully yours,

J. R. LOWELL.

MR. GEORGE BANCROFT TO PARKMAN.

WASHINGTON, D. C., 28 Nov., 1884.

DEAR MR. PARKMAN, — I am delighted at receiving from you under your own hand these two new volumes with which you delight your friends and instruct readers in both worlds. You belong so thoroughly to the same course of life which I have chosen that I follow your career as a fellow soldier, striving to promote the noblest ends, and I take delight in your honors as much or more than I should my own. You have just everything which go to make an historian — persistency in collecting materials, indefatigable industry in using them, swift discernment of the truth, integrity and intrepidity in giving utterance to truth, a kindly humanity which is essential to the true historian, and which gives the key to all hearts, and a clear and graceful and glowing manner of narration. I claim like yourself to have been employed earnestly, and pray you to hold me to be in all sincerity and affectionate regard,

Your fellow laborer and friend,

GEO. BANCROFT.

Mr. Henry Cabot Lodge dedicated his "Historical and Political Essays" to Parkman, —

" To Francis Parkman, in token of admiration
for his great work as an American historian and
for his character as a man " — and at the time
wrote this letter : —

Nov. 11th, [1892].

DEAR MR. PARKMAN, — I send herewith a
little volume of essays, which I have taken the
liberty and given myself the great pleasure of
dedicating to you. . . . I should have liked to
have had time to write an article on the completion of your history, but politics have so engrossed me of late that literature has gone to
the wall. But I wished in some public fashion
to express the great admiration I feel for your
writings and for your services to American history, and also for the character, courage, and
will which have enabled you to do such work
despite the obstacles with which you contended
and which you have so entirely overcome. May
I add that I also wished to express my very
strong personal regard for you. The dedication
cannot possibly give you the pleasure that it
gives me, but I venture to hope that you will
accept it.   Sincerely y'rs,

H. C. LODGE.

Mr. Theodore Roosevelt dedicated " The Winning of the West " to Parkman, having first written this letter to ask permission : —

OYSTER BAY, LONG ISLAND, N. Y.,
April 23d, '88.

MY DEAR SIR, — I suppose that every American who cares at all for the history of his own

country feels a certain personal pride in your
work — it is as if Motley had written about
American instead of European subjects, and so
was doubly our own; but those of us who have
a taste for history, and yet have spent much of
our time on the frontier, perhaps realize even
more keenly than our fellows that your works
stand alone, and that they must be models for
all historical treatment of the founding of new
communities and the growth of the frontier here
in the wilderness. This — even more than the
many pleasant hours I owe you — must be my
excuse for writing.

I am engaged on a work of which the first
part treats of the extension of our frontier westward and southwestward during the twenty odd
years from 1774 to 1796. . . . This first part I
have promised the Putnams for some time in
1889 ; it will be in two volumes, with some such
title as " The Winning of the West and Southwest." . . .

I should like to dedicate this to you. Of course
I know that you would not wish your name to be
connected, in even the most indirect way, with
any but good work ; and I can only say, that I
will do my best to make the work creditable. . . .

Yours very truly,
Theodore Roosevelt.

MR. JUSTIN WINSOR TO PARKMAN.

Cambridge, May 23, '92.

Dear Parkman, — . . . I read your " Pontiac" when I was in college, and I have not failed
to read each succeeding work of yours upon its

publication. In the last ten years I have seldom had them off my study table, for work I have been upon has often — almost constantly — taken me to them; and always with increasing admiration. Believe me faithfully yours,

JUSTIN WINSOR.

Just before his death he was invited to attend the World's Congress of Historians, at the World's Fair, in Chicago, as "The Nestor and most beloved of American Historians." I cite these letters because scholars say that "no one who has not prosecuted some original research on the same lines can have an idea of the extreme care with which he [Parkman] worked, or of the almost petty detail which he was at pains to master, not necessarily to use, but simply to inform himself thoroughly of the circumstances or of the man [of which or whom he was writing]." For though he always wished to make his books delightful to read, he never used his imagination except as a means to discover and to combine the jots and tittles of accurate detail.

There were also tributes from persons less well known.

HON. FRANCIS PARKMAN:
Dear Sir, — Hoping and begging, I write you asking you if you will be so very kind as to give me your "autograph" — please may I have

it? I would feel most highly honored to receive and love dearly to possess your autograph. And if it is pleasing to you, Dear Sir! to favor me with a line or favorite sentiment — I will ever be most grateful for your exquisite kindness — for it will be to me a "precious souvenir" of a "Divinely gifted and most illustrious gentleman" whose name is dearly familiar and whose "noble researches" and "grand and brilliant" Historical writings which ever charm and enlighten the world — have endeared you to all hearts, as the most "famous and brilliantly gifted Historian of the world." . . .

To HON. FRANCIS PARKMAN, "Author," "King of Historians."

CHAPTER XXIII

CANADA AND CANADIAN FRIENDS

PARKMAN'S history is in substance a history of Canada, and in that country aroused great interest and admiration and also some dissatisfaction and dissent. Canadians almost unanimously acknowledged that Canada was greatly indebted to him for fame and honor: for, before Parkman wrote, on the south side of the border there was little information and much prejudice in regard to the past of our northern neighbor; in England there were but hazy ideas of an uninteresting agricultural province, momentarily illuminated by the exploit of an Englishman on the Plains of Abraham; and in France, Canada was but a vague and mortifying memory. English-speakers did not read the books of French Canadians, and for them Parkman put the history of Canada on a level of interest and importance equal to that, as statesmen say, of the most favored nation; before him, there was a history in English by William Smith, and the extent to which Mr. William Smith's history failed to

dispel the general darkness of ignorance holds
out a measure by which we can judge what
Parkman did for Canada.

The criticism which he received, sometimes
bitter, came from French Canadians, not wholly
able to forget that they represented a fallen
cause; they had remained loyal to that cause,
with the loyalty that forgets defects and enhances
virtues. The lost cause was not only that of a
nation, charming even to those whose birth and
breeding cut them off from full appreciation, but
also that of a church, sacred with all the affection that men cherish for their mothers. They
could not enjoy the story which told how that
nation and that church had been vanquished by
their common foe, and, as the story was told,
justly vanquished; for the teller, despite generous and impartial sympathy, believed that the
side upon which the right on the whole prepon-
derated had prevailed. That the victory had
been deserved was, in Parkman's judgment, the
verdict of history; but what man is there, who
belongs to the side which has lost, who can pa-
tiently endure to hear Rhadamanthus say, "You
have received your deserts." Thus there was
some feeling against Parkman, and when in
1878 some of the gentlemen of Laval University, the distinguished Catholic university at
Quebec, wishing to honor him, even if in their

judgment sometimes astray, proposed that the university should confer the degree of Doctor of Letters upon him, there was warm opposition. Hot words were spoken, strong feelings were strongly expressed; the conservatives carried the day, and the degree was denied. On the other hand, in the following year, the English university at Montreal, McGill, gave him the degree of Doctor of Laws. He was also chosen honorary member of the Literary and Historical Society of Quebec, and a corresponding member of the Royal Society of Canada.

The opposition of adverse critics troubled Parkman very little. He took no position on a matter of history until he had studied it with great care, and with all the impartiality that was possible.

On his visits to Canada Parkman naturally visited his friends and not his critics, and from them he always received the kindest hospitality. Quebec, as the historic centre of Canada, was his headquarters, and there he had very warm friends; in earlier days Judge Black, Judge Stuart, and all his life Sir James M. Le Moine, the latter a man of letters and student of history, whose country-seat, Spencer Grange, is not far from the site where the gallant Lévis routed General Murray. In the company of these gentlemen Parkman would wander over the battlefields

from Cap Rouge on the west to the Falls of
Montmorency on the east, examining the historic
spots, such as Sillery, a little village on the north
bank of the river, famous as possessing the oldest
house in Canada, and in the brave days of old
crowned with a French battery. Their friendly
commerce was fittingly accompanied, following
the best Hellenic traditions, by interchange of
gifts. He had friendships, too, with several
French Canadians, gentlemen of Quebec, who
were interested in Canadian history. Such was
M. Hubert La Rue, who always held out a warm
welcome: "Rendez-vous tout droit à la maison, où
votre petite chambre du fonds vous attend avec
impatience." He made a friendly acquaintance
with M. Ferland, Abbé Laverdière, Dr. J. C.
Taché, and other scholars. M. N. E. Dionne, now
librarian of the Parliamentary Library in the
Province of Quebec, did some copying for Parkman in 1871, as he himself tells, in English so
much better than much of our American-French,
that I venture to quote it: "Being poor, I was
glad to gain some dollars, but I was chiefly proud
to accompany this well-known Bostonian through
his peregrinations from the Seminary to the epis-
copal palace, from the registrar office to the Ter-
rier's office, compulsing together every document
which he intended to use." Parkman was well
pleased with the copies; and M. Dionne, himself

a historian, is able to add, "So that I must say, *and everybody can say so*, that if I am something to-day, I owe this to Mr. Parkman."

Among the Catholic clergy he had many friendly acquaintances. M. Audet, chaplain of the Couvent de Jesus et Marie de Sillery, introduced him to a priest at Cape Breton in these terms, "This gentleman, in spite of the difference of faith, has shown in his writings great justice in his estimate of the deeds of Catholics in Canada;" and to another thus, "This gentleman, although he does not share our faith, has in all his writings taken pains to give the most just and favorable testimony to the work of Catholicism in Canada."

Parkman's chief correspondence and most familiar intercourse were with M. l'Abbé H. R. Casgrain, the distinguished historian of Canada. The two were good friends for some twenty-eight years; M. l'Abbé, then a professor in the university, was the chief combatant on Parkman's side in the battle royal over the Laval degree; the friendship had begun by an interchange of letters in 1866, for the Muse of History, taking each by the hand, had brought them together. Parkman wished to subscribe to a Canadian review, "Le Foyer Canadien." Abbé Casgrain, secretary to the board of publication, hearing of this wish, presented him with all the back num-

bers, for, as the French know better than the
rest of us, "little gifts make great friendships."
The Abbé was a descendant of M. Baby, "a
prominent habitant," who lived across the river
from Detroit at the time of Pontiac's attack, and
by his good offices rendered the hard-pressed garrison great service;[1] this ancestry made a natural tie between the two historians. They had
another bond, for the Abbé was afflicted with
a partial blindness that prevented him from
reading or writing. Between them there was
an interchange of maps and documents and of
photographs. The little incidents of history, the
tassels and ornaments of narrative, made their
intercourse very agreeable. For example, Abbé
Casgrain brought together careful documentary
evidence that Champlain's tomb had been erected
on the spot now occupied by the post-office, near
the Château Frontenac, — a feat that aroused
jealousy and disbelief in other antiquarians. On
this occasion Parkman wrote, "A friend in Montreal sent me a newspaper with a notice of your
great discovery. I have long hoped that something might be brought to light on this point,
and wait with interest to hear more." Then follows another letter, disputing the Abbé's opinion
that Brébeuf — the noble Jesuit — should not
have an accent on the first syllable of his name,

[1] *Pontiac*, vol. i. p. 248.

ending, " I hope soon to hear that Champlain's bones are found."

Then Parkman sends a copy of "The Jesuits in North America."

BOSTON, Jan. 30, 1868.

If you are not in Quebec, it will no doubt await your return. Remembering that I am a heretic, you will expect a good deal with which you will be very far from agreeing. The truth is, I am a little surprised that neither Catholics nor Protestants have been very severe in their strictures on the book. I fully expected to be attacked by both — that is by the Calvinistic portion of Protestants. I believe both sides saw that I meant to give a candid view of my subject in the best light in which I could see it.

SAME TO SAME.

BOSTON, Feb. 13, 1868.

MY DEAR ABBÉ, — Many thanks for your most kind and welcome letter. I am truly glad that, as a man of letters and as a Catholic priest, you can find so much to approve in my book, and I set an especial value on your commendation. We are, as you say, at opposite poles of faith — but my faith, such as it is, is strong and earnest, and I have the deepest respect for the heroic self-devotion, the true charity, of the early Jesuits of Canada. . . .

Believe me ever, with great esteem,
Your friend and servant,
F. PARKMAN.

50 Chestnut St., Boston, 10 April, '71.

My dear Abbé, — Many thanks for your most friendly and obliging letter, and for the books which accompanied it. I regret to hear that your eyes still give you so much trouble ; a matter in which I can wholly sympathize with you, my own having been useless for ten years or more, and even now permitting me to write or read only for a few minutes at one time.

Soon after this the Abbé went to Boston and paid Parkman a visit at his country home by Jamaica Pond. The Abbé says, " Les politesses exquises dont je fus l'objet de sa part et de celle de sa famille ont laissé en moi des souvenirs qui ne sont pas effacés ; " and Parkman wrote : " I recall your visit with the greatest pleasure, and congratulate myself that after so long an interval I have at last the good fortune to know you personally." The visit was short, but Parkman took the Abbé to see Harvard College, Mr. Agassiz, and Mr. Longfellow, whose long white beard, falling over his chest, recalled to the Abbé the ancient seers and poets, " Ossian, Baruch, or Camoëns."

One consequence of this visit was the little book, " Francis Parkman, par l'Abbé H. R. Casgrain," published in 1872, which is full of admiration, of compliments, and yet speaks out frankly the author's divergent views.

We have enlarged as far as possible the place of praise, in order to accord to Truth all its rights, to criticism elbow-room. Let us say, without beating about the bush, . . . Mr. Parkman's work is the negation of all religious belief. The author rejects the Protestant theory as well as Catholic dogma ; he is an out-and-out rationalist. We perceive an upright soul, born for the truth, but lost without a compass on a boundless sea. Hence these aspirations towards the true, these flashes of acknowledgment, these words of homage to the truth, followed, alas, by strange fallings off, by fits of fanaticism that are astounding.

The Abbé sent Parkman the proofs of this little book before publication.

PARKMAN TO CASGRAIN.

BOSTON, Jan. 26, 1872.

MY DEAR FRIEND, — The proofs came yesterday. I think you know me too well to doubt that I accept your criticism as frankly as it is given, and that I always listen with interest and satisfaction to the comments of so kind and generous an opponent. I only wonder that, in the opposition of our views on many points of profound importance, you can find so much to commend. When you credit me with loyalty and honor, you give me the praise that I value most of all.

In all that you say of my books and of myself I recognize a warmth of personal regard which would lead me to distrust your praises but for the manifest candor and sincerity which pervade your praise and blame alike. I need not say that I am extremely gratified by the one; and as for the other, I gladly accept it. I know what your views are. You have spoken them openly, but very kindly. As a Catholic you could not have said less, and you might have said more.

I wish you were not in error when you say that I am about finishing my present task. A very long road is still before me. The subject is complicated and difficult, and the time I can give to it each day is short, both from other deviations and the state of my health, which often makes study out of the question. According to the "medical faculty," as the newspapers say, the trouble comes from an abnormal state or partial paralysis of certain arteries of the brain. Whatever it is, it is a nuisance of the first order, and a school of patience by which Job himself might have profited. However, Providence permitting, I will spite the devil yet.

Very sincerely and cordially yours,
F. PARKMAN.

SAME TO SAME.

BOSTON, 17 Nov., '72.

I have just returned [from a trip to France]. I have brought home a large collection of documents. More are to follow, to the amount of about 2500 folio pages. So you see, I did not lose my time.

Let me correct what seems a mistaken impression. In your critique of Chauveau you speak of *dures vérités* which you uttered in regard to my books, and for which I thanked you and still thank you. But this is because I like frank and outspoken criticism, when kindly uttered, not because I recognize as *vérités* the strictures passed upon me. While esteeming my critic, I still believe myself in the right.

[May 23, 1873.]

Of one thing I beg you to be entirely assured, and that is that your article in the " Revue " [criticising Parkman] has not in the slightest degree affected the cordial regard which I entertain for you. I knew that you wrote it with pain and regret, in obedience to a sense of duty ; and besides, I believe that when I feel confident in my position I am not very sensitive to criticism.

After this, Parkman made a return visit to the Abbé, at the Maison d'Airvault, the latter's family place at Rivière Ouelle, a village on the south bank of the St. Lawrence, opposite the mouth of the Murray River. Here Parkman not merely had the pleasure of the society of his host and his host's family, but became familiar with a little village not so very different from what it had been when the fleur-de-lis floated over the citadel of Quebec. Correspondence was taken up again as before. M. l'Abbé wrote a review of the " Old Régime," in which he found sundry expressions of opinion that did not coincide with his own.

PARKMAN TO CASGRAIN.

JAMAICA PLAIN, 9 May, 1875.

MON CHER AMI, — I have read your article on the Old Régime with attention and interest. It is very much what I had expected, knowing your views and the ardor with which you embrace them, as well as the warmth and kindliness of your feelings. I could take issue squarely on the principal points you make, but it would make this letter too long, and I do not care to enter into discussion with a personal friend on matters which he has so much at heart. Moreover, I wish to preserve an entirely judicial, and not controversial frame of mind on all that relates to Canadian matters. Let me set you right, however, on one or two points personal to myself. My acquaintance here would smile to hear me declared an advocate of democracy and a lover of the puritans. I have always declared openly my detestation of the unchecked rule of the masses, that is to say, of universal suffrage, and the corruption which is sure to follow in every large and heterogeneous community. I have also always declared a very cordial dislike of puritanism. I recognize some most respectable and valuable qualities in the settlers of New England, but do not think them or their system to be praised without great qualifications, and I would not spare criticism, if I had to write about them. Nor am I at all an enthusiast for the nineteenth century, many of the tendencies of which I deplore, while admiring much that it has accomplished. It is too democratic, and too much given to the pursuit of material interests at the expense of intellectual and moral greatness, which I hold to be the true end, — to which material progress should be but a means.

My political faith lies between two vicious extremes, democracy and absolute authority, each of which I detest the more because it tends to react into the other. I do not object to a good constitutional monarchy, but prefer a conservative republic, where intelligence and character, and not numbers, hold the reins of power.

I could also point out a good many other mistakes in your article. You say that I see Canadian defects through a microscope, and merits through a diminishing glass. The truth is, I have suppressed a considerable number of statements and observations because I thought that while they would give pain, they were not absolutely necessary to the illustration of the subject ; but I have invariably given every favorable testimony I could find in any authentic quarter. . . .

Very cordially yours,

F. PARKMAN.

SAME TO SAME.

Nov. 2, 1878.

Did you get an attack on the sovereign Demos, which I sent you ? It has drawn on me a great deal of barking and growling, and caused me to be branded as " audacious," a " foe to popular government " etc., — so you see I am shot at from both sides of the line. The article in question, however, has been very widely read, and has received a great deal of approval as well as denunciation.

The following extract relates to the degree which his friends sought to obtain for him from Laval University.

Dec. 10, 1878.

This outbreak is a very curious one. So far as I myself am concerned, I find it rather amusing, and am not annoyed by it in the least. But I regret it extremely on account of the trouble it has given you and Mr. Le Moine; and also on account of the embarrassing position in which I fear that it places the University and the excellent ecclesiastics by whom it is directed. It was to me extremely gratifying that men like these, while differing profoundly from me and disapproving much that I have written, should recognize the sincerity of my work by expressing their intention to honor me with a degree of *Docteur ès Lettres*. It was this generous recognition which gave me particular pleasure; and greatly as I should feel honored by a degree from Laval University, I prize still more the proofs of esteem which its directors have already given me. I trust that they will not feel themselves committed to any course which circumstances may have rendered inexpedient, and that they will be guided simply by the interests of the University.

Thus the correspondence went along, touching on Parkman's gleanings in the archives of Paris, on the Abbé's antiquarian discoveries, on history, on friends, on other matters unimportant, except in the respect most important of all, evidence of good hearts and good friendship. Most of the Abbé's letters unfortunately have been lost or destroyed; Parkman's continue till the year before his death; but the last of his that shall be quoted concerns his health, in answer to inquiries of affectionate interest.

JAMAICA PLAIN, 12 May, 1889.

MON CHER ABBÉ, — For the past five years I have done very little historical work, not so much from laziness as from the effects of insomnia. Two or three hours of sleep in the 24 — which have been until lately my average allowance for long periods together — are not enough to wind up the human machine, especially when exercise is abridged by hereditary gout mixed with rheumatism, produced, according to the doctors, by numerous drenchings in the forests of Maine when I was a collegian (e. g. on one occasion, rain without shelter for three days and nights, just after being wrecked in a rapid of the River Margalloway). Perhaps, however, the rheumatism is a stroke of retributive justice for writing "Montcalm and Wolfe." Though I have slept better in the past year, it is still an open question whether I shall ever manage to supply the missing link between that objectionable work and its predecessor "Count Frontenac." . . .

Que Dieu vous aide —

Tout-à-vous.

We cannot suppose that two historians of divergent views corresponded on such hotspur topics as the peasants of Acadia, the rival merits of

Montcalm and Lévis, or the character of Vaudreuil, not to mention nationality and religion,
without one or the other catching fire and flam-
ing up till the " rash bavin " cause was burned
out, and old friendship returned to its old ways.
But certainly there was no trace of jangling
towards the end; the melody of friendship was
altogether pleasant.

CASGRAIN TO PARKMAN [translated].

QUEBEC, May 23d, 1892.

MY DEAR HISTORIAN, — I make haste to thank
you for the present of your two handsome volumes, "A Half Century of Conflict," which I
have just received. Let me cordially congratulate you upon having set the crown on the great
work to which you have consecrated all your life.
No one values it more than I do. I am now
going to forsake all other reading, in order to
plunge headlong into your two volumes. For me
they have a double attraction : because of the
conscientious researches of which they are the
fruit, and because they are written by a person
who has always been the object of my admiration, and for whom I feel an attachment that I
cannot well express. . . . Je fais des vœux pour
que votre chère santé s'améliore, et je vous prie
de croire à une estime qui n'a d'égale que mon
attachement.   H. R. CASGRAIN.

So they parted with French politeness on their
lips and kind feelings in their hearts. " Croyez

toujours à ma sincère amitié : la votre m'honore infiniment, Casgrain." " Que Dieu vous aide, tout-à-vous, Parkman."

I must not close this correspondence without a passing allusion — my ignorance will not suffer me to do more — to two criticisms which the Abbé Casgrain has made upon Parkman's history. The first is that Parkman was unjust in his account of the poor peasants banished from Acadia by the English in 1755.[1] Parkman did make a mistake in his reliance upon certain documents officially published : " Selections from the Public Documents of the Province of Nova Scotia ; " these were in fact badly garbled, as the Abbé proved by his diligent researches and discoveries in the British Museum and the Record Office in London. The Abbé, relying on this fresh evidence, spoke very warmly in favor of the Acadians in his book "Un pèlerinage au pays d'Evangéline" (1886) ; but other scholars say that the case against the Acadian peasants is not upset by the new documents.

The second criticism is that Parkman made Montcalm the French hero in the final drama at Quebec, whereas this honor should have been bestowed upon Lévis. Several years after Parkman's book was published, Count Raimond de Nicolay, great-grandson of Chevalier Lévis,

[1] *Montcalm and Wolfe*, chap. viii.

through the good offices of Abbé Casgrain, gave permission to the Province of Quebec to publish the journals and letters of his great-grandfather. To these valuable papers Parkman had not access. They were published between 1889 and 1895 under the superintendence of the Abbé, and show that Lévis was a very noble, spirited, and capable man, and, if they do not oust Montcalm from his pedestal, prove that the French had a second hero as well.

During all the years from the beginning of preparation until the "Half Century of Conflict" was sent to the printer, Parkman made from time to time frequent visits to Canada. As Sir James M. Le Moine says, he used to call Quebec his sunny, health-restoring, holiday home. No wonder the St. Lawrence was a river after his own heart, with its long ancestry of lakes, its great seaward flow, its shifting banks, high and low, soft and rugged, its little lines of white villages, and the romantic citadel of Quebec, at whose feet it flows with all the chivalry proper to the prince of rivers. He would go about as always, with a little notebook in pocket, jotting down, not with the prodigality of old, but with a frugal pencil, notes and memoranda, so brief that one little book served for years. But the old love of detail is there.

In Canada, too, after forty lean years of abstinence, he camped out for the last time; on the banks of the Batiscan River, he spent a month with Mr. Farnham, his biographer.

TO MISS PARKMAN.

BATISCAN RIVER, 7 June, [1886].

MY DEAR L., — I am well. Fishing good. Flies bad. Farnham very pleasant. Camp finished and comfortable. Excellent fare. Family consists of selves and our puppy. . . . F. an excellent cook.

F. P.

Parkman could not do much, hobbled by his lame knee, but he was always interested, patient, and cheerful. He enjoyed the "feel" of a rifle once more, and a shot at a handy mark; he tried fishing with a fly, — the worm of his early days having crawled under the protection of fashionable contempt. He liked to get into his little canoe, in which he could mock his lame leg, and paddle down the river, gazing at the green banks, the high bluffs, the close thickets, — all as it were seen in a magic mirror, for he could not enter. This was his last visit to the land he had done so much to honor.

CHAPTER XXIV

LATER LIFE

THERE still remains the duty to chronicle the simple happenings in the life of the scholar invalid, during the thirty years from the war until his death ; they are uneventful, much too undramatic for a reader, but such as they were they made up his life. Random extracts from his sister's diary show the ups and downs over which he passed : —

1862, Jan. 29. F. went to the Baldwins' last ev'g to a small supper given to Mr. W. Hunt, and to-night was able to go to the Club for a short time.

June 11. F. has seemed in very good spirits for a day or two.

Sept. 9. F. is suffering from the most severe attack in his eyes he has had for years. He cannot attend to his gardening at all. Mother feels very anxious.

10th. F., if anything, worse. He seems in very low spirits.

15th. F. seems better.

1863, Jan. 24. F. is highly entertained by " Pickwick," as much as if he had never read it before.

Feb. 11. F. is beginning to work upon his French History, though, as he says, at a snail's pace. His eyes are very troublesome now.

June 27. Rose Show. Grace [his daughter] and I drove in with F. and arranged the flowers. 1st prize, Moss Roses; 2d, June Roses; 3d, Display.

Sept. 20. F. has not slept for some nights, and his head is in a bad state.

Oct. 1. F. still has very poor nights and seems miserably.

2d. F. had very little sleep; head very bad.

1864, June 25. This is the day of the Rose Show. Grace and I went in to help Frank. We worked steadily for two hours, and barely had time to prepare the great quantity of roses. F. took four 1st prizes and a large " gratuity."

1865, June 6th. F. went to Washington this morning.

12th. Frank writes from Washington. He has seen the camps and means to go to Richmond.

20th. Letter from F. at Richmond. He is detained there to collect documents for the Boston Athenæum.

July 18th. Frank and I have been to a reception at the Lymans' to meet Gen. Meade and Staff.

Nov. 7. Frank came down to breakfast very lame; thinks the old trouble is all coming back.

22d. The anxiety about Frank's knee is passing away.

1866, Aug. 10th. F. started for Quebec.

29. F. took the usual prizes at the Hort.

Nov. 16th. F. came in [town] to-day to live.

1867, April 20th. F. came in to spend Sunday.
Grace came to tea. Enthusiasm over cats.

July 10. Frank is going to the Mississippi River;
he is now writing history connected with its discovery, and goes on that account. What a good
summer he has had so far; his book ["Jesuits"]
out this spring and well received, and his
flowers so successful, and he seems so well.

Aug. 15. Frank arrived none the worse for the
5 weeks journey, though he has used head and
eyes much. He has brought many photo's of
Sioux Indians and of Mississippi scenery. [He
saw Henry Chatillon at St. Louis.]

1868, June 30. Drove in with F. to the Rose
Show. F. took 1st prizes.

July 15. F. goes to Cambridge in all the heat.
He is chosen overseer of the college.

Aug. 1st. F. has gone to Rye to spend Sunday
with the children.

10th. F. left this ev'g to spend a fortnight in
Canada.

Sept. 25. Mother is 75 to-day. F. brought in
white roses.

Oct. 29. Frank's head is in a bad state, the first
time for a long time.

Nov. 1. F.'s head is very bad, worse than for
some time; he says, years.

Nov. 27. Frank has determined to go to Paris
for the winter. His head seems a little better,
but he cannot do much with it, and he would
rather be idle there than here. He seems disposed to go, and in good spirits, so we are very
glad to have him, but it leaves a great gap.

PARKMAN TO HIS SISTER.

21 Boulevard St. Michel,
Paris, 15 Jan., 1869.

MY DEAR LIZZIE, — I have rec'd your letter of 8 Dec., but not till a month after its date. . . . There is a little girl in the house, daughter of the concierge, who collects post-stamps, and would be delighted with five or six American and Canadian stamps. Will you inclose them in your next if convenient. I mean to leave here for England early in March, and thence home after a few days in London. . . .

[Jan. 18.]

. . . I have just rec'd all your letters. I am grieved more than I can tell you about mother's accident. Keep me well informed about it. . . . Tell Grace that there are girls here who ride on velocipedes with two wheels in the streets, but that their conduct is not at all approved. . . .

[28 Jan., '69.]

If I do not hear good news soon I shall set out for home, but I trust that mother is getting better. Remember me most affectionately to her and tell her that I think of her continually. I am doing very well indeed, and am far better in health than when I left Boston. . . . I have a good many acquaintances, some of them very pleasant ones, though I refuse dinners, etc.

[Feb. 1, '69.]

I have just rec'd yours of Jan. 16 with news that mother is better, which is an immense relief. I am all right bating a cold in the head.

To-morrow I am going to St. Cloud to breakfast with Count Circourt, a friend of the Ticknors. I see Margry often. He was here the other night, and staid till twelve. . . . I made a journey of 2 miles and more under Paris, through the sewers, partly in a boat, and partly in a sort of rail-car. . . . Give my best love to mother and the children, not forgetting Jack.

[Feb. 24, '69.]

Have been troubled with want of sleep for five or six nights, but otherwise all right. If I accepted invitations, which I do not, I should have the run of the Faubourg St. Germain. I have just declined an invitation from the Prince de Broglie to dine. Yesterday I saw the Marquis de Montcalm, great-grandson of Wolfe's antagonist, who was very civil. The post-stamps were very gratefully received. Don't let the doctor [Dr. Bigelow] think that I am doing anything but amuse myself, for I am not. I meet a few people incidentally, but am very stiff in declining overtures. The Marquis placed his family papers at my disposal. I have not read one of them, but employed a man to copy them, who is now at work.

MISS PARKMAN'S DIARY.

1869. March 27. F. arrived this ev'g. He seems in very good spirits and health.

April 12. Frank's head is almost as bad as before he went away.

1870. Feb. 17. F. has been very sleepless of late. He had his club last night at the Union Club rooms (mother being ill).

March 24. F. is having sleepless nights, and suffering very much.

Sept. 16. F.'s birthday. He got no sleep last night, and I never saw him more affected by it in health or spirits. It is a year since he has been sleepless, more or less.

23d. F. did not sleep at all last night. It is wonderful that he can do anything by day, and he does not do much.

24th. F. slept between 5 and 6 hours. It is such a relief. Yesterday it was mournful enough at breakfast, though he plays with the cats and the children and says nothing.

25th. Mother is 76 to-day. As I came down to breakfast I saw F. coming in with a bunch of roses already tied, and another of ribbons and daisies. He looked so well I knew he had slept, and found he had had a very good night. That alone made mother happy.

1871. March 12. Mother feels very happy that F. has just been chosen professor of Horticulture in the new Bussey Institute of H. C. [Harvard College]. Frank himself likes the appointment, as he thinks he can do the work without giving more time than he can give, and the fact that he can take such a responsibility is a delight as a proof of how much better he is. [He resigned as overseer of the college on the ground of inconsistency between the two positions.]

April 2d. Flora's first kittens appeared, but had a brief existence. F.'s interest was deep, and his disappointment also.

June 8th. Mother moved out of town with great

difficulty (on account of her hip), but at last was safe in her room, rhododendrons and roses of Frank's gathering all about her.

That summer their mother died, while Parkman was in Canada. It was a terrible blow to him, — " poor fellow, how his face looked," — and the brother and sister were left alone to go through life together, for their sister Caroline had married and their sister Mary had died several years before, and their brother Jack — John Eliot, once Elly — died soon afterwards.

In 1872 they went to Paris, as Parkman wished to relieve his insatiable appetite for more documents. Here they saw a good deal of Margry, a person who plays a part in the story of Parkman's difficulties in laying his hands on documents, even on those of which he had definite information. Parkman had known this gentleman for several years, not without forming some opinion of him, as we see from certain phrases in the letters of 1868 to Abbé Casgrain : —

As for Margry, I am fully of your mind concerning him. I am in the midst of La Salle's discoveries. . . . I have a great deal that is new relating to his enterprises ; and but for M. Margry, should have still more. . . . Margry is very intractable, and I can get nothing from him.

M. Pierre Athanase Margry, chef adjoint Archiviste au Ministère de la Marine (in later

years *en retraite*) and Chevalier de la Légion
d'Honneur, had made an immense collection of
documents about La Salle, which he had ferreted
out of the Public Archives under his charge with
great zeal and industry ; these he wished to publish himself, but he had not money enough, and
was not willing that another should reap the har-
vest of his sowing, so he denied Parkman access
to them. As these documents were of great interest in the history of the United States, an
attempt had been made a year or two before to
induce Congress to make an appropriation for the
cost of publication, but in vain. In this collection
were La Salle's own letters, and these Parkman
was most eager to see. This conduct of Margry's
has been harshly blamed. Mr. Justin Winsor
says : " The keeper of an important department
of the French Archives had been so unfaithful to
his trust as to reserve for his own private use some
of its documentary proofs." Be the blame just
or no, — a lawyer might find something to say in
behalf of a right of lien for labor spent in search
and discovery, — Parkman freely forgave him.
Margry was a man with whom it would have
been hard to remain angry, even for a much less
generous person than Parkman ; he was a voluble
Gallic, kindly, smiling, enthusiastic little person,
lively, alert, " sensitive and distrustful," wearing
his mustachios and goatee after the fashion of

the Second Empire.　An amiable, infantile look
of quizzical cunning on his face, with his silk
hat, kid gloves, and loose pantaloons, effectually
disqualified him as an object of indignation.　He
was very friendly, liked to come and sit and chat,
and would stay till cockcrow if permitted ; he was
full of friendly usages, and on this visit celebrated Parkman's birthday with a poem : —

16. 7bre.　1823–1872.

À Francis Parkman, Auteur des Français en
Amérique.

Dans le monde, où vous êtes né
Vos écrits disent notre gloire;
Nul n'a, comme vous, honoré
Les beaux actes de notre histoire.

Cependant presque inaperçu
Vous allez parcourant la France,
Et c'est par hasard que j'ai su
La date de votre naissance.

Aussi je veux pour mon pays
Fêter ce jour, selon l'usage,
Par la même pensée unis
Il m'est cher de vous rendre hommage.

The poem has ten stanzas, is annotated, and
altogether breathes patriotism, hatred of Bis-
marck, and love of Parkman.　The friendship
thus fostered led to a plan, — that Parkman
should try to persuade some American bookseller
to publish the collection, for Margry, in spite of
poetry, firmly declined to sell the documents or

the use of them; but this plan came to nought,
as the great fire in Boston made general economy necessary. Thereupon Parkman pricked on
professors, and the professors stuck spurs into
historical societies — fire, fire, burn stick; stick,
stick, beat pig, — and they, in turn, petitioned
Congress to make the necessary appropriation
of $10,000. Senator Hoar and General Garfield
took the matter up; the act was passed, and the
' Découvertes et Etablissements des Français,
dans l'Ouest et dans le Sud de l'Amérique Sep-
tentrionale (1614–1754), Mémoires et Documents originaux," were published in Paris, and
did good service for a later edition of "La Salle
and the Discovery of the Great West."

There were other friends in Paris, the Marquis
de Montcalm, a nobleman completely indifferent
to that ceremonious deportment which we like
to think accompanies a coronet, but a kindly
little man, always giving full performance in
deeds to the pleasant " expression de ma parfaite
amitié et de mes sentiments les plus distingués ; "
there was M. le Comte de Circourt, and other
gentlemen acquainted with Canadian history,
either through respect for their fighting ancestors, or, by a prodigious cosmopolitan effort, interesting themselves in things outside of Paris.

Parkman enjoyed the beautiful city, he was
diverted by the happy bearing and gay polite-

ness of the people, and he liked to stroll, when
he could, along the *quais*, and examine the rows
of books, always seasonable bait for the foreign
traveler, or see what could be seen from tops of
omnibuses.

There was but one intrusion of unpleasant-
ness into his French relations : a lady, Mme. la
Comtesse de Clermont-Tonnerre, translated into
French " The Pioneers," and " The Jesuits,"
but in such a garbled and wanton manner, as to
suppress facts and opinions which in her judgment
were not so complimentary to the church as the
needs of pious edification required. Mr. Parkman was nettled, and expressed his opinion, but
with much less asperity than the lady deserved.

In contradistinction to this disagreeable im-
propriety, M. Geffroy delivered an intelligent
speech before the Department of Moral and Political Sciences of the French Institute, on the
occasion of presenting a copy of Parkman's
works, and expressed appreciation of the even-
handed justice which Parkman had dealt to so
partisan a subject.

After this visit to Paris in 1872, brother and
sister returned to their old way of life, dividing
the year between Jamaica Plain and 50 Chestnut
Street. He had given up his professorship at
the Bussey Institute, after one year of service,
but he always maintained a deep affection for

the college, and in 1875 was elected one of the
Fellows of the Corporation. He served for thirteen years, and was regular and punctual in his
attendance; sometimes the matters of business
were too severe in their claims on his attention, and he would get up and walk about, or go
out into the fresh air, and then come back to
the business.

In 1880 he made another trip to England and
France. This time the archives and the books
on the banks of the Seine were not his only mo-
tives for going; his younger daughter had married
Mr. John Templeman Coolidge, and was living
in Paris with her husband. This journey was
memorable for the discovery of the letters of
Montcalm to his lieutenant Bourlamaque; these
letters covered all the time from Montcalm's
arrival in Canada to within a few days before
his death, and had long been hidden treasure,
suspected, sought, but undiscovered. For fifteen
years Parkman had been on the scent, and now
that he was approaching the time to publish
"Montcalm and Wolfe," he was doubly eager.
The letters had been traced to England; there
the scent failed. At last they were found to be
a part of a precious collection belonging to Sir
Thomas Phillips, a great buyer of manuscripts in
his day, and from him they had descended to the
Rev. John E. A. Fenwick, and were hid in his

library at Thirlestaine House, Cheltenham. Letters passed rapidly concerning the treasure trove, and it was agreed that Mr. Fenwick's son Fitz Roy, who was "fond of deciphering," should copy the MSS. wanted. The Rev. Mr. Fenwick was obliged to move about, and his travels to Redelston Hall, Derby, and the Crescent Hotel, Buxton, caused several little delays. Then the young gentleman had to hurry back to Oxford for a *cram*, as he was to be examined for his final "school," and a new copyist had to be found. A lady of Atherfield House, Miles Road, Clifton, could not serve. She, however, suggested two ladies of the Brooklands, Gloster Road, but that house was two miles and a half from Cheltenham; finally Mr. Fenwick, a very kind and hospitable man, procured the services of a French lady, Miss Marie Perret, who copied the rest of the documents, " Lettres de Vaudreuil, Lettres de Lévis, Lettres Variarum," at the cost of 3d. for 72 words, as a neat little receipt in her handwriting records. These letters were especially valuable, because they were very intimate, full of frank remarks on Vaudreuil, Bigot, and others, with frequent " brûlez cette lettre," — orders, like many others given by poor Montcalm, disobeyed.

The expenses for copying were often very heavy; the little notebooks record: —

Cost of copying, etc.

Montcalm papers, leave to copy . .	£20
Facsimile to map of Ticonderoga . .	15s.
Book, Conduct of Shirley	2
T. Fitzroy Fenwick, copying	13 2 6
J. E. A. Fenwick, copying (for Miss Perret)	12
Montcalm picture, 60 francs.	
Wolfe "	10s.
Imbry, copying	15 3
Mrs. Bullen, copying	15 1

These expenses obliged Parkman to practice economy, not on a petty scale, but after the manner of a prudent, unostentatious gentleman.

Perhaps it was on this visit that one day he was sitting upon a bench in St. James's Park, somewhat forlorn, missing unconsciously the care he always got at 50 Chestnut Street, when up came friendly aid in the person of Mr. Henry James, who put him down at the Athenæum Club, and gave him a pleasant sense of sympathy, admiration, and fellowship, in the felicitous, evasive way that Parkman liked so much. Mr. James and the Athenæum took off what for Parkman was a rather cold, raw edge in London atmosphere.

There was another visit to Paris the next year; and at divers times there were journeys to Florida, to Acadia, to Canada, which interrupted for a few weeks at a stretch the peaceful life at

Jamaica Pond. His health continued as before, but the lack of sleep grew worse.

PARKMAN TO DR. WEIR MITCHELL.

JAMAICA PLAIN, 5 Nov., 1885.

MY DEAR DR. MITCHELL,—I regret to bother you again with my troubles, but as you have done more for me than anybody else, I am tempted to do so.

For about two years I have observed an increasing tendency to insomnia. This autumn, within about two months, it has become extremely troublesome. Sometimes I do not sleep at all. Often I sleep only from one to three hours. The week before last, the average for seven days was about two hours. Last night I heard every clock but those of eleven and twelve. The preceding night, however, I slept — at intervals and not continuously — to the amount of more than five hours, which was rather rare good luck.

Bromide, etc., produce no effect. . . . Bating sleeplessness and its effects, I have been better than before, with the exception of palpitation of the heart, which is sometimes very troublesome. Throbbing in the ear at night is also annoying at times. The old distress in the head continues, but has been less distressing within the last few years than before I took your advice. Within the last year I have done a very moderate amount of work, and recently none at all. . . . Muscular strength is not exhausted, but nerves are set on edge, and the condition of the head entirely precludes brain-work. I have occasionally had

attacks as severe, or more so, — once four successive nights absolutely without sleep, — but this
is more persistent than any before, and is aggravated by the palpitation of the heart, which
I have reason to believe is not from organic
causes.   Yours very truly,

F. PARKMAN.

The skillful physician could do little or nothing. I must not let myself be betrayed into
too much of malady and medicine. Parkman's
body might be hampered and harassed; there
was no sickness in his spirit. No one who admitted to himself that he was an invalid could
have written so much like a man, belted and
booted, with hand on saddle-bow, as he does in
all his histories.

Neither did he admit that he was cut off from
indoor pleasures. He always enjoyed the meetings of the " Saturday Club," a company of Boston gentlemen, some of great note, — the most
famous club of its kind in America. The club
used to meet at the end of the month to dine together, and pronounce salvation or condemnation,
it was said, upon the intellectual work of Boston.
Parkman was always essentially a sociable person; a man with opinions interesting to hear; a
taker of sides; a man full of likes and dislikes;
a lover of old ways, with delightful variety of
expression between quiet, refined acquiescence

and heady opposition ; a charming companion,
a distinguished presence. John Fiske, who was
a member of the club, and a pretty constant
attendant, never knew that he was an invalid ;
always found him alert, extremely gentle ; and
when he was absent, supposed that a prudence
for digestion or early hours kept him away. "He
never made the slightest allusion to his ill health ;
he would probably have deemed it inconsistent
with good breeding to intrude upon his friends
with such topics, and his appearance was always
most cheerful."

His life had its pleasures, its happiness, its gayeties, the tenderness of deep affection, the cheer
of friendship, the amusement of little comic happenings ; it was a good life, a hundred times
worth the living, if it had been only for the pleasure of daily fight and daily victory ; but there
were history, fame, roses, and a dozen things,
each enough to make him hold life rich. All
these found their way into his daily uneventful
existence, and the years passed on far too quick.

In July, 1886, after his experiment at camping out with Mr. Farnham, he went to the Range-
ley Lakes in Maine, where he lived at Bemis
Camps, "F. C. Barker, Prop'r." He had not
much to do there, and after a time ill health
obliged him to give up even the moderate discomforts of Mr. Barker's proprietorship.

EXTRACTS FROM LETTERS TO MISS PARKMAN.

[Aug., 1886.]

As I am forbidden to take any but the feeblest exercise, and as the light is very strong here, my resources for passing the time are limited. . . .

Aug. 26. Tell Mike I wrote to him to pot the chrysanthemums about Sept. 1, and to order what pots are wanted. . . . I think a little of building a log cabin here, with two small rooms for you, if you should want to come for a week, month, or more. It will cost little, and be independent of the rest. Board at Barker's. No servants needed. Barker will gladly do the job. How does it strike you? — all my affair, of course.

This was a delightful plan, and the log cabin was begun with the happiest expectations, but the grim hand of disease laid hold of him, and the log cabin, half built, was abandoned forever.

The next year he made a visit to Spain and France, in company with Dr. Algernon Coolidge.

The trip was cut short by Parkman's ill health, and he went back to the flowers on the banks of Jamaica Pond, and to the winter life in Boston, where his attendance at the dinners of the Saturday Club, and at the meetings of the St. Botolph Club, became gradually less and less.

In the last summers of his life he used to go to Little Harbour, near Portsmouth, to pay a visit to his son and daughter, Mr. and Mrs. Coolidge, and their children. Mr. Coolidge lived in the Wentworth mansion, which stands on a point of land where the Piscataqua runs into the sea. It is an old house, built in the reign of George II, with a rambling roof and a quaint, romantic aspect, telling stories of ancient days. Round the house are old lilac bushes; on one side is one outlet of the river, on the other a creek, both at low tide almost dry, laying bare sandbank, mussel-bed, seaweed, rocks, and glistening, gleaming mud-flats, — strangely beloved by delicate colors that come as soon as the sea goes and linger till it drives them off again. Here Parkman liked to go a-fishing, — not with the fly of the Canadian camp, but with the homely worm or a vexed grasshopper; on better days he got to the shore with a cane, on worse days with a crutch, but once safely in the little rowboat, he grasped the oars with the comfort of mastery, and rowed for hours at a smartish pace even when against the tide, or sometimes he would throw out his anchor and fish for cod and perch. He enjoyed his grandchildren very much, and his friends; sometimes he had a chat with Mr. Barrett Wendell over Cotton Mather, or with Mr. Howells over that more modern New Englander, Silas Lapham, or, perhaps, in default of other society, he would play with the cat.

PARKMAN TO HIS SISTER — EXTRACTS.

Things are here as usual, — all the worse for your absence; I row every day and fish occasionally. The cat had a temporary seizure, in the nature of a *mal de mer*, in consequence of imprudent indulgence in lobster. The rest of the family are well. My eyes are less sensitive. Knees about as when I last wrote. I sometimes get to the wharf without the one horse shay; but do not like to try it often. Have not slept well for two or three nights. Otherwise well enough. Want very much to see you. . . .

Things go on here as usual. The afternoon of Tuesday was extremely hot, and the night still worse, so that sleep was out of the question. I made up for it last night. All well. I miss you extremely, though Katy [Mrs. Coolidge] has taken her lessons from you very well. . . .

I have received from you a card, a note, and the bundle, of which the last two came yesterday. All were most welcome. I should be a very discreet young man if I were as thoughtful for myself as you are for me. You are the beau ideal of sisterhood; of which I am always affectionately conscious, though I do not say much. I slept last night with the help of "pisen." Eyes better. Miriam [cat] has been suffering, as Molly [his granddaughter] conjectures, from the bite of a spider which she was munching in the grass; but she seems convalescent. Rest of the family well. The shoes were as welcome as unexpected. . . .

It was a great disappointment to learn that you were not coming. Can you not come after your stay with T. ? I took Molly out fishing on Monday. She caught a sculpin and a pollock, which last was served up at tea, and pronounced by her to be one of the best fish she ever tasted. She was delighted with her success. Sleep very uncertain. . . .

After having been able to get about more than for several years past, I was suddenly attacked, three days ago, by a greatly increased lameness of the old knee, and to-day can scarcely get out of the house at all, especially as a severe lumbago is added, which makes my attempts at locomotion rather ridiculous. No cause that I can see. . . .

All right here. The circus came off with éclat, and Molly was conspicuous in gymnastics. A goat race took place with applause. Louise [granddaughter] had a profusion of gifts, to which I made the contribution of an india rubber ball, chosen by her mother as of a safe nature.

Things go as well here as the extreme heat will permit. I have got about more freely, and missing my crutches this morning, sent Molly to look for them. She found them in my room, as I had inadvertently come down without them, which causes me to pass for a bit of a humbug.

Crock [a cat] has caused some moderated sorrow ; but I cannot wear crape as my hat is not adapted to it. Visitors come and go constantly. I am reasonably well and very glad to hear from you.

Thus the simple chronicle of the last years runs away. The "Half Century of Conflict" was published in the spring of 1892; and it is amusing to find the old difficulty about a name that had bothered him with "Pontiac." First he thought of the "Rivals," a dramatic name, then of the "Irrepressible Conflict," a political name, and then at last, the sister, upon whom he had gradually come to depend to a degree that even his strong, independent spirit at last understood, helped him with the happy solution.

His work was then done; there was no reason why he should tarry. After his visit to the Wentworth mansion in the summer of 1893, he returned to Jamaica Plain; he went rowing on a Sunday, came back to the house, felt sick, and went to bed. His life had run its course, and after a brief illness, borne, like all his ills, with dignity, gentleness, and serenity, he died on November 8, 1893.

CHAPTER XXV

CHARACTER AND OPINIONS

A MAN in his innermost core may be a unity, a homogeneous something, which remains always the same; or if it change, changes with a uniform movement, the whole being altering at once. Perhaps by "other eyes than ours" this inmost personality may be seen; but in this world it is invisible, or else appears in such an endless variety of ways that we, guided by a practical philosophy, must face it in an agnostic attitude. Even the outer being shifts with the sun, with the air, with breakfast coffee, with this man's presence or that girl's absence, with hope, tedium, prosperity. A man appears to his acquaintance this, to his neighbors that, to his friends thus and so, to his family different, and perhaps to the woman whom he loves different still. Therefore a biographer but goes a-fishing, seeking which of the many semblances appearing to one or another come in his judgment closer to that inmost self which, though the moving force within, he cannot touch. He must catch, as best

he can, the traits, dispositions, manners, that
have left their imprint here and there and put
them together in some consistent fashion, so
that they shall indicate, if possible, the move-
ments of what he believes is the mainspring
within. This makeshift is likely, at best, to be
a botch. An honest purpose is the only excuse.

The Parkmans, though Boston bred, and an-
cestored by masters in theology, hailed from
Devon, and among their family possessions had
what need never be inquired about too curiously,
— a coat-of-arms. On this there is a chevron,
a field azure, a coronet, a helmet, and various
heraldic appendages; but for us the significant
emblem lies in the crest, which depicts a " horse
hurrant." Here we have the true device for
Francis Parkman. Busy with little things, busy
with big things, as a boy in Medford Fells and
in his chemical laboratory, as a lad in the gymnasium and on the banks of the Margalloway,
as a man in his flower-garden and in his library,
in his quick opinions, in his vigorous speech, in
his wheeled chair or limping on canes, always in
his heart there galloped or chafed the " horse
hurrant."

At Paris, once, on one of the visits made in
later years in pursuit of documents, his friend
M. Margry came to dine with him and his sister. The fête was in honor of his birthday, —

that memorable one crowned by the poem, — for Margry had wished to celebrate it, and the readiest way to forestall his gay proposals was to invite him to the hotel. The voluble little Frenchman talked and stayed, stayed and talked, till Parkman had to betake himself, cane in hand, upstairs for a few minutes' rest; he dashed upstairs with his youthful ardor. Margry caught sight of him, and nicknamed him "le cerf-volant," which is, I take it, a graceful French rendering of "horse hurrant." Thus it was always. Parkman's ardor hurled him on, obstacles stuck spurs into him, difficulties whipped and stung him; onward he dashed, the hot spirit always bullying the body, and the poor body always paying the scot. To his daughter he was a "passionate Puritan," — the phrase is just. Under his stoicism, under his reserve, under his gentleness, all cast in the Puritan mould, was this passionate spirit. *Chi non arde non risplende*, as the Umbrian proverb says. When he was lying on his sick-bed, ill and helpless, a lady came to see him; eager to be of comfort, she said, "Oh, think of what you have done." "Done!" he cried, his head rising from the pillow, "done! there is much more still for me to do!"

The Puritan inheritance mingles with its steadfastness a certain sternness not unbecoming a man. The soldier must be stern; and there are

certain photographs of Parkman that throw into
prominence his fine jaw, and reveal a latent
sternness needful for a lifelong battle with physical ills, and by him well put to use in resistance
to the unseen enemy that robbed him of his eyes,
his legs, and the use of his brain.   That sternness was but his coat of mail; when he came
forth unarmed from his dark chamber, and was
left at ease to enjoy his friends, then, even in
later years when the gifts of youth had left him,
women young and old found him charming,
younger men admired his refined, scholarly face,
his gentle manners, and recognized too his "boyish freshness of feeling and nature." To men of
his own age he was "a most entertaining companion." When some gentlemen in Boston, interested in art and letters, organized the St.
Botolph Club, he was chosen president, not
merely because he was a distinguished man of
letters, but because he was a good fellow and
delightful company.

He belonged to the generation that in creed
represented the reaction against Puritanism; he
could remember the pinch of the vanishing Puritan oppression, and was not born late enough
to look at it with the eyes of the succeeding generation, — those eyes to which that generation
modestly ascribes such perfect vision. He was
strongly averse to the Puritan creed, to their

theocracy, their narrowness, their injustice, and perhaps did not see how closely their virtues resembled his own, — courage, fortitude, love of truth as they saw it, and a passionate ardor in pursuing their ends. Like them, he went untroubled by doubts ; he made up his mind and was indifferent to disagreement. Like them, he was immensely conservative: the inheritance from the past must be held to; the dreams of men, discontented with the lot meted to them and their fellows, — dreams of new forms of society, new conceptions of social order, were to him delusions of vanity rigidly to be pushed away. He deemed New England of a generation or more ago "perhaps the most successful democracy on earth," but the growth and development of modern democracy filled him with detestation ; he beheld in it "organized ignorance, led by unscrupulous craft, and marching, amid the applause of fools, under the flag of equal rights." He felt strongly on new theories, just as his ancestors the Cottons, or their friends the Mathers, would have felt, and he spoke forcibly just as they would have done. "Out of the wholesome fruits of the earth, and the staff of life itself, the perverse chemistry of man distills delirious vapors, which, condensed and bottled, exalt his brain with glorious fantasies, and then leave him in the mud." So it is (for example), he says, with those deluded people who are in favor of woman suffrage.

Not that he did not admire and respect women, — he did, for cause passing common, — but he did not like the notion of woman suffrage. On a loose sheet shut into a notebook kept in Bemis Camps in 1886 is this entry: "The first and fundamental requisites of women, as of men, are physical, moral, and mental health. It is for men to rear the political superstructure; it is for women to lay its foundation. God rules the world by fixed laws, moral and physical; and according as men and women observe or violate these laws will be the destinies of communities and individuals for this world and the next. The higher education is necessary to the higher order of women to the end that they may discharge their function of civilizing agent; but it should be cautiously limited to the methods and degree that consist with the discharge of their functions of maternity. Health of body and mind is the one great essential. In America men are belittled and cramped by the competition of business, from which women are, or ought to be, free. Hence they have opportunities of moral and mental growth better in some respects than those of men."

There was a grim vigor in his speech on these distasteful subjects, that betrayed the Puritan

character. Perhaps this masculine vigor, this
rude immalleability, make a special charm to a
younger generation bred upon a somewhat milk
and water skepticism for principles and theories,
whether old or new. He was masculine in his
outlook on life and on all its chief matters. He
despised effeminacy, self-coddling, comfort-lov-
ing ; hardly less also he disliked the coddling of
others, the " effusive humanitarianism " of New
England " melting into sentimentality at a tale
of woe," as he called it, that tended to concen-
trate interest and sympathy on the feeble rather
than on the strong and self-sustaining. He liked
a masculine judgment, readiness not untempered
by a heady vigor, but devoid of sentimental sur-
charge ; he could not tolerate fanaticism. Therefore in the slavery days he was out of patience
with the abolitionists of Massachusetts, men, as
he thought, of a feminine intemperance, of un-
masculine mawkishness, who neglected the real
ideals of the country for the benefit of a few
scattered fugitives of an inferior race, which
had not the pluck to strike a blow for itself.

It was this belief that men should be masculine that led him to the natural corollary that
women should be feminine. Like other men of
a male temper, he enjoyed the distinctive feminine traits, unreasoning sympathy, instinctive
comprehension, absolute self-abnegation, delicate

sensibility. He took great pleasure in the society of women, and in their company was wont to drop most freely the outer semblance of the warrior, that blending of sternness and determination, which others sometimes found in him. This wish always to keep the two types, mutually complementary, separate and apart, lay at the bottom of his putting Washington so much higher than Lincoln as a hero; for the womanly tenderness of Lincoln seemed to him out of place. He liked a man who could get angry in time of need, and vent his anger in blunt, rough words.

By his creed and by his practice he belonged to the sect of the Stoics, a disciple worthy of the sect's happiest days; his favorite virtue was fortitude, and of all men of philosophic mind, Marcus Aurelius was his accepted pattern. In his youth he jotted down in his private diary his resistance to the strongest temptation that assails the body; and his manhood was a constant obedience to self-restraint, in order that he might fulfill his work. In spirit he was always mindful of the noble emperor's words, "Take care always to remember that you are a man and a Roman; and let every action be done with perfect and unaffected gravity, humanity, freedom, and justice." His friends bear witness that again and again he had to restrain his vehement impulses to rash speech or action; again and again with a calm exterior batten the hatches on a mutinous mood. This antique Puritan, with fire fetched from Devon burning within him, took care to remember that he was a man and a gentleman, and bore himself with gentleness and justice.

Perhaps his aristocratic bent helped him to self-control. In this bent there was no touch of vainglory, no trace of a willingness to live upon the good report of ancestors; but a notion, in part begotten no doubt from the general social theories prevalent in the stately old house in Bowdoin Square, in part based on reasoning, and justified by his purpose to prove that his place was beside the best. We may perceive his views of men, when he speaks of the rose: —

Like all things living, in the world of mind or of matter, the rose is beautified, enlarged, and strengthened by a course of judicious and persevering culture, continued through successive generations. The art of horticulture is no leveler. Its triumphs are achieved by rigid systems of selection and rejection, founded always on the broad basis of intrinsic worth. The good cultivator propagates no plants but the best. He carefully chooses those marked out by conspicuous merit; protects them from the pollen of inferior sorts; intermarries them, perhaps, with other varieties of equal vigor and beauty; saves their seed, and raises from it another generation. From the new plants thus obtained he again chooses the best, and repeats with them the same process. Thus the rose and other plants are brought slowly to their perfect development. It is in vain to look for much improvement by merely cultivating one individual. We cultivate the parent, and look for our reward in the off-spring.

Such was his theory, and if we meet with a little lift of the eyebrows, a little look askant, when he regards *nouveaux riches*, we know that the movement was due not to snobbery, but to what he deemed personal and inherited experience. In a notebook kept while he was overseer of Harvard College, there are memoranda of notes of opinions gathered from the older professors; and among other opinions is this, which evidently squared satisfactorily with his own conclusions, — " The best class of students are those of families of inherited wealth or easy means, sons of *nouveaux riches* do not make scholars." But such a feeling never degenerated into a class spirit. Speaking on a subject in which he took a deep interest, he says : —

The public schools, moreover, are democratic institutions in the best sense of the words ; and, on a broader and more comprehensive scale, they produce the effects which are said to be the peculiar advantages of the great English en-

dowed schools. They bring together children of
different walks in life, and weaken mutual prejudices by force of mutual contact, teach the rich
to know the poor, and the poor to know the rich,
and so sap the foundations of class jealousies
and animosities. The common schools are crucibles in which races, nationalities, and creeds
are fused together till all alike become American.

But his books reveal his character better than
I can suggest it, not only by their obvious admi-
rations, but by their reticence. The historian
never mentions himself except to point a foot-
note; he wears the dignified ermine of historic
impartiality, but a generous heart cannot hide
itself. By his loves he shall be known. Nobody
can read the pages on Champlain, on La Salle,
Brébeuf, or Wolfe, and not know that these are
the heroes whose high deeds quickened a kindred soul.

Yet the reader would not know, nor would an
acquaintance in life have guessed, that this studious gentleman, with his firm jaw and his scholarly brow, of decided views and occasional bursts
of vigorous speech, was tenderly sensitive to sympathy. The show of unwarranted compassion or
officious pity from some person outside the inner
circle of those that loved him was coldly pushed
aside; but real sympathy, offered as one manly
man may offer it to another, or tendered by a

woman who had the right to tender it, when expressed with reticence and restraint, or indicated in action rather than speech, went straight to his heart. It was more acceptable to him even than fame, and he was very ambitious.

CHAPTER XXVI

A MORE INTIMATE CHAPTER

THE story of a scholar is uneventful; it is made up of travels, rummagings, notes, dictation, and printing; it lies far from the madding crowd, remote from the bustle of politics and the creaking machinery of national life. Parkman's infirmities intensified this seclusion; they forced him to sport his oak against all except extreme intimacy, and intimacy is shy of the chronicler; but a biography with no allusion to intimacy is but a shell, a case, a cover, and lets the reader carry away an impression that the man had none of those close affections that reveal themselves in trifling commerce, in looks, in smiles, and silence. This intimacy of Parkman's needs a pen plucked "from an angel's wing," for his deepest feelings radiated from his presence, and no one could say just how they had been expressed; and part of it should be told by Robin Goodfellow, for his playfulness, his fun, his fondness for nonsense, pass in the telling.

He spent his life between the town house —

his mother's during her life, then his sister's —
and his country house at Jamaica Plain; they
were his guests in summer, he theirs in winter.
At 50 Chestnut Street he had the top floor as his
apartment, his bedroom to the south, his study
to the north. The stairs that lead thither have a
half-fulfilled inclination to wind; in later years, a
little elevator for his private use spared him the
stairs he often could not climb. The study was
his home, for illness prevented him from taking
an ordinary part in family life. He came down
to breakfast, lunch, and dinner, but was generally silent, and went up again directly after
the meal was finished. In the study he spent
his time, working when he could. One winter
he employed a young woman, a public school-
teacher, as his amanuensis; she was wholly ignorant of French, and read the copied archives
with a pure Yankee pronunciation. But all the
rest of the time, his sister or some member of
his family wrote for him while he dictated. Insomnia kept him awake at night, and during
these wakeful hours, and also in the long periods
of repose during the day, he would think of his
writing, and put sentence to sentence and paragraph to paragraph, so that when he began to
dictate he proceeded in orderly progress as if he
were reading from a book. Thus, barring the
interruptions of illness, he proceeded day by day,

until chapter was added to chapter, volume to volume, and the whole at last finished.

The "gridirons" were used in earlier years, at times from 1850 to 1860. There were three of these in all, very much alike, the later ones having being made to improve on the earlier model. The last is a little metal frame twelve inches by eight, with wire bars running across like lines on ruled paper, some sixteen in all. Underneath this grill the sheet of paper was slipped in, with a metal back to write on. With this contrivance, following the wire by touch, he could write in the dark without looking. It is an eloquent witness, —

> " Stone walls do not a prison make
> Nor iron bars a cage," —

nor blindness, nor pain, nor manifold privations to the man of heroic temper.

In the evening Miss Parkman would read aloud to him books of various kinds, novels often. He liked a good, strong story, like "Monte Cristo" or "The Wandering Jew," or some classic like Miss Austen's novels or "Evelina;" just as in early days he had loved Cooper and Scott. Poetry he liked, but not all. Wordsworth he could not bear, Byron he enjoyed; but he almost always had a volume of Shakespeare on his table, often open; sometimes he was able to read a few lines, but commonly the silent presence was enough. One of his last gifts to his wife was a fine copy of Milton.

After his mother died, two nieces, the daughters of his sister Caroline, Mrs. Cordner, were frequent inmates of the house, and they, with Miss Parkman, were the only confidantes of his wilder nonsense. To his friends he passed as a man rather lacking in humor, rather inclined to take statements *au pied de la lettre ;* but in the summer time, the tap of the cane coming downstairs was the reveille for jokes and nonsense. The audience was on tiptoe with expectation, and the performance was always received with fullest appreciation ; and even if brother and sister were alone, the humor, if less boisterous, was gay. The cheer was no counterfeit, but born of an honest gratitude for the happy things in life ; it also served to hide his pain from the others, and even from himself, for he could not take part in ordinary conversation, and silence had a painful physical effect on him.

As it was with his nonsense, so too it was with his intimate tenderness, only those who lived under the same roof with him realized it to the full. His daughters and his little nieces used to make him visits twice a year, — two months in the spring and two in the autumn ; they used to be at that breakfast-table, giggling for the nonsense to come, and they knew how to read the tenderness in his eye, and did not need to wait for words, for they knew that the " horse hur-rant " had great difficulty with those most clumsy instruments for expressing tenderness — English monosyllables. The visits were always at Jamaica Pond, and one of them would row with him in the boat, or go a-visiting the roses and the lilies; or he would help them to disentangle the fish-line and bait the hook, or, it might be, arrange the aquatic flora and fauna in their little aqua-rium; or when they said good-by, he would go to the greenhouse to choose a plant for them; and here they found that the language of flowers was also far better than that of the dictionary. These nieces, too, bear witness to his triumphant self-mastery; during all the years from their childhood to womanhood, — in town, when they were not staying in the same house, they lived across the street and ran in daily, — during all these years they never once heard an impatient word fall from his lips, they never once saw an impatient look; they merely could divine that he would not let them be troubled by his pain. This is the triumph of stoicism, of the sweet stoicism of Marcus Aurelius, mingled in no small measure with the teachings of the Gali-lean fisherman.

Thus I come to the end of this uneventful story; but there are a few more pages to complete this little picture of his later life and its intimacies. At Jamaica Plain, in those latter days, — when gardening and horticultural prizes were things of the past, — every morning he and his sister went rowing. This pond is not very big, and does not afford a great variety of scene nor of incident, and the dreary repetition had to be enriched by art. Here Parkman gave loose rein to his boyish imagination. Every afternoon they went for a drive, with Michael, the gardener, — known to his intimates as Mike, — driving. Parkman had no natural love for a carriage ; the "horse hurrant" despised the slow and tedious monotony of the inevitable road, but his fancy filled the borders of the way with historic scenes, and would not permit his helplessness to darken their horizon.

Parkman was very fond of cats, and though they were rigidly excluded from the library, in the evening there was always a cat — Peter or Sarah or Molly — who sat on his lap, or curled on the rug and purred its thoughts into a most sympathetic ear. He had always had a weakness for them. Once when Miss Parkman was in Paris, we find him writing, 1872, a year or two after the siege of Paris, " You are also to be congratulated on the discovery of two Angoras, which I trust were favorable specimens. There used to be a good one in the lodge of the con-

cierge at No. 123 Av. des Champs Elysées, but
the accidents of war may have removed her from
the sphere which she adorned and consigned her
to the frying-pan."

He makes a point of the Angora blood here,
but that is an affectation; good cats, bad cats,
lean cats, fat cats, well-bred or wayfarers, ears
torn, tailless, young and old, had some claim
on his interest. He liked nothing better than to
sit in summer time on the veranda festooned
with wisteria, and stroke a little cat, and listen
to its purring, and help it to make itself perfectly comfortable on his lap. Not only cats,
but pictures of cats, photographs of cats, effigies
of cats abounded. In especial there was one
flannel likeness, whiskered with red silk, eyed
with green beads, and featured pathetically with
cotton thread, presented to him by his little
granddaughter. When he went to Portsmouth
to pay her his summer visit, he tucked this flannel slander of a cat under his coat and brought
it forth triumphantly, she believing that it had
been cherished next his waistcoat all the winter.
He had played the same comedy with the child's
mother when she was a little girl.

My dear Katy, — Me and Creem are wel.
We send u our luv. We do not fite now. We
have milk every day. One day, when i was playing under the evergreens, Creem would not lap

her milk till she had come out and told me that
it was reddy, and we both went and lapped it
together. Papa holds me every night to keep
me tame. . . . Yors till deth,

FLORA, her m × ark [mark].
(I struggled so, my paw has not made a good
mark.)

P. S. Plese bring me a skulpin.

P. P. S. Papa says to thank Grace for her
letter, and he is glad she is having such a good
time.

N. B. This is a lok of my fer, with best luv
of Yors in haste, Puss. [Lock of fur fastened
on.]

The cats returned his affection, and loved to
curl their backs, and rub up against his legs.

His own children, after their mother's death,
had gone to live with their aunt, Miss Bigelow,
who brought them up as if they had been her
own, so that Parkman was spared the care he
could not give and yet had the pleasure of seeing them constantly, for Dr. Bigelow's house was
hard by.   In the early summer and again in the
autumn they made him a visit at Jamaica Plain.
The elder daughter, Grace, took her chief pleasure in the pond and the boat, but the younger,
Katy, liked the garden best, and every morning trudged after her father, basket in hand, as
he walked down the paths with his campstool
under his arm on the matinal expedition to cut

flowers for the house or to send to his friends. Whatever different occupations the three might find during the day, at dusk they met at his sofa in the " ante-room," where he narrated story after story with Grace sitting beside him, and Katy perched on the back of the sofa. He inspired them with deep respect, affection, and admiration.

In later years, after his daughters were married, when on the whole he suffered less and had the sustaining sense that his work was substantially finished, he enjoyed his grandchildren very much, letting them see, perhaps, more of his tender, playful side than he had been able to show to their parents. So his life went by, loved by his cats, his family, his friends, his kindred, and his fellow historians; and it was cheered and brightened by kind and generous expressions of affection, on such occasions as when he resigned from the presidency of the St. Botolph Club, or attained his seventieth year.

I am not sure that I have spoken enough of his gentleness, and I have said too little of his modesty. John Fiske was once delivering a lecture on " America's Place in History," at Hawthorne Hall, in Boston; he alluded to Pontiac and his conspiracy, and said that it was memorable as " the theme of one of the most brilliant and fascinating books that have ever been writ-

ten by any historian since the days of Herodotus."
The words were hardly out of his mouth when
he caught sight of Parkman in the audience. He
says, " I shall never forget the sudden start which
he gave, and the heightened color of his noble
face, with its curious look of surprise and pleasure, an expression as honest and simple as one
might witness in a rather shy schoolboy suddenly singled out for praise. I was so glad that
I had said what I did without thinking of his
hearing me."

Parkman's memory is linked forever with the
first great epoch in American history; and a
memorial in stone is to be placed near the edge
of Jamaica Pond hard by the dock from which
he used to push his little boat when he and his
sister went for their daily row around the pond.
Two great monoliths will stand, one on each
side of a stone seat; in one the sculptor has
carved the figure of an Indian, in the other an
image of the Spirit of the Woods,— the comrades of Parkman's boyhood.

After this it was noised abroad that Mr. Valiant-for-Truth was taken with a summons. . . .
When he understood it, he called for his friends,
and told them of it. Then said he, . . . " though
with great difficulty I have got hither, yet now
I do not repent me of all the trouble I have been
at to arrive where I am. My sword I give to

him that shall succeed me in my pilgrimage, and my courage and skill to him that can get it. My marks and scars I carry with me." . . .

When the day that he must go hence was come, many accompanied him to the river-side, into which as he went he said, "Death, where is thy sting?" And as he went down deeper, he said, "Grave, where is thy victory?" So he passed over, and all the trumpets sounded on the other side.

APPENDIX

LETTER written to Mr. Martin Brimmer in 1886, with instructions to be kept until after Parkman's death, and then to be given to the Massachusetts Historical Society : —

MY DEAR BRIMMER, — I once told you that I should give you some account of the circumstances under which my books were written. Here it is, with some preliminary pages to explain the rest. I am sorry there is so much of it : —

Causes antedating my birth gave me constitutional liabilities to which I largely ascribe the mischief that ensued. As a child I was sensitive and restless, rarely ill, but never robust. At eight years I was sent to a farm belonging to my maternal grandfather on the outskirts of the extensive tract of wild and rough woodland now called Middlesex Fells. I walked twice a day to a school of high but undeserved reputation about a mile distant, in the town of Medford. Here I learned very little, and spent the intervals of schooling more profitably in collecting eggs, insects, and reptiles, trapping squirrels and woodchucks, and making persistent though rarely fortunate attempts to kill birds with arrows. After four years of this rustication I was brought back to Boston, when I was unhappily seized with a mania for experiments in chemistry involving a lonely, confined, unwholesome sort of life, baneful to body and mind. This lasted till the critical age of fifteen, when a complete change came over me — I renounced crucibles and retorts and took to books; read poetry and fancied for a while that I could write it; conceived literary ambitions, and, at the same time, began to despise a literary life and to become enamored of the backwoods. This new passion — which proved permanent — was no doubt traceable in part to fond recollections of the Middlesex Fells, as well as to one or two journeys which I was permitted to make into some of the wilder parts of New England. It soon got full possession of me, and mixed itself with all my literary aspirations. In this state of mind I went to college, where I divided my time about equally between books and active exercises, of which last I grew inordinately fond, and in which I was ambitious beyond measure to excel.

My favorite backwoods were always in my thoughts. At first I tried to persuade myself that I could woo this new mistress in verse; then I came down to fiction, and at last reached the sage though not flattering conclusion that if I wanted to build in her honor any monument that would stand, I must found on solid fact. Before the end of the sophomore year my various schemes had crystallized into a plan of writing the story of what was thus known as the "Old French

War;" that is, the war that ended in the conquest
of Canada; for here, as it seemed to me, the forest
drama was more stirring and the forest stage more
thronged with appropriate actors than in any other
passage of our history. It was not till some years
later that I enlarged the plan to include the whole
course of the American conflict between France and
England; or, in other words, the history of the American forest; for this was the light in which I regarded
it. My theme fascinated me, and I was haunted with
wilderness images day and night.

From this time forward, two ideas possessed me.
One was to paint the forest and its tenants in true
and vivid colors; the other was to realize a certain
ideal of manhood, a little mediæval, but nevertheless
good. Feeling that I fell far short of it, I proceeded
in extreme dissatisfaction to apply heroic remedies.
I held the creed that the more hard knocks a man
gets, whether in mind or body, the better for him,
provided always that he takes them without flinching;
and as the means of forcing myself up to the required
standard, I put my faith in persistent violence which
I thought energy. I held that the true aim of life
was not happiness but achievement; had profound respect for physical strength and hardihood when joined
with corresponding qualities of character; took pleasure in any moderate hardship, scorned invalidism of
all kinds, and was full of the notion, common enough
with boys of a certain sort, that the body will always
harden and toughen with exercise and exposure. I
remember to have had a special aversion for the Rev.

Dr. Channing, not for his heresies, but for his meager proportions, sedentary habits, environment of close air and female parishioners, and his preachments of the superiority of mind over matter; for, while I had no disposition to gainsay his proposition in the abstract, it was a cardinal point with me that while the mind remains a habitant of earth, it cannot dispense with a sound material basis, and that to neglect and decry the corporeal part in the imagined interest of the spiritual is proof of a nature either emasculate or fanatical. For my own part, instead of neglecting, I fell to lashing and spurring it into vigor and prosperity.

Meanwhile I diligently pursued my literary scheme. While not exaggerating the importance of my subject, I felt that it had a peculiar life of its own, of which I caught tantalizing glimpses, to me irresistibly attractive. I felt far from sure that I was equal to the task of rekindling it, calling out of the dust the soul and body of it and making it a breathing reality. I was like some smitten youth plagued with harrowing doubts as to whether he can win the mistress of his fancy. I tried to gauge my own faculties, and was displeased with the result. Nevertheless, I resolved that if my steed was not a thoroughbred, I would at least get his best paces out of him, and I set myself to a strenuous course of training for the end in view. A prime condition of success was an unwearied delving into dusty books and papers, a kind of work which I detested; and I came to the agreeable yet correct conclusion that the time for this drudgery was not come; that my present business was, so to speak, to impregnate myself with my theme, fill my mind with impressions from real life, range the woods, mix with Indians and frontiersmen, visit the scenes of the events I meant to describe, and so bring myself as near as might be to the times with which I was to deal. Accordingly, I spent all my summer vacations in the woods or in Canada, at the same time reading such books as I thought suited, in a general way, to help me towards my object. I pursued these lucubrations with a pernicious intensity, keeping my plans and purposes to myself, while passing among my companions as an outspoken fellow.

The danger into which I was drifting rose from the excessive stimulus applied to nerves which had too much stimulus of their own. I was not, however, at all nervous in the sense in which that term is commonly understood, and I regarded nervous people with more pity than esteem. The mischief was working underground. If it had come to the surface, the effects would probably have been less injurious. I flattered myself I was living wisely because I avoided the more usual excesses, but I fell into others quite as baneful, riding my hobbies with unintermitting vehemence, and carrying bodily exercise to a point where it fatigues instead of strengthening. In short, I burned the candle at both ends.

The first hint that my method of life was not to prove a success occurred in my junior year, in the shape of a serious disturbance in the action of the heart, of which the immediate cause was too violent

exercise in the gymnasium. I was thereupon ordered
to Europe, where I spent the greater part of a year,
never losing sight of my plans and learning much
that helped to forward them. Returning in time to
graduate with my class, I was confronted with the
inevitable question, What next ? The strong wish of
my father that I should adopt one of the so-called regular professions determined me to enter the Harvard
Law School.

Here, while following the prescribed courses at a
quiet pace, I entered in earnest on two other courses,
one of general history, the other of Indian history and
ethnology, and at the same time studied diligently the
models of English style ; which various pursuits were
far from excluding the pleasures of society. In the
way of preparation and preliminary to my principal
undertaking, I now resolved to write the history of
the Indian War under Pontiac, as offering peculiar
opportunities for exhibiting forest life and Indian
character ; and to this end I began to collect materials by travel and correspondence. The labor was not
slight, for the documents were widely scattered on
both sides of the Atlantic ; but at the beginning of
1846 the collection was nearly complete.

I had been conscious for some time of an over-
stimulated condition of the brain. While constantly
reminding myself that the task before me was a long
one, that haste was folly, and that the slow way was
the surer and better one, I felt myself spurred forward irresistibly. It was like a rider whose horse has
got the bit between his teeth, and who, while seeing

his danger, cannot stop. As the mischief gave no
outward sign, nobody was aware of it but myself. At
last, however, a weakness of the eyes, which was one
of its symptoms, increased so fast that I was forced
to work with the eyes of others. I now resolved to
execute a scheme which I had long meditated. This
was to visit the wild tribes of the far West, and live
among them for a time, as a necessary part of training for my work. I hoped by exchanging books and
documents for horse and rifle to gain three objects at
once — health, use of sight, and personal knowledge
of savage life. The attempt did not prosper. I was
attacked on the plains by a wasting and dangerous
disorder, which had not ceased when I returned to
the frontier five months later. In the interval I was
for some weeks encamped with a roving band of Sioux
at the Rocky Mountains, with one rough though not
unfaithful attendant. It would have been suicidal
to accept the part of an invalid, and I was sometimes
all day in the saddle, when in civilized life complete
rest would have been thought indispensable. I lived
like my red companions, and sometimes joined them
in their hunting, with the fatiguing necessity of being
always armed and on the watch. To one often giddy
with the exhaustion of disease, the strain on the system was great. After going back to civilization, the
malady gradually subsided, after setting in action a
train of other disorders which continued its work. In
a year or more I was brought to a state of nervous
prostration that debarred all mental effort, and was
attended with a weakness of sight that for a time

threatened blindness. Before reaching this pass I
wrote the "Oregon Trail" by dictation. Complete
repose, to me the most detestable of prescriptions, was
enjoined upon me, and from intense activity I found
myself doomed to helpless inaction. Such chance of
success as was left lay in time, patience, and a studied
tranquillity of spirit; and I felt, with extreme disgust,
that there was nothing for it but to renounce past
maxims and habits and embrace others precisely the
opposite. An impulse seized me to return to the
Rocky Mountains, try a hair of the dog that bit me,
and settle squarely the question to be or not to be. It
was the time of the Mexican War, and I well remember with what envious bitterness I looked at a col-
ored print in a shop window, representing officers
and men carrying a field battery into action at the
battle of Buena Vista. I believe that I would willingly have borne any amount of bodily pain, provided only I could have brought with it the power
of action.

After a while — as anything was better than idleness — I resolved on cautiously attempting to make
use of the documents already collected for the "Conspiracy of Pontiac." They were read to me by friends
and relatives at times when the brain was least rebel-
lious, and I wrote without use of sight, by means of
a sort of literary gridiron or frame of parallel wires,
laid on the page to guide the hand. For some months
the average rate of progress did not exceed three or
four lines a day, and the chapters thus composed were
afterwards rewritten. If, as I was told, brain work

was poison, the dose was homeopathic and the effect
was good, for within a year I could generally work,
with the eyes of others, two hours or more a day, and
in about three years the book was finished.

I then began to gather materials for the earlier
volumes of the series of France and England in North
America, though, as I was prevented from traveling
by an extreme sensitiveness of the retina which made
sunlight insupportable, the task of collection seemed
hopeless. I began, however, an extensive correspondence, and was flattering myself that I might succeed
at last, when I was attacked with an effusion of water
on the knee, which subsided in two or three months,
then returned, kept me a prisoner for two years, and
deprived me of necessary exercise for several years
more. The consequence was that the devil which had
been partially exorcised returned triumphant. The
evil now centred in the head, producing cerebral
symptoms of such a nature that, in 1853, the physician who attended me at the time, after cautious cir-
cumlocution, said in a low and solemn voice that his
duty required him to warn me that death would probably follow within six months, and stood amazed at
the smile of incredulity with which the announcement
was received. I had known my enemy longer than
he, and learned that its mission was not death, but
only torment. Five years later another physician —
an eminent physiologist of Paris, where I then was —
tried during the whole winter to discover the particular manifestations of the insanity which he was
convinced must needs attend the symptoms he had

observed, and told me at last what he had been about. "What conclusion have you reached?" I asked. "That I never knew a saner man in my life." "But," said I, "what is the chance that this brain of mine will ever get into working order again?" He shook his head and replied, "It is not impossible" — with which I was forced to content myself.

Between 1852 and 1860 this cerebral rebellion passed through great and seemingly capricious fluctuations. It had its ebbs and floods. Slight and sometimes imperceptible causes would produce an access which sometimes lasted with little respite for months. When it was in its milder moods I used the opportunity to collect material and prepare ground for future work, should work ever become practicable. When it was at its worst the condition was not enviable. I could neither listen to reading nor engage in conversation, even of the lightest. Sleep was difficult and was often banished entirely for one or two nights, during which the brain was apt to be in a state of abnormal activity, which had to be repressed at any cost, since thought produced the intensest torture. The effort required to keep the irritated organ quiet was so fatiguing that I occasionally rose and spent hours in the open air, where I found distraction and relief in watching the policemen and the tramps on the malls of Boston Common, at the risk of passing for a tramp myself. Towards the end of the night this cerebral excitation would seem to tire itself out, and gave place to a condition of weight and oppression much easier to bear.

Having been inclined to look with slight esteem on invalidism, the plight in which I found myself was mortifying; but I may fairly say that I never called on others to bear the burden of it, and always kept up a show of equanimity and good humor. The worst strain on these was when the Civil War broke out and I was doomed to sit an idle looker on.

After it became clear that literary work must be indefinitely suspended, I found a substitute in horticulture; and am confident that I owe it in good measure to the kindly influence of that gracious pursuit that the demon in the brain was gradually soothed into comparative quiet. In 1861 I was able, with frequent interruptions, to take up my work again. At the same time there was such amendment as regards sight that I could bear the sunlight without blinking, and read for several minutes at once without stopping to rest the eyes, though my chief dependence was still in those of others. In 1865 "The Pioneers" was finished, and the capacity of work both of brain and eye had much increased. "The Jesuits" was finished in 1867; "The Discovery of the Great West," in 1869; "The Old Régime," in 1874; and "Frontenac," in 1877. "Montcalm and Wolfe," which involved more labor, was not ready till 1884.

While engaged on these books I made many journeys in the United States and Canada in search of material, and went four times to Europe with a similar object. The task of exploring archives and collecting documents, to me repulsive at the best, was, under the circumstances, difficult, and would have been impossible but for the aid of competent assistants working under my direction.

Taking the last forty years as a whole, the capacity of literary work which during that time has fallen to my share has, I am confident, been considerably less than a fourth part of what it would have been under normal conditions. Whether the historical series in hand will ever be finished I do not know, but I shall finish it if I can. Yours faithfully,

F. PARKMAN.

JAMAICA PLAIN, 28 Oct., 1886.

POEM BY DR. OLIVER WENDELL HOLMES

Read at the Special Meeting of the Massachusetts Historical
Society in Memory of Francis Parkman, November 21, 1893.

He rests from toil ; the portals of the tomb
　　Close on the last of those unwearying hands
That wove their pictured webs in History's loom,
　　Rich with the memories of three mighty lands.

One wrought the record of the Royal Pair
　　Who saw the great Discoverer's sail unfurled,
Happy his more than regal prize to share,
　　The spoils, the wonders of the sunset world.

There, too, he found his theme ; upreared anew,
　　Our eyes beheld the vanished Aztec shrines,
And all the silver splendors of Peru
　　That lured the conqueror to her fatal mines.

No less remembered he who told the tale
　　Of empire wrested from the strangling sea ;
Of Leyden's woe, that turned his readers pale,
　　The price of unborn freedom yet to be ;

Who taught the New World what the Old could teach ;
　　Whose silent hero, peerless as our own,
By deeds that mocked the feeble breath of speech
　　Called up to life a State without a Throne.

As year by year his tapestry unrolled,
　　What varied wealth its growing length displayed !
What long processions flamed in cloth of gold !
　　What stately forms their flowing robes arrayed !

Not such the scenes our later craftsman drew ;
　　Not such the shapes his darker pattern held ;

A deeper shadow lent its sober hue,
  A sadder tale his tragic task compelled.

He told the red man's story; far and wide
  He searched the unwritten records of his race;
He sat a listener at the Sachem's side,
  He tracked the hunter through his wildwood chase.

High o'er his head the soaring eagle screamed;
  The wolf's long howl rang nightly; through the vale
Tramped the lone bear; the panther's eyeballs gleamed;
  The bison's gallop thundered on the gale.

Soon o'er the horizon rose the cloud of strife, —
  Two proud, strong nations battling for the prize,
Which swarming host should mould a nation's life;
  Which royal banner flout the western skies.

Long raged the conflict; on the crimson sod
  Native and alien joined their hosts in vain;
The lilies withered where the Lion trod,
  Till Peace lay panting on the ravaged plain.

A nobler task was theirs who strove to win
  The blood-stained heathen to the Christian fold,
To free from Satan's clutch the slaves of sin;
  Their labors, too, with loving grace he told.

Halting with feeble step, or bending o'er
  The sweet-breathed roses which he loved so well,
While through long years his burdening cross he bore,
  From those firm lips no coward accents fell.

A brave, bright memory! his the stainless shield
  No shame defaces and no envy mars!
When our far future's record is unsealed,
  His name will shine among its morning stars.

INDEX

INDEX